LOUIS ARMSTRONG
&
PAUL WHITEMAN

LOUIS ARMSTRONG

&

PAUL WHITEMAN

TWO KINGS OF JAZZ

JOSHUA BERRETT

YALE UNIVERSITY PRESS / NEW HAVEN & LONDON

Published with assistance from the foundation established in memory of Philip Hamilton McMillan of the Class of 1894, Yale College.

Designed by Mary Valencia
Set in Futura and Meridien type by The Composing Room of Michigan, Inc.
Printed in the United States of America by Vail-Ballou Press.

Library of Congress Cataloging-in-Publication Data

Berrett, Joshua.
  Louis Armstrong and Paul Whiteman : two kings of jazz / Joshua Berrett.
        p.   cm.
  Includes bibliographical references and index.
  ISBN 0-300-10384-0 (cloth : alk. paper)
  1. Armstrong, Louis, 1901–1971.   2. Whiteman, Paul, 1890–1967.   3. Jazz musicians—United States—Biography.   I. Title.
  ML419.A75B46 2004
  781.65′092′2—dc22

                                                    2004004217

A catalogue record for this book is available from the British Library.

The paper in this book meets the guidelines for permanence and durability of the Committee on Production Guidelines for Book Longevity of the Council on Library Resources.

10 9 8 7 6 5 4 3 2 1

To my beloved Lynne

CONTENTS

ACKNOWLEDGMENTS

A critical mass of colleagues and friends provided much valued help in the writing of this book. Chris Albertson and Larry Gushee shared vital information about Lillian Hardin, her studies at Chicago College of Music, and her pianistic accomplishments as a protégé of Louis Victor Saar. Richard Sudhalter sharpened my understanding of Whiteman and his arrangers; Dan Morgenstern provided special insight into the relationship between Louis Armstrong and Fletcher Henderson; Krin Gabbard shared copies of rare film footage; and Michael Cogswell and Peggy Alexander of the Louis Armstrong Archive offered much information about Armstrong and his use of Selmer trumpets as well as his product endorsements. Sylvia Kennick-Brown of Williams College was most helpful in making available materials in the Paul Whiteman Collection; Don Rayno filled in details of Whiteman's early Denver days and other vital background; Cynthia Magill, Paul Whiteman's granddaughter, very kindly provided some rare photographs; and Julia Scott shared the results of her research into Jazz at Lincoln Center. Lewis Porter, as always, was a much-appreciated sounding board for many issues in jazz history and style.

Jim Maher deserves special thanks for the cherished hours spent with me, generously sharing his personal reminiscences and unpublished work covering so many topics of this book. The irrepressible Ira Wolff was always there with yet another rare picking from a book sale. My son Jesse provided valuable pointers with regard to such matters as "Muscular Christianity," the labor movement, and the Scottsboro trial. My beloved wife, Lynne, and close family members stood by me throughout this roller-coaster ride to make sure I did not lose my balance. And Mercy College is to be thanked for the sabbatical leave that helped move things along.

In many ways this book is a tribute to the initiative and quiet determination of Harry Haskell, formerly of Yale University Press. It was he who first contacted me about a book and then waited patiently while I completed two others—on Louis Armstrong and J. J. Johnson. His encouragement and gentle nudging were essential in bringing the manuscript to completion. Following his departure it has been my pleasure to work with Larisa Heimert, Keith Condon, Dan Heaton, and Susan Laity.

INTRODUCTION

"THERE'S GLORY FOR YOU!"

"I DON'T KNOW WHAT YOU MEAN BY 'GLORY,'" ALICE SAID.

HUMPTY DUMPTY SMILED CONTEMPTUOUSLY. "OF COURSE YOU DON'T—TILL I TELL YOU. I MEANT 'THERE'S A NICE KNOCK-DOWN ARGUMENT FOR YOU!'"

"BUT 'GLORY' DOESN'T MEAN A 'NICE KNOCK-DOWN ARGUMENT,'" ALICE OBJECTED.

"WHEN I USE A WORD," HUMPTY DUMPTY SAID, IN A RATHER SCORNFUL TONE, "IT MEANS JUST WHAT I CHOOSE IT TO MEAN—NEITHER MORE NOR LESS."

"THE QUESTION IS," SAID ALICE, "WHETHER YOU CAN MAKE WORDS MEAN SO MANY DIFFERENT THINGS."

What is jazz? By its very nature, the apocryphal answer "If you have to ask, you'll never know" sows doubt about our ever being able to arrive at a definitive answer. If anything, it implies an attitude of exclusion, "a nice knock-down argument for you," signifying a certain "glory" for an in-group playing by its own rules. What's more, perhaps the label *jazz* is not to be trusted all that much. In 1969 Duke Ellington, for example, was quoted as saying: "If 'jazz' means anything at all, which is questionable, it means the same thing it meant to musicians fifty years ago—freedom of expression. I used to have a definition, but I don't think I have one any more, unless it is a music with an African foundation which came out of an American environment."[1]

This book revisits the world of early jazz to examine just how it came to encompass the careers of both Paul Whiteman and Louis Armstrong—two musicians, both affectionately known to fans and colleagues alike as "Pops." In the words of cultural essayist Gerald Early: "These are the twin father figures of American popular music . . . both heavy and both popular as personalities as much as for their musical abilities . . . two fathers, one black and one white."[2] They came from opposite sides of the tracks and inhabited worlds that would seem to be mutually exclusive. But closer scrutiny of their work, and of the contributions of those who fell within their respective orbits, reveals significant overlap and reciprocity. What is more—if this jazz-parsing process, focused on roughly the first four decades of the twentieth century, is to mean anything at all—it is imperative to confront issues of race, not to mention critical factors of class, category, and commerce. And as a corollary, there is the daunting challenge of confronting the very nature of jazz historiography as well as theories of the etymology of *jazz*—that is, the invention of the term itself and changes in its meaning over time. It is a challenge that brings one face to face with the issues of defining jazz history as an African-American narrative of appropriation and exploitation by whites. This effort to elevate a victimized race brings to mind the "noble lie" of Plato's *Republic*—a connection compellingly made by Arthur M. Schlesinger in *The Disuniting of America*, a collection of his musings on multiculturalism: "People live by their myths, and some may argue that the facts can be justifiably embroidered if embroiderment serves a higher good, such as the nurture of a nation or the elevation of a race. It may seem more important to maintain a beneficial fiction than to keep history pure—especially when there is no such thing as pure history anyway. This may have been what Plato had in mind when he proposed the idea of the 'noble lie' in *The Republic*."[3]

Armstrong's supreme position in the jazz pantheon as the first great soloist has never been in doubt. As Dan Morgenstern has put it: "Though he was never billed as the King of Jazz, Armstrong is the only legitimate claimant to that title. Without him there would of course have been the music called jazz, but how it might have developed is guesswork. This extraordinary trumpeter and singer was the key creator of the mature working language of jazz."[4] That regal title was at one time bestowed on Whiteman, first as part of an advertising campaign for brass instruments and later in a 1930 movie. Yet his role as an outstanding pioneer has generally been far more problematic, especially starting in the 1930s; more often than not he has been condemned in jazz history as a usurper or else been expunged from the record altogether. In 1990, for example, the centennial of his birth, there were no known celebrations in his honor. And the following excerpt from a 1996 double issue of *The New Yorker* entitled "Black in America" typifies the whacking of Whiteman:

> In the early decades of the century, Negro music came to dominate the new technologies of sound recording and radio so thoroughly that, in 1924, an

alarmed music establishment sought out a syncopationally challenged band-leader by the comically apt name of Paul Whiteman and designated him "the King of Jazz." But jazz and its offshoots could not be so easily tamed. The wildly creative creolization of African-American and European-American strains produced a profusion of mulatto musics.[5]

The issue of race has indeed bedeviled the discussion of jazz for almost one hundred years and continues to drive much of the recent discussion of the music and its performance. As the quintessential creation of the African-American twentieth century, jazz has by its very nature inspired fierce debate on both sides of the hyphenated epithet. By the same token, the claims of cultural ownership inflamed by the passions of ideology have all too often undermined any effort to dispassionately analyze the facts of jazz's origins or examine the sources of the word itself, let alone consider the multiple styles that the word describes. Certainly, the glib and derisive remarks of Hendrik Hertzberg and Henry Louis Gates, Jr., about Whiteman, while scoring points for an Afrocentrist position, fail to identify "an alarmed music establishment" or to explain how it came to seek out "a syncopationally challenged bandleader." And how in fact did Whiteman acquire his "King of Jazz" crown and continue to rule his kingdom?

In seeking answers one should do no less than reexamine a legacy reaching back to the early years of the twentieth century, when it seems that the towering presence of Paul Whiteman was almost everywhere. The trajectory of his career carries us on a path from west to east, providing a bicoastal view of jazz that draws attention to simultaneous and sometimes contradictory developments in San Francisco, Los Angeles, Atlantic City, and New York. Through it all Whiteman was the entrepreneur par excellence, with extraordinary access to money and media, the supreme purveyor of dance music in his capacity as "The King of Jazz"—a catalyst for far-reaching developments. It was on his bandstand that some three hundred musicians over the course of about two decades honed their craft, among them Bix Beiderbecke, Frank Trumbauer, Joe Venuti, Eddie Lang, Bing Crosby, Jack Teagarden, and Jimmy and Tommy Dorsey, performing a broad spectrum of arrangements by Ferde Grofé, Bill Challis, and others. In the words of Joe Venuti: "Don't ever make fun of Paul Whiteman. He took pride in having the finest musicians in the world and paid the highest salaries ever paid."[6]

Then again, pointed comparison of selected Whiteman recordings of the 1920s with those of King Oliver, Louis Armstrong, Fletcher Henderson, and Duke Ellington from the same general period lead any open-minded, perceptive listener to conclude that Whiteman was more often the leader than the follower. What is more, in countries beyond the United States—England, Germany, and Russia, to name a few—his stature was immense. Most illustrative is the case of the Russian pianist Leopold Teplitsky. He arrived in the United States in early 1926 with a directive from the Commissariat of Public Enlightenment to "master the techniques of American jazz, buy up stock arrangements and all the necessary musical instruments, and then put all to use in a new jazz orchestra for the city of Lenin's revolution." Upon his return to Leningrad in 1927 Teplitsky was carrying crates of recordings, more than twenty Paul Whiteman arrangements, and more than forty instruments.[7]

Much to his credit, Whiteman helped break racial barriers, hiring Don Redman and William Grant Still as arrangers and commissioning Duke Ellington to compose *Blue Belles of Harlem*. In moments of crisis he came to the defense of a Louis Armstrong or an Earl Hines. By the late 1930s Whiteman had such musicians as Benny Carter, Louis Armstrong, and Roy Eldridge on the same stage. For his part, Armstrong was able to breach such barriers as well, sharing the spotlight with such Whiteman alumni as Mildred Bailey, Bing Crosby, Jack Teagarden, Eddie Lang, Joe Venuti, and the Dorsey Brothers. In the process jazz and popular styles came to be melded and a common core repertoire shared: such standards as "Ain't Misbehavin'," "Body and Soul," "Dinah," "Basin Street Blues," "Jeepers Creepers," "Rockin' Chair," and "St. Louis Blues." Whiteman and Armstrong became icons of mainstreaming, always committed to their public—"laying it on them," as Armstrong would have put it—energizing the world of mass entertainment.

1 BEGINNINGS

WE FIRST MET . . . JAZZ AND I . . . AT A DANCE DIVE ON THE BARBARY COAST. IT SCREECHED AND BELLOWED AT ME FROM A TRICK PLATFORM IN THE MIDDLE OF A SMOKE-HAZED, BEER-FUMED ROOM. . . . MY WHOLE BODY BEGAN TO SIT UP AND TAKE NOTICE. IT WAS LIKE COMING OUT OF BLACKNESS INTO BRIGHT LIGHT. . . . I WANTED TO WHOOP. I WANTED TO DANCE.

Paul Whiteman's confession harks back to a time in 1917 when he was adrift in San Francisco, often "blue all day," frustrated with dead-end symphony work, yet on the cusp of the most dramatic change in his life. He was not long out of Denver, where he had grown up as the son of Wilberforce Whiteman. His father, named after the great English abolitionist William Wilberforce (1759–1833), was a stern man who made no bones about his disgust with Paul's lack of direction.[1] On his son's twenty-fourth birthday, March 28, 1914, Wilberforce had served the floundering youth with what was in effect an eviction notice from the family home. Paul reportedly overheard his father say to his mother: "It seems that our son has his mind set upon not amounting to anything. I've tried to see that he have a proper start. I've led the horse to water, as the saying is. But what do we see? A lazy fellow who indifferently plays a viola in a theater orchestra, and then drives a taxicab the rest of the night in the most immoral part of the city. . . . His proper place is no longer here with us, Mother. We've done all we can for the boy. The truth is I don't want him around any longer."[2]

Soon after, with the help of five hundred dollars surreptitiously given him by his mother, Paul Whiteman packed his bags and left Denver for good, heading west to San Francisco. He hoped to find work there as a symphony musician, another foray into the classical music world which he hoped, fruitlessly, would win his father's respect. Job prospects on the West Coast looked especially promising that year. The Panama-Pacific International Exposition, a 288-day wonder in 1915, was drawing crowds from all over the world. Rising like a phoenix from the ashes of the 1906 earthquake, San Francisco was also celebrating the opening of the Panama Canal. Paul Whiteman had the good luck to get a position in the viola section of the eighty-piece San Francisco Exposition Orchestra performing at the Union Pacific Railroad exhibit on the fairgrounds. The repertoire was far-ranging. One of the stars was the octogenarian Camille Saint-Saëns, visiting from France, who conducted several of his own works. There was also an American Composers' Day, featuring native composers like Amy Marcy Beach and George Chadwick, both of Boston, and Horatio Parker, teacher of Charles Ives from Yale. And there were added attractions, like performances by the charismatic dancer-choreographer of the day Loie Fuller and her company, beguiling audiences with such presentations as "A Thousand and One Nights."

The young Whiteman, knowing that his nights in the orchestra would necessarily number fewer than a thousand, kept his eye out for other work and was fortunate to be given a seat in the San Francisco Symphony under Alfred Hertz in September. But that too would be short-lived. With guaranteed earnings during the 1915–16 season of only $25 a week for sixteen weeks—subsequently raised to the munificent sum of $40 per week—he was constantly on the alert for other opportunities to make money. Convinced that the orchestra was a dead end financially, he resigned at the end of the 1917–18 season and turned to playing popular numbers and ragtime novelties with a combo he organized, performing mostly at such venues as an ice rink and various San Francisco hotels. He was surprised to discover how much he could earn by playing jazz fiddle, and how much he liked playing this new kind of music.

San Francisco's Barbary Coast was the hotbed of this brand of music, coming from a "stagnant pool of immorality and crime spread[ing] its contaminating vapors over the surrounding blocks on either side . . . the haunt of the low and vile of every kind," who could be found thronging at dance houses, concert saloons, gambling houses, and opium dens.[3] The district—located in the northwestern area of the city bounded by Broadway and Pacific Streets, and extending from Stockton east to the waterfront of San Francisco Bay—had, by "the Gay Nineties," given San Francisco notoriety as "The Wickedest City in the World."

In order to fully enter his new life, the rebel son had to consciously reject the moral high ground of his early Denver roots and the possibility of his father's approval. Wilberforce's attitude toward jazz has been widely quoted. In 1938, when his son was a well-established international celebrity, Wilberforce remained the inveterate curmudgeon: "When it comes to 'swing music,' you can have my portion. I have always been addicted to frank speech, and I say plainly that I DO NOT LIKE swing or jazz or ragtime or whatever you choose to call it. . . . They say swing started with the savages back in the wilds of Darkest Africa. As far as I am concerned, they can have it right back. I am not a jungle chieftain, and I don't see why I should have to listen to jungle music any more than I have to eat jungle food."[4]

Whiteman himself implies that his painful experience of depression and his strong determination to make something of himself in the burgeoning world of jazz were related to his growing up the son of Wilberforce Whiteman at the end of the nineteenth century. A child of the frontier, Paul was born in Denver on March 28, 1890, the eighty-seventh day of "the Gay Nineties," a decade that brought a surge in the popularity of ragtime. It was also only fourteen years since the Colorado Territory had been admitted to the Union as the thirty-eighth state, and memories were still fresh of the "fifty-niners" striking gold in Cripple Creek, and very soon also silver and lead elsewhere. In 1894, when Paul was four years old, his father assumed a position of considerable local authority when he was appointed superintendent of music for Denver's entire school system, a position he was to occupy for thirty years until his retirement in 1924. Even afterward he continued to be a force on the local scene until his death in 1939. It is ironic, considering his low opinion of jazz, that two notable African-American jazz musicians, Andy Kirk (1898–1992) and Jimmie Lunceford (1902–47), received their first musical training in Denver schools on Wilberforce's watch. Another member of this generation was the pianist Harry Barris, who with his New York Jewish family relocated to Denver when he was in his teens. Not only did he study music in high school with Wilberforce Whiteman, he, Al Rinker, and Bing Crosby later also became an exciting part of Paul Whiteman's act as the Rhythm Boys.

Wilberforce was an American "type" of his time. He believed in the work ethic. He was known for his weekly official visits to area high schools, never missing the Monday morning assembly. His ritual on the first Monday morning of each new school year was particularly memorable. Gene Fowler, a contemporary of Paul Whiteman's who passed through the local school system, vividly recalls:

Wilberforce would pass from desk to desk, at which the students sat in threes, to select a chorus to occupy the rostrum of the assembly hall. During the master's march along the aisles, pianist Sue Miller would play "America" over and over. Mr. Whiteman would pause briefly, now with a tuning fork instead of a pitch pipe in hand, diagnose a voice, leaning over a candidate like a specialist in lung diseases. . . . Mr. Whiteman leaned above me and my two friends. He endured my phrasing . . . then turned to Sullivan, taking everything but his blood pressure. Then he crooked a finger, not at Sullivan but at me, and motioned for me to take a chair on the platform.[5]

This emphasis on the work ethic perhaps best explains Wilberforce's obsession with drawing up formal contracts between himself and Paul. This seems to have started when the boy was all of seven. One of Paul's hobbies was woodworking, which carried with it written obligations specified by Wilberforce:

1. Paul Whiteman, herein known as the party of the second part, agrees to take the best care of all tools provided by the party of the first part, Wilberforce J. Whiteman.
2. Said tools will be kept sharp and clean and well oiled after each time they are used.
3. Said party of the second part agrees and promises to put tools away after use, sweep all sawdust and shavings from the bench and floor, look out for fire hazards, and not waste nails, screws, or wood.[6]

However Paul might have bridled at his father's autocratic ways, he did learn some valuable lessons for later in life; for it is no secret that his acumen in the handling of business contracts was formidable, what with the hundreds of sidemen, singers, arrangers, publishers, and media moguls with whom he had to deal over several decades. It comes as no surprise that when Paul was learning to play the violin or viola at a tender age, his father once again had him sign a written agreement. This specified, among other things, that the party of the first part would spend a total of sixty-five dollars on an instrument and cover the cost of lessons during the year. Paul, in return, would owe his father one hour's practice a day; any day he failed to keep his end of the bargain, he would owe his father an hour's service.

Matters came to a head one summer's day around 1901, when Paul was about eleven years of age. It came at a point when he would just as soon have been outdoors playing ball or swimming. Besides, he had already protested by threatening to run away, but no one paid heed. True to form, Wilberforce, rigidly following the letter of the law he had imposed, was simply not going to yield one iota. "We can't get around something we both signed. I haven't quite decided what I want you to do during the time you owe me. So, until then, suppose you spend it in your mother's sewing room."[7]

Once locked in the room, Paul discovered that his violin and a book of études had been deliberately placed there . . . a further form of humiliation by his father. Understandably enraged, Paul smashed the instrument over his mother's sewing machine, only to have his father come into the room and insist that Paul pay back the sixty-five dollars spent on the instrument: "damages, you know." And before long Wilberforce was back with a lawnmower and shears, not to mention a new contract: mowing lawns for the next two years was Paul's immediate fate. The labor apparently traumatized him so that the smell of newly cut grass forever reminded him of the rage he felt at having been imprisoned in that sewing room.

Wilberforce had strong opinions on the importance of channeling boyhood aggression and cultivating manliness. He was a man with powerful forearms who had been a champion cornhusker in his native Ohio, one who would put on the boxing gloves with his son every day except Sunday. This commitment to physical activity would seem to have taken a leaf or two from the immensely popular book of Thomas Hughes, *Tom Brown's Schooldays*. In Hughes's book, Thomas Arnold, the legendary headmaster of Rugby School, is a proponent of the idea of a hardy masculinity, dubbed Muscular Christianity. In the words of the baseball pro turned star evangelist, Billy Sunday, Jesus was "no dough-faced, lick-spittle proposition" but rather "the greatest scrapper who ever lived."[8] Paul's formative teenage years coincided exactly with the two presidential terms of Theodore Roosevelt, the preeminent public figure of the day and quintessential muscular model, who occupied the White House from 1901 to 1909. Wilberforce Whiteman might not "speak softly and carry a big stick," regularly go on the mat with a pair of judo experts, or engage in pillow fights with his children, but he did take boxing very seriously.

Fists indeed helped define young Paul, muscle sometimes superseding music. He grew up imbibing a form of muscular Christianity on the frontier that promoted the development of manliness and self-discipline through sports, athletic organizations, the branches of the Young Men's Christian Association, the Boy Scouts, and the like. These values are broadly hinted at by Paul Whiteman in the course of his 1926 book *Jazz*: "Wilberforce J. Whiteman, my father, is the best balanced man I know. For thirty years, he was director of music education in the Denver schools. He never had a drink until he was fifty-five and never smoked until he was sixty. Yet he wasn't priggish in the least. He was always keen on athletics and was really proud of me the time the Denver Y.M.C.A. named me among a dozen physically perfect fellows in the gym class. He was plumb disgusted when I began to get fat and used to try to make me box it off."[9]

Thirty years later, in 1956, reminiscing about those years on the occasion of the dedication of Denver's Wilberforce J. Whiteman Elementary School, Whiteman injected a note of boyhood realism: "The Denver kids then, including myself, weren't exactly what you would call music lovers. They used to call dad 'Willie Willie Whiteman, do-mi-so.' Naturally they called me that too. That's how I learned to fight."[10] We learn also that Wilberforce himself could make a news splash, readily resorting to fisticuffs outside of the home to settle scores. Writing in 1933 as a Broadway columnist, Ed Sullivan recounted an episode on Denver's West Side:

> The elder Whiteman, a slender and wiry gentleman, was popular in all Denver schools, but on the West Side he loomed a hero. In 1905 he incurred the dislike of an especially tough gangster at the Elmwood School. Professor Whiteman had decided that the young thug was a tenor, whereas the affronted young man decided he would sing bass or not at all. One word led to another, and when school let out for the day, it was reported that the young man was waiting to paste the professor in the nose. "I'd leave by the side door if I were you," the principal advised Whiteman. "If you were I," said the professor, "you'd leave by the front door and that's how I'm leaving." When he reached the street he found a hundred boys waiting to witness the massacre. As the disgruntled young tough stepped up, raising a right fist, Paul Whiteman's dad countered with the nicest left hook ever delivered, until Jack Dempsey, another Colorado product, began to make pugilistic history. The professor received an ovation as he walked calmly away to catch a Lawrence Street car. From that time on a male pupil would even sing falsetto if Professor Whiteman counseled that register.[11]

Yet except for a few occasions, attaining a robust manliness was something that eluded Paul. Indeed, during his teen years we find his physical problems multiplying. Stricken with typhoid fever, he permanently lost most of his hair and during recovery developed an insatiable craving for food. Chronic weight problems and baldness were to dog him for the rest of his life. When he eventually returned to school, he did poorly, attending at least three different high schools between 1903 and 1907. Failing grades and difficulties with his father were coupled with confrontations with teachers and administrators. And it was not long before he landed in juvenile court charged with greasing the city's trolley tracks with butter. A subsequent brief stint at the University of Denver meant taking "physics, football and my lunch."

Careening as he did through his teens, Paul did nevertheless find a measure of stability in his music making . . . a source of fulfillment to both his father and himself. In fact, in a sanitized family history, dated 1936, Wilberforce Whiteman makes a point of praising his son, who, following the violin-smashing episode in his mother's sewing room, had taken up the viola. Referring to a performance of *Messiah* which he directed, Wilberforce writes of his son: "Although only 12 years old . . . after seven lessons [he] played the viola parts perfectly."[12] In addition, as a big booster of the musicians' local, Wilberforce ensured that his Paul became a member of the union. Under existing rules orchestras had to exhaust the supply of local talent before importing musicians from elsewhere.

Accordingly, some two years later we find Paul, only fourteen years old, playing viola in Raffaelo Cavallo's symphony orchestra, in various groups at Denver's Brown Palace Hotel, the Broadway Theater, and other venues. But what clearly dominated the music making of the Whitemans as a family was performing the Anglo-German Handel-Haydn-Mendelssohn oratorio repertoire, the vital Victorian manifestation of an evangelism that defined much of musical life on both sides of the Atlantic. Music seems to have been an integral part of family life, with Wilberforce also serving as musical director of Trinity Methodist Church and both parents giving private lessons in their home on South First Street. Elfrida Whiteman, in particular, was well known in the Denver area for her solo work in major oratorio repertoire; staples included such works as Handel's *Messiah, Judas Maccabeus,* Samson, Haydn's *Creation,* and Mendelssohn's *Elijah.* Elfrida invariably joined her husband and the Trinity Choir, 150 to 250 strong, augmented by singers and players from area high schools. She would also on occasion appear further afield, in such locales as New York and most notably Boston, bastion of the Handel and Haydn Society.

By 1908 the opposite sex, rather than visions of the hereafter, came to influence much of Paul Whiteman's life; he had developed enough of a roving eye to plan to elope with a touring chorus girl some six or seven years his senior. Meanwhile, the relationship between father and son had sunk to a new low, epitomized by what reportedly transpired one morning at breakfast. Recovering from a nervous breakdown following the ordeal of organizing a mammoth fund-raising concert, Wilberforce leaned across the table to say in a choked voice: "I don't like the way you are holding your mouth. Put it back the way it ought to be." When Paul stood up and left the table, his father grabbed a chair and broke it across his son's back. As Paul dashed for the door, his father is said to have yelled: "And don't think you'll ever be old enough or big enough to lick me!"[13]

Whiteman decided he had had enough of his father's tyranny and made plans to join his chorus-girl sweetheart, Nellie Stack, now back on the road with her show, in New York. He told his father that he wanted to make the trip to New York to explore opportunities for studying music. The ruse worked. With his father's money in his pocket for train fare and a hotel room, he made his way to Manhattan. Yet only two weeks later he was mysteriously back in Denver, very quiet and dejected. It was only about two years later, when a "Dear Sir" letter arrived addressed to Wilberforce Whiteman, that the mystery was solved. Nellie Stack wanted the marriage annulled. It seems that Paul had been a minor at the time of the ceremony, and "it would be no great trouble to you to have the annulment procured."

How his father reacted to this news we can only surmise. It certainly did not strengthen the father-son bond. Whiteman was to endure some six more years in Denver, including a stint as first-chair violist in the local symphony, until his father's frustrated "I don't want him around any longer" precipitated his departure for San Francisco. He was rebellious and also depressed—out on his own. When he tells us how he first encountered jazz, saying "it hit me hard," we feel that he is touching a raw nerve. Much of the intensity of this impact has to be understood against the background of not only the vicissitudes of his prior musical experience, but also the issues of the exalted pedigree that his father claimed. It seemed to widen the gap between father and son even more. Nothing could be further removed from "the middle of a smoke-hazed, beer-fumed room" on the Barbary Coast than Wilberforce Whiteman's musings on family lineage and accomplishment, jottings dating from his final years:

> The Whiteman family has for generations been endowed with an exceptional talent for music. Not only has this blessing been bestowed upon them, but they have been given self-control and qualities of leadership. . . .
>
> Wilberforce J. Whiteman, through his paternal grandmother, Rebecca Lackey Whiteman, traces his ancestry back to the early nobility of Scotland, in one case to Bruce, in another to Wallace, and still further back to the Norman knights. He is a direct descendant of Andrew Stewart of the House of Ochiltree of Scotland. Andrew Stewart, son of the second Lord of Avondale, was ordained by an Act of Parliament, March 13, 1542, to be called Lord of Ochiltree.

Sir Walter Scott in his *Lady of the Lake* mentions the house of Lord Stewart of Ochiltree. The lives of the Stewarts, Lords of Ochiltree, read like romance.[14]

Paul Whiteman's encounter with the music of the Barbary Coast came not a moment too early. Campaigns to close down the Coast—with slogans like "A Clean City for a Clean People"—were already under way by 1913. The district finally succumbed in November 1921, a casualty of the crusading *San Francisco Examiner* of William Randolph Hearst, local Methodists, World War I, and Prohibition. But the young Whiteman was still able to see plenty of action, much of it generated by the fervor for popular dance music. The decade between 1910 and 1920 has been described as "the period in which America went dance mad." In its October 1913 issue, for example, the magazine *Current Opinion* breathlessly described the dancing mania: "People who have not danced before in twenty years have been dancing during the past summer, afternoons as well as evenings. Up-to-date restaurants provide a dancing floor so that patrons may lose no time while the waiter is changing plates. Cabaret artists are disappearing except as interludes while people recover their breaths for the following number."

Animal dances were the rage, "as if Uncle Remus had joined high society."[15] They made up a menagerie that included the turkey trot, the bunny hug, the chicken glide, the grizzly bear, and more. Starting in the honky-tonks, dance halls, and tenderloin districts in the West and South, these dances developed on San Francisco's Barbary Coast before shaking up the status quo in cities like New York. Anna Pavlova, the famous Russian ballerina of the day, was on a slumming tour with society folk when she visited one of the dance halls on Pacific Street, the main stem of the Barbary Coast. She tried the turkey trot and was positively enthralled. She declared: "The turkey trot is a wonderful dance. It is something quite different from anything I have ever known before. . . . I am going to dance it and introduce it in Russia and throughout all Europe. It is full of possibilities. . . . I will have a great and beautiful ballet made of it . . . that will astonish the world."[16]

By 1912 dances like the turkey trot made it to New York as part of a vaudeville production from San Francisco entitled *Over the River*. The show gave audiences the thrill of seeing dancers perform the "fast, marching one-step, arms pumping at the side, with occasional arm-flappings emulating a crazed turkey." Adding to the excitement was the tune "Everybody's Doing It," containing the refrain "It's a bear," at which point "the dancers are supposed to lurch like a grizzly bear—another dance from the West."[17] There were denunciations by churchmen, even condemnation by the Vatican.[18]

Publications such as *Harper's Weekly* stoked the fires of controversy by printing such sensationalist pieces as "Where Is Your Daughter This Afternoon?"—a dire warning that some young miss dancing at the local hotel might be trotting her way to hell.[19]

The animal dance craze was a manifestation of something much bigger—a fascination with the exotic, with the Other, placing us astride the fault line separating black and white, and the challenges of making jazz "acceptable." Straddling that line is a vast body of literature and attendant scandal, from around the 1850s and continuing through the 1920s, involving the psychology of sex. Names like Havelock Ellis, Richard von Krafft-Ebing, Lord Alfred Douglas, Walt Whitman, Oscar Wilde, and Sigmund Freud are perhaps the most prominent. Often implicit in their writings is the colonial vision of the "noble savage," typifying the mysterious lure of the remote and unknown that came to profoundly shape the thinking of novelists like Joseph Conrad in such works as *Lord Jim* (1900) and *Heart of Darkness* (1902). But nothing could equal the subsequent mass appeal of the series of Tarzan stories that Edgar Rice Burroughs of Chicago's Oak Park published between 1912 and 1916. The inspiration for some fifty films, the story of Tarzan, the orphaned white-skinned baby lovingly raised by a family of apes in the jungle of French Equatorial Africa, is an explicitly colonial narrative caught between the worlds of the "primitive" and the civilized. The arrival of a human expedition makes Tarzan painfully aware not only that he is one of them but also that a member of his newly found family is about to cause the apes grievous harm. In addition, the trope of primitivism can be traced in the visual arts through the paintings of Henri Rousseau—his *Snake Charmer* and *Dream of the Gipsy* come to mind—not to mention Pablo Picasso's seminal cubist-primitive 1907 masterpiece *Les Demoiselles d'Avignon*. These works, in turn, provide a rich aesthetic context within which to situate such works as Igor Stravinsky's *Rite of Spring*, not to mention Darius Milhaud's Afrocentric ballet *La Création du Monde*, a work which, for Paul Whiteman, validated his efforts in the area of "symphonic jazz" and his avowed goal to "make a lady out of jazz."

The musical world that Whiteman entered during the years of World War I brought with it some heavy cultural baggage. And nothing more vividly dramatizes the divide that both separates and binds black and white than the tradition of the minstrel show. With its core of five performers, originally whites in blackface seated in semicircle, the minstrel show has been a disturbing part of the American consciousness from the 1820s to latter-day movies like Spike Lee's *Bamboozled*. In his study *Love and Theft*, Eric Lott examines the mindset of the masses, departing from what most others writing about minstrelsy have argued: that minstrel-show mimicry is based on a deep racial aversion. Rather, says Lott, "it was cross-racial desire that coupled a nearly insupportable fascination and a self-protective derision with respect to black people and their cultural practices, and that made blackface minstrelsy less a sign of absolute white power and control than of panic, anxiety, terror, and pleasure."[20] How else even to hazard an explanation of how the craze for early jazz around the time of World War I could be purveyed in a world governed by blatant segregationist laws of "separate but equal" associated with the *Plessy v. Ferguson* decision of 1896, a world in which lynchings were commonplace and D. W. Griffith's 1915 racist movie *Birth of a Nation* could prompt Woodrow Wilson, the twenty-eighth president of the United States, to say, "It is like writing history with lightning, and it is all so terribly true"?

Nowhere was the animal dance craze better promoted as a naughty-but-nice novelty for the white middle and upper classes than in New York City. It all came together when the attractive Anglo-American husband-and-wife dancing couple Vernon and Irene Castle joined forces in 1913 with the band of James Reese Europe (1881–1919). A native of Washington, D.C., where he grew up a few houses away from John Philip Sousa and received a solid grounding in violin and piano, Europe had made his initial mark around 1905 in Manhattan's world of all-black musical comedy, working with such notables as Will Marion Cook, Ernest Hogan, and Bob Cole. The infectious rhythms of ragtime and "syncopated" music, whether vocal or instrumental, seemed to be everywhere. And from 1912 to 1914 Europe made history by bringing ragtime or "syncopated" music into Carnegie Hall. Keenly attuned to the growing need for his brand of music, in 1910 Europe established a professional booking agency, the Clef Club, dispatching his musical forces throughout the city and the greater New York area to cater to the "smart set"—among them the Astors and the Vanderbilts—and their need for mildly risqué, more gentrified versions of such animal dances as the turkey trot, grizzly bear, or bunny hug. In its issue of November 22, 1914, the *New York Tribune* introduced James Reese Europe to its readers as the Castles' composer and bandleader, the man who, depending on an ensemble of violins, cornets, clarinets, mandolins, drum, and piano, had "all but secured complete control of the cabaret and dance field in the city."

Even though these were very largely note-reading, "straight" players who rarely improvised, they caught the pulse of the times to perfection. It was Europe's rendition of W. C. Handy's "Memphis Blues," in particular, that inspired Irene and Vernon Castle to create the fox-trot box step embellished with a few elegant glides and turns. As a result, the blues-inflected idiom of the fox-trot was soon to make its way into the mainstream of American popular culture, largely through the influence of Paul Whiteman.

Naughtier and more raucous was the music of the contemporaneous all-white Original Dixieland Jazz Band, the first commercially successful "hot" Dixieland ensemble. This five-piece combo, part of a fad for the frenzied music making of New Orleans novelty orchestras, was rattling the rafters of the Paradise Room at Reisenweber's, New York's "newest, largest and best-equipped restaurant," at Eighth Avenue and 58th Street. Primarily "ear" musicians rather than note-readers, the ODJB—"untuneful harmonists playing peppery melodies"—had a certain stilted rhythmic intensity coupled with a penchant for breaks offering rather crude barnyard imitations. Some of this can be heard in their first recordings, dating from 1917, in such numbers as "Livery Stable Blues," "Barnyard Blues," and "Ostrich Walk." Opinions differ on the matter of their significance. Louis Armstrong, for example, remembered them as one of his favorites when he started buying records around 1917 or 1918. A contrasting view comes in 1924, on the occasion of the historic February 12 concert featuring the world premiere of Gershwin's *Rhapsody in Blue* conducted by Paul Whiteman with his Palais Royal Orchestra, the composer himself at the piano. The primary object of Whiteman's concert, as stated proudly in the program, was to demonstrate "the tremendous strides which have been made in popular music from the day of the discordant jazz"—strides achieved through the art of "legitimate scoring" in "symphonic jazz"—a development, as we shall soon see, made possible by the decisive contributions of Ferde Grofé. In this brave new world, the music making of ODJB is seen as part of a primitive past: "'Livery Stable Blues' is one of the many popular Jazz tunes of the past. The shrieking clarinet, thumping piano and the clattering traps describe vividly a husky hostler dragging his wife by the hair around their squalid hut behind the stable. The 'G-r-r-r!' of the cornet and the moan of the trombone are Fido and Towser barking, yapping and howling outside the door, eager to get into the fray. This tune is Jazz in its true, naked form."[21]

The first appearance of ODJB in New York, almost exactly seven years earlier, had created a sensation, prompting the youthful Damon Runyon to pen some ringing verses in his capacity as a new columnist for the *New York American*. A later companion to Al Capone, Jack Dempsey, and Babe Ruth, Runyon would become widely known for his racy tales of the underworld, not to mention such works as *Guys and Dolls* (1932).

I hear a far away tap, tap, tapping,
That fills my soul with joy.
It's from the Levee; the Levee—
The Mississippi Levee,
And it's wonderful—Oh, BOY!
There's a shuff-shuff, shuff-shuff shuffle;
Grab your partner by the hand—
It's that
    hazy,
    mazy,
    drive-you-crazy
    music of the old Jaz band!
It makes your backbone feel peculiar,
It makes your spare ribs tingle so
Oh, your hands are shaking
And your heart is aching
When you hear that sweet jazboe.
It makes your feet go slip-slip sliding—
Hit 'em a lick! Buh—LAM!
It's that moany, groany, saxophony
music of the old Jaz band![22]

The dancing riffs of Runyon's lines, the images of the old South, the idio-syncratic spelling of *jaz*, not to mention the allusion to the seductive call of the saxophone, are all most compelling. Runyon's usage, at a time before the word became standardized as the universally familiar four-letter *jazz*, raises crucial questions about the very nature of the form and the origins of the word. Typical of the time is the promotional copy touting the "Original Dix-ieland Jass Band" that appeared on the front cover of the March 1917 Victor Records catalog: "Spell it Jass, Jas, Jaz or Jazz—nothing can spoil a Jass band. Some say the Jass band originated in Chicago. Chicago says it comes from San Francisco—San Francisco being away off across the continent. Anyway, a Jass band is the newest thing in the cabarets."[23]

Clearly lacking here is any consistent spelling for *jazz*, a fact that points to the origins of the word in the folk tradition—something which has prompted many theories about its possible etymology, none of them definitive. But ori-gins are not the only issue. Even more daunting is clearly separating the strands of pre-1920 jazz—ragtime dance music, the one-step, and the me-nagerie of animal dances, not to mention blues. In addition, there were ap-

1.1 Front cover of Victor Records catalog of March 1917, promoting a wild new music to a world unsure of its spelling. Courtesy of the Hogan Jazz Archive, Tulane University.

parently regional differences in semantics rather than actual musical style, so that "there is overwhelming agreement among New Orleans musicians who were playing before 1920 that 'jazz' was just a fashionable, Northern name for New Orleans instrumental ragtime."[24] Compounding the challenge is the fact that both blues and ragtime could refer to discrete written forms as well as to unwritten styles of performance; this was a general rule that was to gradually change in the 1920s as the first concerted efforts were made to notate what had previously been unwritten.

So through it all, *jazz* was a loose term in the teens of the twentieth century, often used simply to mean popular dance music, the kind of jazz that so deeply touched the impressionable young Paul Whiteman. This was the brand of music making that he honed during his critical formative years as bandleader on the West Coast, from about 1917 to 1920, when he looked to musicians such as the Oakland-born Art Hickman (1886–1930) as a role model. It was Hickman who inspired the sonority of lead trumpet and trombone, sweetened by the addition of saxophone and violin, with the underpinning of a rhythm section consisting of piano, bass, and drums.

The youthful Art Hickman had been smitten by the sounds of the Barbary Coast, when he worked as a Western Union messenger. As he recalled in a 1928 interview: "I used to greet with joy the chance to deliver a message to some hop joint, or honky-tonky in the Barbary Coast. There was music. Negroes playing it. Eye shades, sleeves up, cigars in mouth. Gin, and liquor and smoke and filth. But music! There is where all jazz originated."[25]

Art Hickman's ensemble had provided the dance music in Boyes Hot Springs, where the San Francisco Seals baseball team was in spring training back in March 1913. Most fascinating is that these Hickman performances are associated with the first known appearances in print of the word *jazz*, in the sports pages of the *San Francisco Bulletin*. On March 3, for example, the paper ran a story by "Scoop" Gleeson about a promising rookie by the name of George McCarl: "McCarl has been heralded all along as a 'busher' [a clumsy novice], but now it develops that this dope is very much to the jazz. He has more boosters right now than any other two players at the Spa." Continuing in a similar vein, Gleeson writes three days later: "Everybody has come back full of the old 'jazz.' What is the 'jazz'? Why, it's a little of that 'old life,' the 'gin-i-ker,' the 'pep,' otherwise known as the enthusiasalum [*sic*]. The team, which speeded into town this morning, comes pretty close to representing the pick of the army. Its members have trained on ragtime and 'jazz' and Manger Del Howard says there's no stopping them."[26]

It was there and then that Art Hickman and his combo caught the attention of James Woods, the manager of one of San Francisco's most luxurious hotels, who hired them to perform at the St. Francis on Union Square in the summer of 1913—a move that set a precedent for Paul Whiteman and later bands on the hotel circuit. What Hickman brought to these venues was the timbre of the two saxophones added to his ensemble. The presence of the instruments themselves was not that unusual, given the number of stock arrangements from the period that include saxophones or the rosters of Mexican-American bands for the period from 1913 to 1916. What made the difference in Hickman's case was the addition of two players with distinctive personalities—Bert Ralton and Clyde Doerr.

Hickman's innovation was far-reaching in its effect in that the military-band, Dixieland model of cornet lead, trombone countermelody, and clarinet obbligato was modified in favor of a warmer and more varied texture. All of this was made possible by the dividing of the brass and reeds into sections, having countermelodies accompany statements by the brass, and inserting orchestrated "breaks"—that is, disruptions of the established rhythm, often filled with syncopated saxophone figures. In much of this Hickman was inspired by the example of Ferde Grofé (1892–1972), "a leading architect of the modern dance orchestra" and a man whose work was to have the most profound implications for Whiteman's own future.[27] Here was a highly accomplished, versatile musician bearing the seed of "symphonic jazz," who had the experience of working both sides of the tracks—a multi-instrumentalist who had played viola in the Los Angeles Philharmonic as well as pursuing an active career as pianist and conductor in assorted theaters, cafés, dance halls, and mining camps, as well as on silent movie lots (where his music set the mood for the actors).[28] Best known for his later orchestration of Gershwin's *Rhapsody in Blue* and such musical travelogues as *Grand Canyon Suite,* Grofé first entered Whiteman's life around 1915, when Whiteman sought him out at Porta La Louvre, a night spot outside of the Barbary Coast district, at the corner of Powell and Market Streets.

Whiteman was intrigued by Grofé's improvisations and arrangements, particularly his adeptness in turning classical staples into dance numbers. A close relationship soon developed. Even though Whiteman was fired after sitting in for two nights with the house band at Tait's Restaurant—he was told he simply could not play jazz—he remained undaunted. Hanging around the Barbary Coast's dives and restaurants and their environs, he soaked up all that he could of the new music, especially the way each player improvised or "faked" each part for himself. Part of his learning curve meant figuring out how to best capture the flavor of jazz improvisation as he had heard it, accurately notating it as an integral part of a dance band orchestration—an area where Grofé's expertise was to prove invaluable. Indeed, it was musicians like Grofé who helped define the sound of Whiteman's fledgling group that soon began performing on the hotel circuit, at venues like the Alexandria in Los Angeles, San Francisco's Fairmont, and Santa Barbara's Belvedere.

1.2 Paul Whiteman and his Jazz Classique Orchestra at the time of their opening at the Alexandria Hotel, Los Angeles, late December 1919. From left, Henry Busse (trumpet), Harold McDonald (drums), T. E. "Buster" Johnson (trombone), J. K. "Spike" Wallace (bass), Paul Whiteman (violin), Charles Caldwell (piano), Leslie Canfield (saxophone), Charles Dornberger (saxophone), Mike Pingitore (banjo). Courtesy of Cynthia Magill.

No account of Paul Whiteman's formative California years would be complete without some mention of his service in the U.S. Navy toward the end of World War I. It provided valuable experience in developing self-discipline and in honing his leadership skills. He was stationed during 1918 (April 27–June 21 and June 26–December 13) on Mare Island, Vallejo, "Uncle Sam's principal seat of Pacific Coast defense," some twenty-five miles northeast of San Francisco in San Pablo Bay. There he directed a twelve-piece ensemble, the Naval Training Camp Symphony. According to the *Mare Island Bulletin* of October 17, Whiteman's group "played at practically every theater in San Francisco, together with two weeks at the Columbia Theater. . . . [It] is in great demand for the Red Cross drives [and] Liberty Loan pageants, and plays at all picture shows on the island and at the three services on Sunday."

One of the few of Whiteman's early letters to survive can be dated from mid-June 1918, a little more than a week before his five-day leave. In it he shares with his mother sundry tidbits of naval life as well as some of his plans once he makes it back to the mainland.

> My dearest Mother:
>
> You ask what my duties are. Well, at present nothing. I have charge of the upper barracks and just boss the other fellows. The meals are fine, by the way. The sailors call it chow. But when I get out of here I am to lead the vaudeville show and play viola in a string quartet. I don't have to play in the band, so it is very soft unless I get shipped on a boat. Then I shall have to take up a brass instrument, but it isn't likely. I shall have to leave for a while. I get out of Detention a week from Monday. The bandmaster is very nice to me. He's come to me a couple of times and is going to give me leave for five days. . . .
> Love to both you and father.
> Paul.

On Mare Island, Paul Whiteman also crossed paths with musicians such as Art Landry, a classically trained violin prodigy from Montreal and Minneapolis, who subsequently found his niche in the world of jazz and dance music.[29] Around 1918 Art Landry and the saxophonist Rudy Wiedoeft took shore leave to go sit in with a number of hotel orchestras, particularly Art Hickman's in the Rose Room of San Francisco's St. Francis Hotel. In addition, Landry sat in with black orchestras on the Barbary Coast and played hotel tea dances with a small combo put together by Paul Whiteman.

Toward the end of 1919 Whiteman, now fronting a nine-piece orchestra—a front line of trumpet, trombone, violin, and two saxophones, with a rhythm section of drums, string bass, piano, and banjo—became a major presence on the California fancy hotel circuit. Starting at the Fairmont Hotel in San Francisco, he was soon heard at the Alexandria Hotel in Los Angeles, where on December 22 he began an auspicious run; and it was there that he became the darling of the movie colony. Among his admirers were D. W. Griffith (Whiteman had provided musical accompaniment for his 1916 movie *Intolerance*), Charlie Chaplin, Fatty Arbuckle, Mabel Normand, Harold Lloyd, and Cecil B. DeMille. Performances followed at hotels in Santa Barbara and Pasadena, where his band entertained the King of Belgium.

Paul Whiteman's acclaimed appearances with his orchestra at upscale area hotels soon caught the attention of one of the major real estate developers of the day, Simon William Straus. Straus, generally recognized as the originator of the modern real estate mortgage bond, was to later underwrite the construction of some of New York City's best-known landmarks, among them the Chrysler Building and Chanin Building, not to mention the Ziegfeld Theater. His immediate interest in Whiteman, however, arose from his desire to hire a dance band for his newly built (1919) Ambassador Hotel in Atlantic City. The largest hotel of the day on the Boardwalk, it fast became the vacation spot of choice for such notables as Enrico Caruso, President Warren Harding, and Sir Arthur Conan Doyle. Times were booming and Atlantic City's preeminence as the center of "ocean madness" was made secure in September 1921 with the first Miss America beauty pageant. And so it was that Paul Whiteman and his nine-piece band headed east, guaranteed a one-year contract for $1,200 per week, with $2,600 advanced for the train trip—big money for those days.[30]

One good thing led to another—a case of serendipity at its best. In the course of the final three days of June 1920 the National Association of Talking Machine Jobbers held its convention in Atlantic City. Meanwhile a representative of the Victor Phonograph Company happened to lunch at the Ambassador Hotel, where he heard the band play and was impressed enough to offer them a contract. As a result, Whiteman and his Orchestra found themselves in Victor's Camden, N.J., studios on August 9, making their first recordings, with two more sessions following that same month. In fact, Whiteman was soon to strike it rich as a Victor artist, scoring hits with such fox-trots as "Whispering" and "The Japanese Sandman"; "Avalon—Just Like a Gypsy," a medley fox-trot; and the one-step "Best Ever Medley."[31]

Whiteman's success attested to his savvy in cultivating the suave two-saxophone sonority with full rhythm section, a model inspired by the example of Art Hickman and the skill of Ferde Grofé's arrangements. Here was the essence of the syncopated dance orchestra. His rise also was fueled by changes in the dance band business as a whole in the larger New York area starting in the late teens—in particular, the untimely death on May 9, 1919, of James Reese Europe. The evidence is overwhelming that before around 1919, black and Creole musicians maintained a virtual monopoly in supplying dance music for whites. Talking about the Boston scene of the time, one musician recalled, "Well you see, up till the First World War there was nothing but black musicians. White musicians didn't have a chance."[32] White band members were frustrated by a pervasive preference for black musicians. As one Eugene de Bueris complained bitterly in a letter to the Boston *Globe*, it "will not be long before the poor white musician will be obliged to blacken his face to make a livelihood or starve."[33] Much the same conditions prevailed in New

York, where the bands of James Reese Europe, Ford Dabney, and Luckey Roberts, among others, had cornered the market for the best society gigs. Even in the mid-twenties Roberts, for example, is known to have been whisked down to Florida, hired by the well-heeled to perform for special occasions at Palm Beach.[34] Nor did it help the cause of racial harmony when, on July 27, 1919, a black teenager drowned at Chicago's Twenty-Ninth Street beach after being stoned by angry whites for accidentally floating across an unmarked barrier separating the races. Some six days of rioting and bloodshed in the Windy City made national headlines and left no doubt about the brutality born of segregation and discrimination. Race riots erupted in many other U.S. cities during that "Red Summer." Mounting xenophobia was reflected in the resurgence of the Ku Klux Klan and the passage of the Immigration Act of 1924 that enforced strict national quotas.

In young Louis Armstrong's New Orleans, segregation based on race and class was a long-standing reality. It was, after all, an incident on a New Orleans railroad car that had, in the case of *Plessy vs. Ferguson* in 1896, prompted the Supreme Court to uphold a Louisiana law creating separate carriages for black passengers. Legalized segregation—"separate but equal"—throughout the South, and many places elsewhere, was an ugly fact of daily life. What added color and tension to the Crescent City's distinctive complexion was the long-established caste system defined by color and language. Within the black community there were two distinct groups: the French-speaking, and sometimes Spanish-speaking, lighter-skinned Creoles lived downtown, while in the uptown neighborhoods were found the darker-skinned English speakers, many of them migrants from the rural hinterlands. The social statuses of these two groups were very different. The Creoles, originally from the West Indies, who lived east of Canal Street in the area of the French Quarter, enjoyed a tradition of relative freedom extending back to 1803 and 1812, when as a result of the Louisiana Purchase and Louisiana's statehood, they became Americans. At the turn of the twentieth century the city could boast of a sizable number of conservatory-trained "legitimate" Creole musicians, who performed at the Opera House, in chamber ensembles, and in upscale society bands—musicians, as we shall see, who showed some striking affinities with Paul Whiteman.

In sharp contrast to the Creoles, and in a totally different universe from Paul Whiteman, Louis Armstrong hailed from squalid Jane Alley, located in the poorest area of the city, west of Canal Street, in the "Back o' Town" slum. His parents were anything but socially prominent. He was born to the fifteen-year-old daughter of a former slave, Mary Albert (better known as Mayann), and her largely absent common-law husband, William Armstrong, who, by the time Louis was baptized at three weeks, had already abandoned mother and child. William Armstrong worked as a stoker at a local turpentine factory, had children by at least one other woman, and "was a freak for being the Grand Marshall for the Old Fellows Lodge, especially when they had funerals."[35]

There is another part of Louis Armstrong's family history which he himself barely knew about. Digging deeply into local property and notarial records, Tad Jones has traced Armstrong's ancestry back to 1818, at a time when New Orleans was one of the largest slave markets in the South. What apparently prompted the whole search was the name of a Catherine Walker, listed as baptismal sponsor of infant Louis at the Sacred Heart of Jesus Church. In fact, these baptismal records, authenticated in 1988, helped establish Armstrong's actual birth date as August 4, 1901, effectively discrediting the mythic date to which Armstrong held until his dying day: "I was a Southern Doodle dandy, born on the Fourth of July, 1900." And Catherine Walker, it turns out, rather than "a white neighbor whom the Armstrongs might have worked for," was Louis's great-grandmother.

It was thanks to a bulky volume entitled "Acts, Jan.–July 1818, Marc Lafitte, Notary" that Tad Jones was able to put it all together:

> On May 18, 1818, a slaveowner named Antoine Turcas purchased Daniel Walker, 32, from Richmond for about $600, a substantial price at the time. Walker, a further search of records showed, had a son, also named Daniel, who married Catherine Washington, born in 1837 and brought with her mother and sister from a plantation in Madison County, Miss., to New Orleans, where they were auctioned off together. Catherine and Daniel Walker had a daughter named Josephine who later married Ephraim Armstrong. They had a son named Willie, the father of Louis Armstrong. Catherine Walker, Louis's great-grandmother, attended the baby's baptism in 1901 as sponsor.[36]

Utterly amazing and profoundly moving was Armstrong's capacity to rise above this family history of slavery and privation to become an international icon, a human being of ebullient personality and often irrepressible humor, yet with a core of solid common sense. His personal memoir, *Satchmo: My Life in New Orleans,* was first published in 1954 and subsequently translated into a number of languages. Spanning the years from his childhood through the time of his arrival in Chicago in August 1922, the memoir stands as a remarkable document of a man of minimal education who was born on a dirt street in the poorest section of New Orleans. From the age of five until his departure for Chicago, Armstrong lived mostly at Liberty and Perdido in the heart of the black vice district—a world of pimps, hustlers, prostitutes, saloons, and gambling joints. His unique mix of personal attributes—toughness, sensitivity, drive, an innate optimism, and strength of character—helped make possible a truly inspiring rags-to-riches story told by a discerning critic of human nature.

Armstrong once summed up his experiences by saying: "My whole life has been happiness. Through all the misfortunes . . . I did not plan anything. Life was there for me, and I accepted it."[37] At the same time, he always felt indebted to Grandmother Josephine and his mother, Mayann Albert, for instilling in him a core of homespun, deceptively simple values that carried him through life: "I didn't go any further than fifth grade in school myself. But with my good sense and mother-wit, and knowing how to treat and respect the feelings of other people, that's all I've needed through life."[38]

Among the most inclusive and tolerant of music's immortals, Armstrong displayed an exemplary generosity of spirit, whether in matters of faith or of musical taste. "As far as religion, I'm a Baptist and a good friend of the Pope, and I always wear a Jewish star for luck. Those people who make the restrictions, they don't know nothing about music; it's no crime for cats of any color to get together and blow."[39] His idea of jazz, in particular, as "anything you can express to the public" is typical of the early twentieth century, just as his acceptance of music, in general, showed little concern for the boundaries of category. For example, when around 1917–18 he began collecting records, Armstrong gravitated toward leading pop and opera singers as well as the Original Dixieland Jazz Band, a fact borne out by his comments to Richard Meryman: "Big event for me then was buying a wind-up victrola. Most of my records were the Original Dixieland Jazz band—Larry Shields and his bunch. They were the first to record the music I played. I had Caruso records too, and Henry Burr, Galli-Curci, Tetrazzini—they were all my favorites. Then there was the Irish tenor McCormack—beautiful phrasing."[40]

Even many years later, in 1960, when he was interviewed on a Tampa radio station, Armstrong revealed an amazing openness to a broad range of styles. "I buy everybody's records. I carry two tape recorders and hi-fi portables. . . . I got all kinds of music—Beethoven and Bach and rock 'n' roll." Asked whether his first love is Dixieland, Armstrong retorted: "No, my first love is music."

Unlike Paul Whiteman, Louis Armstrong did not have an omnipresent, authoritarian father against whom to rebel. In fact, his having a largely ab-

1

Louis Armstrong + the Jewish Family
in New Orleans La.
The year of 1907

Written by Louis Armstrong — Ill in his Bed at the
Beth Isreal Hospital
March 31, 1969
New York City N.y.

A Real life story and Experiences.
At the age of seven years old
with the KORNORFSKY FAMILY (Jewish family)
The year of 1907.

All Scenes happened in New Orleans La.
Where Armstrong was Born.
The year 1900.

The Neighborhood was Consisted of NEGROS,
Jewish People And lots of CHINESE. But The
Jewish People in those early days were having
Problems of their own. Along with Hard
Times; from the other white Folks and
nationalities who felt
that they were better than the Jewish
Race. And took Advantage of every Chance
that they had to prove it.

1.3 Title page of "Louis Armstrong + the Jewish Family in New Orleans La. The
year of 1907." Courtesy of Louis Armstrong House and Archives.

sentee father was a blessing in disguise in that he sought out a series of surrogate fathers, even a surrogate family, who supported him in profound ways at crucial points in his career. On March 31, 1969, ill in his bed at Beth Israel Hospital, New York, and acutely aware of his own mortality, Armstrong began writing in longhand what would become a seventy-seven page confession, "Louis Armstrong and the Jewish Family in New Orleans La. The year of 1907." In "a real life story and experiences at the age of seven years old with the Kornorfsky [*sic*] family" (he was probably closer to six years of age), Armstrong writes a far-ranging memoir, characterized by Gary Giddins as "achingly candid."

He pays tribute to the Russian-Jewish family of junk dealers who were responsible for giving him his first job and who taught him so much—among other things, the virtues of a strong work ethic. "Working for these fine people I learned to be an early riser just like them. I noticed they believed in being on the move. Up early every morning, making hay while the sun shone. In Soulville, where I lived on the other side of town, the Negroes were just the opposite."[41]

This work ethic came to define his life and his need to connect with his public until the very end. Even though he was suffering from congestive heart failure and shortness of breath, he did not worry about dying onstage during what was to be his last gig, in March 1971 at the Waldorf Astoria's Empire Room. His dedication to his public was undiminished in its fervor. His personal physician, Dr. Gary Zucker, who attended him in his hotel suite, has recalled feeling a chill go up and down his spine as Armstrong, assuming the position of holding the trumpet and looking up at the ceiling, said: "Doctor, you don't understand. My whole life, my whole soul, my whole spirit, is to b-l-o-w this h-o-r-n. My people are waiting for me. I cannot let them down."[42]

That horn, by whatever name we call it—cornet, bugle, or trumpet—was inseparable from Louis Armstrong for virtually his whole life: the trumpet as talisman. Most revealing are those intimate, candid moments describing his earliest contacts with his chosen instrument; no contracts of a Wilberforce Whiteman were needed to get him to practice: "I had a lot of lucky moments with the Karnofskys. After blowing my tin horn [on the junk wagon] so long I wondered how I would do blowing a real horn; a cornet was what I had in mind. Sure enough, I saw a little cornet in a pawn shop window. Five dollars. My luck was just right. With the Karnofskys loaning me on my salary, I saved fifty cents a week and bought the horn, all dirty. But it was soon pretty to me."[43]

But a few years later, on New Year's Eve, December 31, 1912, his world changed. Louis had since left the Karnofskys—the family that had seen that he "had music in his soul"—and started delivering coal to the cribs in Storyville. He had dropped out of Fisk School and begun singing tenor in a quartet that did its share of hustling on Rampart Street and thereabouts. Usually they "would draw down a nice little taste" (make a little money). Only this time he had with him a .38-caliber pistol he had found at the bottom of Mayann's trunk. Egged on by his "gang," Armstrong began firing in the air, and had just finished firing his last blank cartridge "when a couple of strong arms came from behind me." As he puts it: "It was cold enough that night, but I broke out into a sweat that was even colder."[44] He found himself locked up overnight in the New Orleans Juvenile Court House, only to be sentenced the following day to the Colored Waif's Home, where he was to remain eighteen months. He was eleven years old.

Even though the Colored Waif's Home was a reformatory run by Captain Joseph Jones along strict military lines, there were some shining moments for Louis there, especially when he assumed the role of bugler and was asked to become leader of the band: "I jumped straight into the air." The band of the home, directed by Peter Davis, was the pride of the institution, a source of considerable status to its members, in that it performed in city parades and at picnics. Something of the change in Louis's fortunes is vividly communicated in the following recollection: "I took up the bugle at once and began to shine it up. The other bugler had never shined the instrument and the brass was dirty and green. The kids gave me a big hand when they saw the gleaming bright instrument instead of the filthy green one. I felt proud of my position as bugler. . . . The whole place seemed to change. Satisfied with my tone, Mr. Davis gave me a cornet and taught me how to play 'Home, Sweet Home.' I was in seventh heaven."[45]

In his later years Louis looked back on his eighteen months in the Colored Waif's Home with a great deal of gratitude; that phase of his life provided the much-needed structure that helped set him on the proper course. As he commented perceptively, it was time to stop running around and start learning something. By all appearances, he seems to have thrived on the sometimes harsh discipline, building upon the sense of commitment to task and the work ethic instilled in him earlier when he was working for the Karnofskys. What is more, so unlike Paul Whiteman, the rebel son of a disapproving father, he received attention from older men, part of a series of surrogate fathers that he craved.

In his later years, when he might be relaxing in his den at home in

1.4 An eleven-year-old Louis Armstrong, center rear, in the Colored Waif's Home Brass Band under Peter Davis. Frank Driggs Collection.

Corona, Queens, reminiscing with his wife, Lucille, and playing recorded music, or else socializing backstage or elsewhere, Armstrong developed the habit of having a reel-to-reel tape recorder running. The resulting reels of many recorded hours have come to represent a remarkably vivid soundtrack of his private and public lives—a recorded legacy which he would store in boxes all lovingly decorated with collages created from news clippings, photographs, and such. Among them is a revealing tape of a visit to Vancouver, B.C. On it, a member of the host family is reading to Armstrong a letter of thanks that Captain Jones wrote him after receiving his congratulatory telegram on the occasion of his retirement from the Colored Waif's Home. Jones calls Armstrong "my favorite son," and says that he ("Pops") and "Mom" will always have the spare room waiting every time they strike town. Deeply touched, Armstrong is heard to remark, "I'm so glad you read that letter. I'll keep it forever."[46]

Soon after he was released from the Colored Waif's Home on June 16, 1914, the young Armstrong found other older men to bond with, each of whom in his own way helped guide Louis on his journey. The most vividly drawn among them is Black Benny Williams, hustler, six-foot-six muscleman, part-time drummer, and protector, who in crowded places would handcuff "Little Louis" with a handkerchief so that he wouldn't get lost. The New Orleans trombonist Edward "Kid" Ory has recalled how Black Benny brought Armstrong to a local picnic where Ory was playing. "Remembering the kid from the street parade," Ory let him sit in with his band. "Everyone in the park went wild over this boy in knee trousers who could play so great."[47]

In another defining moment, Black Benny brought "Little Louis" and Sidney Bechet together. This contact was to have profound implications for Louis, particularly in the adaptation of the great Creole musician's virtuosic extension of the New Orleans clarinet tradition to the cornet and trumpet. Their meeting is captured in the following charming anecdote in Bechet's autobiography: "[Black Benny] said to me one day, 'You think you can play. But I know a little boy around the corner from my place; he can play "High Society" better than you.' So I said, 'Well, I'd like to see that boy.' He said, 'All right, come over with me.' And we went, and it was Louis. And I'll be doggone if he didn't play 'High Society' on the cornet. . . . It was very hard for clarinet to do, and really unthinkable for cornet to do at those times. But Louis, he did it. So I was very pleased about it."[48]

In Armstrong's eyes, and to his ears, the most compelling surrogate father in those early years was Joe Oliver. While it is unclear exactly where and when they first met, Armstrong came to revere Oliver as a divine presence, "the greatest of them all . . . a creator with unlimited ideas . . . and a heart as big as a whale . . . helping the underdog in music such as me." He illustrates the experience of playing with Oliver by telling a story of "the Sister in our Church in N.O." One Sunday when their beloved pastor took the day off and sent in another preacher who was not as good, everyone in the congregation frowned on him, except one woman, who later explained: "Well, when our pastor preach, I can look right through him and see Jesus. And when I hear a preacher who's not as good as ours—I just look over his shoulder and see Jesus just the same." Similarly, when playing with musicians who were not that good but were trying their best, Armstrong said he would look "over their shoulders and see Joe Oliver and several other great musicians from my home town."[49]

In terms of actual music making, Armstrong always took a vital cue from Oliver, who said: "If a cat can swing a lead and play a melody, that's what counts." And swing he did, coming to transform the nature of jazz, particularly hot jazz, from a music of ensemble improvisation to one defined by a theme-solo(s)-theme format. As the first indisputably great soloist, Armstrong helped write the very history of the world of jazz; he led the way by expanding upon "breaks" and embellishing melodies to create memorable improvised solos lasting a whole chorus or more—all of it animated by a distinctive "swing" to create a music of passion, excitement, and intensity.

The earliest phase of this process in New Orleans necessarily led to conflict between the darker "ear" musicians from uptown and their lighter-skinned "eye" (score-reading) Creole counterparts from downtown. In the course of a lengthy 1941 letter, Armstrong compares his reception when passing through New Orleans during the early years of World War II with what he had experienced as "Little Louis":

> Gee, they came runnin' from every direction when they heard that Louiee [sic] Armstrong's bus was parked at Dumaine and Claiborne Avenues, two popular streets. I remember way back in the days when the Odd Fellows and the Labor Day parades used to pass that corner—I was quite a youngster then—but I still can remember that I had to do a lot of runnin' [and] second lining behind those parades—just to hear Joe King Oliver or Bunk Johnson or Emanuel Perez blow those trumpets. Those Creoles were certainly bad in those days. The downtown boys would not let the uptown boys pass Dumaine and Claiborne without putting up a fight or getting sapped up.[50]

While Armstrong is clearly speaking in generalities of the "bad" Creoles, there are indeed names to be named. One is Isidore Barbarin, a cornet, mellophone, and alto horn player associated for many years with two of the best marching bands in New Orleans, the Onward Brass Band and the Excelsior Brass Band; he dismissed those playing by ear as "routine" musicians catering to "ratty people"—that is, those who frequented joints and dives, out to dance and have a good time.[51] But when it came to funerals, that was another story. Armstrong has recounted an instance of how most of "those big shots"—reading musicians in John Robichaux's band—were working during the day at other jobs, and were simply not available. So members of Kid Ory's band, Armstrong included, were engaged to take their place. Upon showing up at the lodge, however, they "noticed all those stuck-up guys giving . . . lots of ice." Unfazed by all of this, Louis Armstrong reportedly nudged Kid Ory as if to say, "You dig what I'm diggin'?" Starting out with a medium fast march on the way to the home of the deceased, they continued with "real slow funeral marches" to the cemetery. But once the body was lowered six feet under and the drummer played his roll, Ory, Armstrong, and company were in their element, the swinging ragtime march giving them the competitive edge: "Those old fossils just couldn't cut it."[52]

Yet there is evidence that uptown musicians were able to mix with their downtown colleagues if they were deemed good enough—that is, able to read proficiently. This appears to have been the case shortly before Armstrong's departure from New Orleans for Chicago in August 1922, when he apparently played alongside Isidore Barbarin himself in the Tuxedo Brass Band. These Creole musicians came out of a nineteenth-century tradition that helps give us a broader picture of the world of popular dance music. Like Paul Whiteman, these were literate, classically trained "eye" musicians coming out of an earlier, preragtime tradition of quadrilles, polkas, waltzes, mazurkas, schottisches—musicians who, like Whiteman, often played violin but were able to double on other instruments as well. These so-called "Creoles of Color," often associated with New Orleans but not unique to the Crescent City, were as a rule free mulattos, quadroons, or octoroons—musicians from "downtown" who prided themselves on their ability to "play legitimately," generally seeing themselves as standing apart from the "uptown" black "ear" musicians. These were musicians who, for their time, traveled widely, contributing mightily to the diffusion of the multiple popular styles of the day.

Consider the case of Armand J. Piron (1888–1943), violinist, bandleader, and composer who effectively straddled the worlds of both Paul Whiteman and Louis Armstrong. For some sixteen years, from 1918 to 1934, Piron led ensembles—A. J. Piron and his Non-Pareil Orchestra, Armand J. Piron and his Novelty Orchestra, and Piron's New Orleans Orchestra, among others. His bands played at posh places like the Parisian Roof Garden, Tranchina's Restaurant at the New Orleans Spanish Fort, and the New Orleans Country Club, where he never hired a player who could not pass for white.[53] In 1923 Piron and his band were engaged to perform at both New York's Roseland Ballroom and the Cotton Club. He was so popular that Paul Whiteman reportedly wanted to hire him away. But Piron became homesick; besides, he owned the Crescent City's society ballroom scene.

Piron was a man of many parts. Around 1916 he joined forces with Clarence Williams, pianist, entrepreneur, composer, and publisher, to create a vaudeville trio performing song-and-dance routines, with Jimmy Noone on clarinet. In addition, Piron and Williams opened a small publishing company that year, and their first hit was very soon in coming—"I Wish I Could Shimmy Like My Sister Kate." Louis Armstrong remembered crossing paths for the first time with sharpie Clarence Williams in 1917 at Pete Lala's Cabaret. The young Louis, all of sixteen at the time, had recently been hired by Kid Ory, who had urged him "to work up a number so we can feature you once in a while." As Armstrong put it to the publicist and jazz buff Ernie Anderson in a posthumously published interview:

> So I put a new piece together. Words and music. Even put in a little dance. . . . One night, as I did the number, I saw this cat writing it all down on music paper. He was quick, man; he could write as fast as I could play and sing. When I had finished he asked me if I'd sell the number to him. He mentioned twenty-five dollars. When you're making only a couple of bucks a night that's a lot of money. But what really put the deal over was that I had just seen a hard-hitting steel gray overcoat that I wanted for those cold nights. So I said, "Okay," and he handed me some forms to sign and I signed them. He said he'd be back with the cash. But he never did come back.[54]

Nevertheless, this bittersweet encounter at Pete Lala's did not prevent Armstrong from subsequently making some of his major early recordings with Clarence Williams's Blue Five—a precursor of Armstrong's own Hot Five. From November 1924 to October 1925, in the course of his tenure with Fletcher Henderson in New York, he put on disc a total of seventeen titles under the Williams banner in the company of such musicians as Sidney Bechet, Buster Bailey, and Sippie Wallace. So it was that the worlds of Armand Piron, Clarence Williams, Louis Armstrong, and Paul Whiteman overlapped.

Revisiting the West Coast at the turn of the twentieth century, it is striking just how many New Orleans musicians—both uptown black and downtown Creole—were drawn to the West Coast, not only by the climate and possibly by the promise of less racial prejudice, but also by the prospects of jobs as cooks and waiters aboard the relatively new Southern Pacific Railroad. In fact, since 1883 New Orleans had been the eastern terminus of the railroad. One line extended all the way north to Promontory, Utah, where the Southern Pacific joined the Union Pacific to form the first transcontinental link. In a major study covering the years 1908–25, Lawrence Gushee has identified some fifty New Orleans–area musicians who were active on the West Coast.[55] His findings force us to reevaluate the received wisdom regarding the spread of southern dance music throughout the United States; it was not limited to Kansas City, Chicago, and New York. Starting in 1905, such musicians as the cornetist Bunk Johnson and the ragtime pianist Tom Turpin were appearing on the West Coast as well. And by 1920 the trumpeter Papa Mutt Carey, the cornetist Freddie Keppard and his Creole Band, and the trombonist-bandleader Kid Ory were performing in San Francisco. Perhaps the flashiest of all was the bandleader and pianist Ferdinand "Jelly Roll" Morton, who, in February 1919, arrived in San Francisco in his twelve-cylinder touring car after a series of performances in such West Coast locales as Los Angeles, San Diego, and Oakland.

The trajectory of Paul Whiteman's early career, passing from Denver, to San Francisco, to Los Angeles, to Atlantic City, clearly gives the lie to the geographical stereotype. Similarly, in scrutinizing the roughly parallel period of Louis Armstrong's life, we are confronted with comparable challenges to standard assumptions about the dissemination of jazz. The Barbary Coast experience of Armstrong's mentor, Joe Oliver, is instructive here. Oliver came out to San Francisco in May 1921 from Chicago with the encouragement of Kid Ory. By the beginning of August 1922 we find Oliver back in Chicago, suddenly sending a telegram to his protégé Armstrong, down in New Orleans, inviting him to join him in the Windy City as second cornet in his band.

From his initial arrival in Chicago, sometime in February 1919, until his departure for California in May 1921, Joe Oliver's first turn in the Windy City had been one wild ride. During most of 1919 Oliver regularly performed at both the Dreamland and the Royal Gardens. But the managements of these two black-owned clubs, located in the heart of the black entertainment district called the Stroll, had slightly different ways of reading cabaret law. Whereas one obeyed the law in an effort to curb vice, the other flouted it. Newspapers announced that the Dreamland was "running the regular way, from 8.00 P.M. to 1.00 A.M.," while the Royal Gardens, by contrast, advertised dancing until 4.00 A.M.[56] In addition, Oliver and his band had the distinction of being part of two highly publicized events. The first was an elaborate "Decoration Day" tribute held at the Royal Gardens on May 31, 1919, honoring the memory of James Reese Europe, who had been fatally stabbed earlier that month. The *Chicago Defender* announced that day: "Our Hero's Night, featuring Eleanor Wilson and the Royal Gardens big beauty chorus of 25, and a platoon of real soldiers. See the big girlie revue, with Allegretti and Margaret, and the Midnight Follies under the direction of Clarence E. Muse. Magnificent costumes and lighting effects. Come early. Dance late. Hear the world's greatest jazz band."

Even though in October of that year Oliver and his ensemble from the Dreamland were heard at the "Black Sox" World Series in Chicago's Comiskey Park, later that fall business at the Dreamland was in a slump.[57] Remodeling the dance floor, engaging the best vaudeville acts, and hiring a new chef failed to effect a recovery. The owner, Bill Bottoms, apparently blamed Oliver for the decline in his fortunes and promptly hired replacements, only to hire Oliver back in early April 1920. At this point Oliver was playing at the Pekin Café, an infamous black-and-tan establishment—one, that is, frequented by both blacks and whites—which was located on State Street, some seven blocks north of the Dreamland. Later that year, in the early hours of August 23, this "house of a thousand crimes"—as *Chicago Defender* readers came to know it—was the scene of a double murder, when members of the "whiskey ring" killed two detectives at the café. With the Pekin soon permanently closed, Oliver went back to the Royal Gardens, working as cornetist.

A year after its supposed slump, the Dreamland announced a grand reopening to celebrate its resplendent, newly remodeled interior. The *Chicago Whip* of November 19, 1920, vividly described the appointments:

> In the large dome in the center of the ceiling hangs a beautiful bunch of green foliage, in which blaze red, white, and blue incandescent electric lights, with the initial "D." Hanging from the ceiling there are four lights covered with shades, hand painted. Gold decorations are the color scheme and on the floor is a new Brussels carpet. In the center is a glass flooring, five feet square, under which brilliant lights burn with stunning effect. On each table is an electric shade. The new addition is the balcony which can be reached at the four corners of the room. At the west end is placed the special balcony for the New Orleans Jazz Band under the direction of Professor Joe Oliver.

Meanwhile, the press was awash with glowing reviews: Oliver's band was touted as a "distinct feature," "justly celebrated," and "the talk of the town."[58] But such hype was cause for suspicion, especially once rumors began circulating in early April 1921 that Bottoms had put the Dreamland up for sale.[59] Even though negotiations for the sale ultimately fell through, Oliver was sufficiently anxious about job security to accept an invitation to go to the San Francisco area.

Oliver's vital connection with California was with Kid Ory, who had been on the West Coast since 1919. One of the most successful bandleaders of the day, Ory had been among the first in New Orleans to publicize his band by attaching his name as leader. During the period 1910–19 his name seemed to be everywhere, whether at Pete Lala's in Storyville, white society parties at the Yacht Club, colored picnics at the West End, or Tulane University fraternity parties. In short, he "played in every hole that could be played in."[60] Both King Oliver and Louis Armstrong had been Ory's sidemen during the period 1917– 19, including the occasion at Pete Lala's when Clarence Williams and Armand J. Piron reportedly stole Armstrong's "I Wish I Could Shimmy Like My Sister Kate"; this was shortly before the two of them made a splash on the New York scene and caught the attention of Paul Whiteman. Here again Louis Armstrong and Paul Whiteman were moving in intersecting orbits.

Sometime in 1920, during an engagement at the Creole Café in West Oakland, Kid Ory was approached by the management of the Pergola Dancing Pavilion at 949 Market Street in San Francisco and offered a contract. Ory turned them down because of a prior commitment but recommended Joe Oliver instead. Honoring Ory's suggestion, the Pergola extended an invitation to Oliver and his Creole band to come out to the West Coast. Finally, on May 21, 1921, Oliver departed Chicago for California, accompanied by his front line of Johnny Dodds on clarinet, James Palao on violin, and Honoré Dutrey on trombone, and his rhythm section of Ed Garland, Minor Hall, and Lillian Hardin on bass, drums, and piano, respectively.

Unfortunately, after only about two months things began to fall apart for Oliver. There was simply not enough work, so he tried to release Palao, his most dispensable sideman. But drummer Hall, loyal to Palao's family, with whom he had grown up in New Orleans, protested and threatened to quit if Oliver went through with his plan. Enraged by Hall's mutiny, Oliver summarily dismissed him and promptly sent for a replacement in the person of Warren "Baby" Dodds, Johnny Dodds's younger brother. But repercussions soon followed when Hall complained to the musicians union, arguing that Oliver had failed to consult them before hiring Baby Dodds. The upshot was that Oliver was assessed a fine, which he reportedly "neglected" to pay; and he was apparently "forced" by the union to cover the cost of Minor Hall's return trip to Chicago.

The period through April 1922 saw Oliver and some holdouts like Ed

Garland and Johnny and Baby Dodds—Lillian Hardin had been replaced and returned home to Chicago—joining forces with Kid Ory, scrambling to find enough work. The *Oakland Sunshine* was probably referring to this aggregation when it gave billing to "King Oliver's and Ory's Celebrated Creole Orchestra," a group which, on February 28, 1922, provided music for a Mardi Gras ball at Oakland's Municipal Auditorium. Oliver's final public appearance in California presumably took place on April 22 to help mark the opening of "Ragtime" Billy Tucker's Hiawatha Dancing Academy in Los Angeles. Tucker himself, the California correspondent for the *Chicago Defender*, reported on the event as follows: "As an extra added attraction we are featuring 'King' Joe Oliver, the world's greatest cornetist, who is in town en route to Chicago. He has been up in San Francisco a few months. When he came to Los Angeles a few days ago, Jelly Roll Morton entertained him at Wayside Park, and I'll chirp to the whole continent [that] he set Los Angeles on fire. . . . Matt Lewis (my partner) and myself have offered him all kinds of inducements to stay in Los Angeles and take charge of our bands at the Hiawatha, but he has already made his contract."[61]

The "contract" was for Oliver's engagement in Chicago at the recently renovated former Royal Gardens, operating under the name of Lincoln Gardens since May 1921. Indeed, Oliver's return to Chicago was soon making news, with the *Chicago Defender* of June 17, 1922, including this announcement: "Dance to the music of Joe Oliver's Creole Jazz Band just back from a great year on the coast." Yet problems with the musicians union continued to haunt Oliver. Ed Garland has told the story of how the band was on the verge of starting its performance at Lincoln Gardens when a union representative entered the cabaret to call a halt to the proceedings. Before the band could continue, Mrs. Major, the white owner, reportedly had to pay a fine assessed at $100 per player in addition to a penalty of $200.[62]

This kind of experience, we can assume, must have been profoundly embarrassing, if not downright humiliating, to Joe Oliver. If nothing else, it dramatized just how vulnerable he was, answerable to his sidemen as well as the musicians union—a bitter reminder of how things had soured for him and his band in California. It is likely that Joe Oliver now felt an acute need to have a semblance of stability in his professional life in the person of a highly gifted, supportive, eager, deferential young man who looked to him as a father; hence his sending that telegram to Louis Armstrong in early August to come join him up north. It is somewhat baffling, on purely musical grounds, to understand why Oliver called upon Armstrong to join him as second cornet, since this additional instrument was extremely rare in the New Orleans hot bands of the period. What we do know is that on August 8 Armstrong was already aboard the 7 P.M. Illinois Central bound for Chicago, part of the Great Migration, eager to join "Papa Joe" at Lincoln Gardens, and soon to change the course of jazz history.

What drove Armstrong on his journey to Chicago that summer was, of course, a personal history profoundly different from anything that had shaped Whiteman's early life. And in his search for surrogate fathers none filled the shoes of that absentee parent better than Joe Oliver. The bond was deep and long-lasting, and Armstrong's own words are most telling in recounting his debt: "Joe Oliver has always been my inspiration and my idol. No trumpet player ever had the fire that Oliver had. Man, he really could *punch* a number. . . . I was very young when I first heard Joe Oliver. He was in the Onward Band, a brass band they had down there in New Orleans. . . . When Joe would get through playing I'd carry his horn. I guess I was about 14. Joe gave me cornet lessons, and when I was a kid I ran errands for his wife."[63]

For Armstrong, Oliver "was a Creator." But *Creator* could also take on the more biological meaning of *procreator*, with Oliver reportedly being "cute fresh," even down in New Orleans, about how he was actually Armstrong's father. It is a joke that went on for some time. An especially amusing moment occurred when Louis's mother, a panicked Mayann, having heard rumors of her son's death, showed up in Chicago's Lincoln Gardens from the Crescent City only to discover that her boy was doing just fine. As Armstrong recalled: "So when May Ann came on the stand I whispered into Joe's ear, 'Well, Papa Joe—Mother's here—shall I tell her what you've been saying?' I Gosh, you should have seen Papa Joe blush all over the place. And May Ann thanked him for being so Swell to her son—UMP—I thought he'd—Just 'Swoon'—or something like that.—It was really 'Cute' to see the 'shy' Expression on Joe Oliver's Face—when I asked him about how he was 'Ribbing' me about he was my 'Stepfather' in the presence of my 'Mother May Ann.'"[64]

The style of music making learned at "Papa" Joe's side was indeed to last a lifetime—swinging a lead, playing a melody, and helping develop an approach to jazz improvisation that was defined, as we have seen, by a theme-solo(s)-theme format. It was an achievement analogous to what Ferde Grofé had accomplished for Paul Whiteman, using sectional choirs to delineate contrasting timbres and voicings in his arrangements for big band. On April 5, 1923, just under eight months after his arrival in Chicago, Armstrong was in the studios of Gennett in Richmond, Indiana, making his very first recordings, with King Oliver and his Creole Jazz Band.

Owned at the time by the Starr Piano Company of that city, Gennett had recently entered the "race record" market, a market active between 1920 and 1932 that produced and merchandised records for African-American consumers. As the pioneer record producer Perry Bradford put it in 1920: "There's fourteen million Negroes in our great country, and they will buy records if recorded by one of their own, because we are the only folks that can sing and interpret hot jazz songs just off the griddle correctly."[65]

Louis Armstrong was paralleling the recording achievements of Paul Whiteman and his Ambassador Orchestra, which, flush with success at Atlantic City's Ambassador Hotel, had three years earlier first entered Victor's studios in Camden, N.J. Even though these two historic recording sessions point up sharp differences in marketing and distribution, there is a vivid symmetry in what these two musicians had recently achieved. Indeed, the critical transcontinental journeys of Paul Whiteman and Louis Armstrong, some three years apart—Whiteman's from the West Coast to Atlantic City, Armstrong's from New Orleans to Chicago—might be seen as defining trajectories in the history of jazz, intersecting axes that linked major centers for this new music in the United States. And the many ways these paths, separated by race and class, were to diverge and cross are critical to the story of the future of jazz.

2 CIVILIZATION ON TRIAL

The paths that brought Whiteman to Atlantic City and Armstrong to Chicago marked the beginning of major developments in each man's career. Whiteman's success at Atlantic City's Ambassador Hotel, coupled with spectacular sales of recordings of "Whispering" (1.8 million copies), "Avalon," and "Japanese Sandman" for Victor, led to his being hired with his nine-piece band for New York's Palais Royal dance and supper club. Opening on October 1, 1920, at this elegant locale in midtown Manhattan, he gave the right swing and lilt to the lives of its well-heeled clientele—the Vanderbilts, Drexels, Biddles, Goulds, Lord and Lady Mountbatten. Timing was of the essence. Whiteman was unwittingly cashing in on a radical change in the music business. Sheet music sales were beginning to lose their market share because of rising production costs associated with a printer's strike and a paper shortage. And moguls of the music industry were discovering the enormous potential in "mechanical royalties"—that is, the brave new world of recordings.

For his part, Armstrong became second cornet in King Oliver's Creole Jazz Band at Chicago's Lincoln Gardens on the city's South Side. A huge venue accommodating more than a thousand dancers, it represented for Armstrong the big time. Oliver's group had also begun to make recordings on the Gennett label. Even though Gennett's initial recordings, predating those of King Oliver's group, featured performances by such white bands as the Original Memphis Five, the "race record" industry, effectively active from 1920 to 1932, represented an early form of niche marketing, targeting a wide range of ethnic or national groups, whether Jewish, Russian, Polish, Irish, or black. Ralph Peer, an executive associated with Okeh, another prominent "race" label, remembered the label *race* as a way of catering to "all foreign groups. . . . We were afraid to advertise Negro records. So I listed them in the catalogue as 'race' records, and they are still known as that."[1] Others of a more idealistic bent have seen the term as signifying a new market for "Negro citizens" who, buoyed by a certain optimism following World War I, "found both comfort and support in references to a commonality of black people."[2]

Yet amid the headlong rush of the "Jazz Age" there were darker forces lurking that gave a special tension to the times and that help one more fully appreciate what Armstrong and Whiteman were able to achieve. In *The Great Gatsby,* published in 1925, F. Scott Fitzgerald has Tom Buchanan make a pessimistic outburst that hints at an impending doom. "'Civilization's going to pieces,' broke out Tom violently. 'I've gotten to be a terrible pessimist about things. Have you read *The Rise of the Colored Empires* by this man Goddard? The idea is if we don't look out the white race will be—will be utterly submerged. It's all scientific stuff; it's all been proved. It's up to us, who are the dominant race, to watch out or these other races will have control of things.'"[3]

For all the dynamic modernism of the Jazz Age—its Stutz Bearcats, speakeasies, airplanes, skyscrapers, telephones, and radios—there was also the ugliness of racial bigotry and the intolerance of any threat to the established order. Certainly, the rioting and bloodshed of the "Red Summer" of 1919, which had started in Chicago and spread to many other U.S. cities, was still a fresh memory. And there was further unrest that year as the activities of radicals in the labor movement led many citizens to identify unionism and strikes with the threat of communist revolution. Soon after there was a closing of conservative ranks with the resurgence of the Ku Klux Klan and the passage of the Immigration Act of 1924 which mandated strict quotas. Similarly we find the perpetuation of old plantation stereotypes in the "Negro" entry of the contemporary *Encyclopaedia Britannica.* Dubious scientific evidence is invoked to suggest that in the negro "the growth of the brain is . . . arrested by the premature closing of the cranial structures and the lateral pressure on the frontal bone," and that "the mental constitution of the negro is very similar to that of a child, normally good-natured and cheerful, but subject to fits of emotion and passion during which he is capable of performing acts of singular atrocity." According to this line of reasoning, it is not too much of a stretch to think of the negro as "the savage underneath the smile," a menace to white women, perhaps even a cannibal.[4] In essence, this perception of the black man marked an intensification of attitudes that are traceable to the cross-racial desire associated with minstrel-show mimicry—a darker variation on the theme of "panic, anxiety, terror, and pleasure."

The potent mix of science, race, and religion came to the boiling point the following summer, in July 1925, in a sweltering courthouse in Dayton, Tennessee, when John T. Scopes, a twenty-four-year-old teacher of science at the local high school, agreed to be a defendant in a case testing a new state law forbidding the teaching of evolution. This so-called Monkey Trial brought together the Great Commoner, William Jennings Bryan, defending the cause of religious fundamentalism among Baptists and Methodists of the rural South, and Clarence Darrow, chief counsel for the defendant and champion of the modern urban view, that of evolution. As Darrow cogently put it: "Scopes isn't on trial; civilization is on trial." Amid all this, Bryan-baiter and gadfly H. L. Mencken came to Tennessee to make sport of the fundamentalists, and a new breed of broadcasters had a feeding frenzy.

But the religious fundamentalism of the rural South was just part of a larger phenomenon. The developments that ultimately gave rise to the Monkey Trial roughly coincided with the cultural awakening in the black community known as the Harlem Renaissance—a movement associated with a mass migration from the rural South to such centers in the urban North as New York, Pittsburgh, Detroit, and Chicago. This human flood has been attributed to multiple causes, among them the demands of the war industry, coupled with the imposition of strict foreign quotas, the terror wrought by the Ku Klux Klan, and the depredations of the scourge of the South, the boll weevil. It was Harlem, the area north of New York City's West 110th Street, that saw the fullest flowering of African-American creativity in poetry, prose, drama, the visual arts, and music, and that gave its name to the national movement. Alain Locke, the quintessential voice of the Harlem Renaissance, wrote in his definitive 1925 anthology *The New Negro:* "The mind of the Negro seems suddenly to have slipped from under the tyranny of social intimidation and to be shaking off the psychology of imitation and implied inferiority. By shedding the old chrysalis of the Negro problem we are achieving something like a spiritual emancipation. . . . The day of 'aunties,' 'uncles' and 'mammies' is equally gone. Uncle Tom and Sambo have passed on."[5]

Speaking for the majority, Locke was seeking to emulate the values of high European culture. In that scheme of things the idioms of blues and jazz were properly to be transformed and incorporated into symphonic music or symphonic jazz. Yet included in the same anthology is an essay entitled "Jazz at Home" by Joel Augustus Rogers, who is quick to celebrate the liberating powers of the music: "The true spirit of jazz is a joyous revolt from convention, custom, authority, boredom, even sorrow—from everything that would confine the soul of man and hinder its riding free on air." For Rogers, even though there is a link with the "barbaric rhythm and exuberance" of the African and Haitian bamboula, we learn that "jazz time is faster and more complex than African music. With its cowbells, auto horns, calliopes, rattle, dinner gongs, kitchen utensils, cymbals, screams, crashes, clankings and monotonous rhythm it bears all the marks of a nerve-strung, strident, mechanized civilization. It is a thing of the jungles—modern man-made jungles."[6]

Remember, it was also the era of Prohibition. With the expansion of nightlife and the promotion of jazz came a proliferation of such nightclubs in Harlem as Connie's Inn, Small's Paradise, and the Cotton Club, as well as theaters like the Apollo, Lincoln, and Lafayette—virtually all of them white-owned. Prohibition also provided the setting for whites "slumming" in areas like Chicago's South Side or New York's Harlem. "Jazz Age Harlem was thought to put touring Caucasians in touch with their real selves, to be a place of primal authenticity where fingers could feel the pulse of life."[7] Duke Ellington, during his residency at the Cotton Club (1927–31), purveyed a kind of jazz called "jungle music," replete with pounding tom-toms, exotic scales, muted growling brass lines, and other coloristic effects to accompany the elaborate floor shows, with their dancers scantily clad in leopard skins.

Perhaps the poetic flame that burned brightest in this jungle was Edna St. Vincent Millay. Her poem "First Fig" became a veritable anthem of the Jazz Age, capturing the spirit of wild abandon that drove a generation of white women who were experiencing free love, drugs, and alcohol for the first time.

> My candle burns at both ends;
> It will not last the night;
> But ah, my foes, and oh, my friends—
> It gives a lovely light!

Such women were among the thousands who flocked to ballrooms, dance halls, and clubs, not to mention those who listened to records and the radio at home. They made up a public expecting to hear a broad repertoire from a jazz orchestra, which could be hired for a residency in a ballroom or booked for a theater appearance, radio hour, or record date. The repertoire could range from novelty tunes like "Yes, We Have No Bananas," to numbers like "Copenhagen" or "Changes," to selections from a musical like *Show Boat*, to "Song of India" or "Meditation."

Within this giddy world there were complex changes under way in jazz—changes a lot more involved than a two-step process. Yet there are those who have argued that until around 1926 the symphonic jazz of Paul Whiteman held sway, with its fully worked out scores and notated parts assigned to individual sections of the orchestra—strings, reeds, brass, and so on—by such arrangers as Ferde Grofé and Don Redman. This was a style of music for those who could read scores rather than simply "fake" their parts. This early period was followed by a phase during which "Henderson, Ellington, Goldkette and the rest souped up the symphonic jazz with good jazz solos, stronger rhythm sections, and . . . arranged passages that captured a true jazz feeling, to produce a music hotter than Whiteman would, or could, make it."[8] An immediate problem with this simplistic picture is that in 1927 Whiteman himself raided the orchestra of Jean Goldkette for its hot soloists, most notably Bix Beiderbecke and Goldkette's arranger, Bill Challis. This second phase also coincided with the period when Louis Armstrong made his now-canonized recordings with the Hot Five and Hot Seven.

In fact, a close look at the respective worlds of Armstrong and Whiteman throughout the decade of the twenties gives us a far more nuanced portrait of each jazzman—portraits defined by the imperatives of class and commerce rather than simply race alone. What is more, "jazz" was from the first an inclusive music without any distinct stylistic boundaries. As George Gershwin succinctly put it in 1926: "The word [jazz] has been used for so many different things that it has ceased to have any definite meaning."[9] We can begin to fill in these portraits by taking as points of reference two proximate defining events early in the year of 1924, separated by the distance between Chicago and New York. On February 5 Louis Armstrong married Lil Hardin in the Windy City, and exactly one week later Paul Whiteman made history by premiering Gershwin's *Rhapsody in Blue* at New York's Aeolian Hall at a concert famously billed, using scientific jargon, as "An Experiment in Modern Music." It is something of a cliché in musical surveys of the 1920s to describe the Whiteman concert as the momentous occasion when he "made a lady out of jazz" by bringing it into the concert hall.[10] In Armstrong's case, even though his marriage to Hardin did not immediately bring him into the concert hall, it was nevertheless a decisive event, leading eventually to his break as sideman to Joe Oliver and his being "civilized" by Lil Hardin, who groomed him to become the upwardly mobile star soloist and a commodity in his own right. Hardin was indeed a critical catalyst, prompting the analogous image of Armstrong as "jazzman made by a lady."

Lil Hardin was very much the urban sophisticate, willful and assertive,

2.1 "Making Jazz Respectable." Cartoon by George Hager in *Musical America,* February 13, 1926. Musical America Archives.

the third in a line of tough, independent matriarchs who had come north from Mississippi and Tennessee. She was apt to call the shots when it came to matters of Armstrong's wardrobe, weight loss, and, most important, career moves. It was Hardin who persuaded Armstrong to leave King Oliver to strike out on his own. And it was at the beginning of October 1924, at a point when Paul Whiteman was on his symphonic jazz crusade, that Armstrong joined the Fletcher Henderson Orchestra in New York. Lil Hardin's critical role in redirecting Armstrong at this juncture in his career should not be underestimated. A literate rather than purely "ear" musician who had briefly attended Fisk University in Nashville, Tennessee, she had already made a name for herself in Chicago by the time Armstrong came to town on August 8, 1922, to join King Oliver's Creole Jazz Band at Lincoln Gardens.

She had graduated from demonstrating sheet music—everything from

J. S. Bach to W. C. Handy—at Jones's Music Store on South State Street to become a valued pianist in Oliver's band. State Street was a major artery through the very heart of Chicago's South Side in an area bounded by 12th and 31st Streets. That stretch of State was a black street teeming with theaters, restaurants, and cabarets—a dramatic manifestation of a swelling population that had migrated north since the end of the Great War in search of jobs in Chicago's slaughterhouses, factories, and railyards.

Lil Hardin's first meeting with her future husband, just two days after his arrival in Chicago, was apparently not the greatest thrill of her life. Oliver had already whetted Armstrong's appetite by sending photographs of Hardin to him in New Orleans. Now here she was in the flesh, performing at the Dreamland Café at 3520 State Street, an upscale establishment touted by the city's nationally distributed black newspaper, the *Chicago Defender,* as a "first class resort owned by a member of the Race." What she saw was a 226-pound man called "Little Louis" by fellow musicians. "I said 'Little Louis?' I wonder why they call him 'Little Louis' as fat as he is? Well, I was disappointed all round 'cause I didn't like the way he dressed, I didn't like his hairdo; he had bangs— that was the style in New Orleans . . . and they were sticking right straight out." What is more, even Armstrong's cornet playing failed to grab her attention at this point. "I must admit that from a musical standpoint jazz didn't mean anything too much to me. Maybe it's because I was as young as I was, and was interested in the money . . . no taxes; my mother didn't take any money, nothing. Just buy ice cream and clothes."[11]

But others were listening intently, sensing the uniqueness of Armstrong's sound. It so happens that in the fall of 1922 Paul Whiteman and his Orchestra were at Chicago's all-white Trianon Ballroom, where the band reportedly netted $25,000 for six nights' work—a record in the band business of the day. After hours they could be found "slumming" at the city's Lincoln Gardens at 459 East 31st Street. As Lil Hardin put it: "A bunch of white musicians—ten, twelve, fifteen, sometimes twenty, would come and they would roll up in front of the bandstand to listen. I used to wonder to myself what they were listening [to] . . . what particular thing. That's how much I knew about what they were doing. Louis and Joe said . . . that they were some of Paul Whiteman's band and that Bix [Beiderbecke] was in the bunch. They were in that bunch that used to come. . . . They used to talk to Louis and King Oliver and Johnny [Dodds]."[12]

The drummer Baby Dodds, Johnny Dodds's kid brother, claimed that King Oliver was intent on frustrating his white competition by cutting the titles off the music his band played. "They had tuxedos on, and on the cuffs of their sleeves they'd jot down different notes we played. . . . No one could come up and look at the number to get it for his own outfit. Sometimes they asked Joe what a certain number was called and he would say anything that came into his mind."[13]

Oliver's disdain for the white musicians hovering around the bandstand was perhaps typical of Chicago's attitude at the time toward anyone associated with Paul Whiteman. And a sense of the chilly local reception accorded Whiteman and his musicians was conveyed by an unnamed member of his orchestra, who remarked: "My God, they just wouldn't dance to our music."[14] The problem was not simply that Whiteman's "symphonic syncopation" fell flat. He was faulted for not providing what was now being sought by Chicagoans in social dance music—"that steady hammering rhythm" and the prized value of keeping "good time."[15] Others, like Oliver and company, were clearly delivering the goods. "In a dance hall, amidst hundreds of feet, the special arrangements are literally lost in the shuffle, while the 'hot' band with no pretense at symphonic qualities, blares forth the rhythmic jazz in a manner to please the masses."[16]

Driving much of this rhythm was a moral crusade for "politely peppy dance music" in a setting which provided "carefully engineered and sanitized musical and dance experiences." A watchdog organization, the Juvenile Protective Association, had recently been formed to monitor the music making at virtually all of Chicago's largest dance halls. And owners, in turn, had banded together to establish the National Association of Ball Room Proprietors and Managers in an effort to resolve differences with the JPA. One of the first reforms to be implemented in 1921 was to speed up the music. "Within twenty-four hours, every orchestra in the ballroom group had doubled the tempo of its melodies. The toddle, the shimmy and kindred slow syncopated motions were impossible at the brisk pace the music set, and the managers found most of the bad dancing eliminated."[17]

So as far as the Chicagoans were concerned, Paul Whiteman, unlike King Oliver and his star protégé, was clearly not up to speed. But Oliver's mix of paranoia and overweening pride could have its downside. According to Hardin, one night he made an offhand remark to her that ultimately led to his undoing. He admitted that Armstrong could play better than he could, but that "as long as I keep him with me he won't be able to get ahead of me; I'll still be the King." But now Lil Hardin, who had by this time joined King Oliver's Creole Jazz Band, began to pay serious attention, especially at the band's first Gennett recording session, on April 5, 1923, in Richmond, Indiana. With the band members clustered around "the great big horn," there

2.2 King Oliver's Creole Jazz Band, 1923. From left, Baby Dodds (drums), Honoré Dutrey (trombone), Joe Oliver (cornet), Bill Johnson (bass), Louis Armstrong (cornet), Johnny Dodds (clarinet), Lil Hardin (piano). Institute of Jazz Studies, Rutgers University.

were apparently such problems of balance that Joe Oliver's playing was simply inaudible. The solution, it turned out, was to have Armstrong stand some twelve to fifteen feet away from the rest of the group; such was the power and intensity of his sound. At the same time there were the first stirrings of a strong mutual attraction between Lil Hardin and Louis Armstrong. "He thought it was bad for him to be away from the band. He was looking so sad and I'd look back at him, smile, you know. . . . So then I was convinced. H'm yes, he really can play better because if his tone overshadows Joe that much he's got to be better. . . . I comes to feeling sorry for him. . . . That's a bad sign when you start to feel sorry for a man."[18]

Before long, as they were "getting to be sweethearts," going to dances and doing things together, Armstrong's wardrobe came under her scrutiny. "Everything he had on was secondhand." Inevitably talk of money came up, and a remark of Armstrong's proves a clue to future events: "Joe [Oliver] keeps my money. . . . I'm working for Mr. Joe. . . . He sent for me. . . . He looks after me."[19] Rebellion in the ranks was at hand. Defections from the band soon followed, when Johnny Dodds and his brother Baby Dodds discovered that Oliver had for a long time been collecting ninety-five dollars a week for each band member and pocketing twenty. Reportedly the Dodds brothers threatened to beat up Joe Oliver, who began carrying a pistol in his trumpet case. Amid all this strife Hardin and Armstrong clung to Oliver's band a while longer, until June 1924. Armstrong experienced a growing frustration at having to play second cornet to Oliver and to imitate the older man's style, particularly in such numbers as "Dippermouth Blues," while Hardin was more and more firmly convinced that Armstrong should be his own man, especially after she could hear the clear evidence of his gifts as he'd come home "whistling much more than a block away." Hearing all those amazing riffs, trills, and runs finally prompted her ultimatum: "You can't be married to Joe and to me." Determined to build his self-confidence, she would spend time with him at the piano, helping him refine his skills in sight reading and develop his knowledge of scales and harmony.

Many years later Armstrong himself freely acknowledged how vital a part Lil Hardin had played in his progress: "If she did engineer my life, she had a perfect right to. We married and heard the preacher when he said to love, honor, and obey. And to me that's what was happening. . . . I listened very careful when Lil told me I should play first cornet. Play second to no one, she told me. They don't get great enough. She proved she was right, didn't she?"[20] After Armstrong quit the band he found himself casting about for a while. He even briefly had thoughts about rejoining Joe Oliver when the fateful call came from Fletcher Henderson to join him as first trumpet in his big band at the prestigious Roseland Ballroom. By the beginning of October 1924 he was already in New York.

Closer scrutiny of the kind of world that Armstrong was about to enter can tell us a great deal about the complex interplay of race, class, and commerce in the early development of jazz. It diminishes Henderson's achievement, let alone Armstrong's contributions, to suggest that Henderson's band somehow "sold out" by playing a venue like Roseland. Henderson has been criticized as making "commercial concessions, especially at his debut, when he attempted to be the 'Paul Whiteman of the race.'"[21] Such a condescending view serves only to polarize the discussion of jazz, promoting the cliché that jazz "black" and "hot" is "the primitive art of Negroid improvisation" and epitomizes the "true" expression of the music, whereas "white" jazz and its commercial band arrangements exemplifies all that is sterile and bland.[22] It is a simplistic essentialist dichotomy that does not hold up.

Located at Broadway and West 51st Street, Roseland was the playground of Louis J. Brecker, a graduate of the Wharton Business School and a big fan of Irene and Vernon Castle. The grand opening of his sumptuously decorated showplace had taken place on New Year's Eve, 1919. Serving an exclusively white clientele, including such notables as Billie Burke, Flo Ziegfeld, and Will Rogers, it offered the added attraction of pretty dance hostesses who were to be available most nights to "any sober and orderly male partner" willing to pay. The club was promoted "as a place for wholesome entertainment, with continuous music for dancing of the fox-trot/waltz/tango/rhumba variety. It was never noted as haven for the Charleston fan or, ten years later, the jitterbug."[23] This is the context in which to read the original advertisement for the position that Henderson's ensemble eventually filled as the resident black band, performing in alternate sets with its white counterpart, Sam Lanin and his Orchestra. Henderson was hired as a replacement for the recently departed New Orleans Creole bandleader Armand J. Piron, a man whose popularity was so great that Paul Whiteman had tried to lure him into remaining in New York. "We have an opening for TWO VERSATILE BANDS. Two high-grade Dance Orchestras . . . wanted by a high-class New York ballroom to play for the evening sessions. Jazz bands will not be considered."[24]

Henderson had all the right credentials to enter many areas of the black music business as it sought to mainstream itself for popular Broadway consumption. Of light complexion and born into a middle-class black Georgia family, he had been exposed early on to European art music, had studied piano, and had been effectively insulated by his parents from "low" black music like ragtime and blues. He earned a bachelor's degree in chemistry and mathematics at Atlanta University only to find jobs closed to him when he came north to New York. Fortunately, he was able to find work as house pianist, demonstrating songs and serving as musical factotum, organizing combos and such for the black-owned publishing firm of Handy and Pace. When Harry Pace parted company with W. C. Handy to form the record label Black Swan, Henderson joined him as house accompanist. The first label to be run and owned by black businessmen, it appropriated the nickname of the opera singer Elizabeth Taylor Greenfield. The label included a catalogue of overlapping categories, with material ranging from European classical music to blues, for their clientele, the black "race record" market.

The climate was right for mainstreaming: the memory was still fresh of the Broadway premiere on May 23, 1921, of *Shuffle Along*—something of a miracle in that never before had a musical written, performed, and directed by blacks been presented there. It had had a run there of 504 performances, until July 22, 1922, a staggering number for its time, to be followed by several road companies touring the country until well into 1924. A collaboration involving principally the talents of Eubie Blake and Noble Sissle, it was a show packed with virtually every current dance step except the waltz, and it included the showstopper "I'm Just Wild About Harry." This particular number, by the way, came to have a firm place in Paul Whiteman's repertoire, especially in the arrangement of Roy Bargy. And speaking of arrangers, the pit band for *Shuffle Along* included a young oboist by the name of William Grant Still, later to become one of Paul Whiteman's principal arrangers and "the dean of black American composers." Such were some of the ways in which black and white musical worlds intermingled.

But at the same time, certain racial stereotypes persisted and were duly catered to. Consider the orchestra for *Shuffle Along;* they all committed the entire score to memory. As Eubie Blake later explained: "We did that because it was expected of us. People didn't believe that black people could read music—they wanted to think that our ability was just natural talent."[25] A wickedly clever routine, and a variation on this theme, promoting the image of blacks as "instinctive" musical illiterates, was attributed by Eubie Blake to James Reese Europe:

> Europe would buy full, stock arrangements of the popular hits of the day and rehearse his musicians, all of whom were good readers, extensively in this material, adding a few distinctive touches to make the arrangement fit the band. Once the arrangement was worked over, however, it would be memorized and the music would not be brought to the job. . . . Europe, when taking requests, would ask the patrons to sing a few bars of the melody and ask for a few minutes to "work it out with the boys." Then he would have the orchestra play the tune exactly as it had been rehearsed, to the accompaniment of amazed remarks by the audience about the natural talent of these Negroes.[26]

Henderson himself, however, was the child of a new age, a beneficiary of the Harlem Renaissance. Nathan Irvin Huggins, a major scholar of this period, has suggested that this was a time when "inequities due to race might best be removed, when reasonable men saw that black men were thinkers, strivers, doers, and were cultivated, like themselves."[27] Henderson and his sidemen, unlike many slightly older black musicians of the day, were perfectly open about being skilled readers, eminently capable of playing dance arrangements in the manner of white society orchestras such as those of Vincent Lopez and Paul Whiteman. As a bandleader, Henderson was sleek and polished, somewhat aloof, and very concerned about appearances. Howard Scott, a member of the trumpet section during Armstrong's time with the band, recalls Henderson as "a very strict leader. Every night you had to . . . stand inspection. He'd look at your hair, your face, see if you shaved, your shoes, see if they're shined. You had to be perfect to suit him. . . . He was strict and nice and exact in everything he did."[28] Even more important, he was uncanny in his ability to spot outstanding young talent. In fact, much of the creative energy of the ensemble flowed from its sidemen and arrangers, such as Coleman Hawkins on tenor saxophone, Louis Armstrong on trumpet, and Don Redman, reed player and arranger. Redman's charts were as vital to Henderson's early success as Ferde Grofé's were to Paul Whiteman; and in Redman's case especially we hear the beginnings of later big band swing.

Dave Peyton of the *Chicago Defender* published a glowing review of the ensemble shortly after Armstrong had joined it, without ever mentioning him by name; he compared the group to the best white orchestras. As leader of a dance orchestra catering to a white clientele, the upwardly mobile, assimilationist Peyton deplored the crudities of "hot" jazz, which, in his view, served only to perpetuate the primitive stereotype of purely "ear" black musicians. Better to aspire to a level of musical literacy that required reading from meticulously worked out written arrangements. As Dave Peyton put it: "On the Atlantic coast we have Fletcher Henderson's and Leroy Smith's famous orchestras, both recording units that we are proud of. . . . These orchestras stand shoulder to shoulder with the best American orchestras in the dance field. Let these orchestras be an example to follow. Get their programs, read them, and when possible, hear them play, and you will hear and understand just what the public wants."[29]

Paul Whiteman himself praised the group highly. In the words of Howard Scott: "Paul Whiteman came himself to hear Fletcher's band, and he said if Fletcher was a white man, he would be a millionaire. That's just what he said. I heard him."[30] In fact, Whiteman soon put his money where his mouth was by commissioning from Fletcher Henderson the number "Whiteman Stomp," which is actually credited to Paul Whiteman, Fats Waller, and Alphonso Trent. In its arrangement by Don Redman, the piece comes across as a tour de force of nervous energy, rich in timbral and textural variety "inside the strain" or within a given chorus. There are those who have heard this style as the epitome of Redman's "experimental" period as an arranger while others have considered the arrangement a parody of the Whiteman style with "its humorously complicated changes of mood and rhythm."[31] No matter. Whiteman himself relished this general kind of orchestration, pointing out in his book *Jazz:* "After the tune is set the instrumentation shall be changed for each half chorus. . . . The new demand is for change and novelty."[32] The piece came to be included in the band "book" of both Whiteman and Henderson, becoming something of a repertoire staple. Then again, there is Henderson's self-revealing piece, "Dicty Blues," with an oxymoron of a title if ever there was one. Certainly the characteristic psychological message of *blues* as earthy, "down-home," melancholic, or as an expression of survival, seems incompatible with the idea of *dicty*, a synonym for the elegant and upscale. What adds to the effect is the use of chimes as a refrain to signify classy living—a quality attributed by Armstrong to Henderson. There is also the feature—and a highly unusual one for a blues—of the piece ending with the opening strain in the subdominant key: that is, four steps above the initial key, representing perhaps a metaphor for upward mobility. This is fully consistent with Fletcher Henderson's reputation as the "Ivy League prom king"—in the words of *Variety*—because he so often played at fraternity gigs at Cornell, Yale, and Princeton. Giving his account of a summer spent with the Henderson outfit, Armstrong conveys his own enjoyment of the good life, a world far removed from the abject poverty of his early New Orleans years or from his strong work ethic: "I stayed with Fletcher's band from the last part of 1924 to almost [the end of] 1925. We played at the Roseland Ballroom for over Six Months, then we went on tour. We were the First Colored Big Band to Hit the Road. We went All through the New England States. We spent our First Summer up in Lawrence Mass—That was our Headquarters, while we played dances to all the Surrounding Towns. Was quite a Thrilling Experience to have most of my days off and we would go 'Swimming' etc."[33]

Quite predictably, the addition of Armstrong to the band of Fletcher Henderson meant the meeting of two different musical cultures, as Armstrong's account of the first rehearsal makes vividly clear:

> When I arrived in New York I had to go straight to rehearsal—I felt so funny. I walked up to old "Smack" [Henderson's nickname] and said: "Er, wa, I'm that boy you sent for to blow the trumpet in your band." And "Smack," all sharp as a Norwegian with that hard-hitting steel-gray suit he had on, said, "Oh, yes, we're waiting for you. Your part's up there" (meaning the bandstand). I said, "Yassuh," and went up there with my eyes closed. When I opened them I looked square into the faces of Coleman Hawkins, Don Redman, Kaiser Marshall. . . . They all casually looked out of the corner of their eyes. . . . I said to myself these boys look like a bunch of nice fellows, but they seem a little stuckup. . . . Where I had come from I wasn't used to playing in bands where there were a lot of parts for everybody to read. Shucks, all one man in the band had to do was go to some show and hear a good number. He keeps it in

his head until he reaches us. He hums it a couple of times, and from then on we had a new number.[34]

We also pick up some other telling clues about the repertoire of Henderson's big band and the blurring of category from the inclusion of such popular Indian ditties of the day as "By the Waters of Minnetonka"—the first number Armstrong actually played with them. There is the amusing anecdote told by Henderson himself about a rehearsal of a medley of Irish waltzes that highlights Armstrong's unfamiliarity at the time with the basic elements of notated dynamic markings. Apparently Armstrong seemed a little perplexed by the written part given him, even though the dynamics were clearly marked, indicating among other things a diminuendo down to *pp* following a *fff*. Everyone in the band proceeded to dutifully observe these markings, except Armstrong, who was still playing his part at full volume. Stopping the band, Henderson said: "'Louis, you are not following the arrangement.' Louis objected, saying, 'I'm reading everything on this sheet.' I said, 'But, Louis, how about that *pp*?' and Louis broke us all up by replying, 'Oh, I thought that meant "pound plenty."' There was no tension after that."[35]

Armstrong did not remember things quite that way. In fact, the tension between the two of them was very real for him. He felt that he was effectively put in a straitjacket, limited in all of his Henderson recordings to eight- or sixteen-bar solos, occasional breaks, and in one notable instance, a complete chorus—hardly space enough to spread his improvisational wings. However, it should be said that a recent major reexamination of Fletcher Henderson, his musical methods, and his musical world, yields a different conclusion: that the role of improvised "hot" solos by players such as Armstrong was to add variety to an arrangement inside the strain (or chorus).[36] This was just one example of how bandleaders of the time such as Henderson and Whiteman came to relish the practice of introducing variety within a chorus by frequently shifting between instruments and sections of the band—a feature for which the "Whiteman Stomp" is notable.

Yet Armstrong's expressions of general frustration are understandable. He claimed that he was allowed to play only third cornet, even though when occasion demanded it, he would "hit those high notes that the big primadonnas, first chair men, couldn't hit." And as a vocalist he fared even worse, complaining about Henderson, who was acutely sensitive to how he was perceived by his exclusively white clientele: "As far as Fletcher was concerned he wouldn't even listen to me sing nothing."[37] Henderson's version, dating from many years later, very shortly before his death in 1951, gives a slightly different spin while still communicating a certain condescension. "About three weeks after he joined us, he asked me if he could sing a number. I know I wondered what he could possibly do with that big fish horn voice of his, but finally I told him to try it. He was great. The band loved it, and the crowd just ate it up."[38]

The realities of Armstrong's workaday world were considerably more complex and intense than his recorded legacy with Henderson might suggest. For one thing, there were those occasional appearances he made with the group up in Harlem, where he could strut his stuff. His debut in that part of town was at the Lafayette Theater, Seventh Avenue at West 131st Street, when, onstage with the Fletcher Henderson Orchestra, he unleashed several choruses of "Whatcha-Cal-'Em Blues" to wild applause. But in terms of posterity, his other work in the recording studio, quite separate from that with Henderson, demonstrates ever so clearly how much creative energy the young man had to burn.

Days after his arrival in New York he had been propositioned by Clarence Williams, the ambitious pianist-composer-entrepreneur who knew Armstrong from his New Orleans days. Now ensconced as head of the Clarence Williams Publishing Company in the Gaiety Theater Building at 1547 Broadway, a few blocks down from the Roseland Ballroom, Williams was operating out of a building that was a beehive of activity in African-American entertainment. Bert Williams, Will Vodery, Pace and Handy, and Perry Bradford were among the notables of the day with offices there. Clarence Williams supervised artists and repertoire operations in New York for Okeh, a major race record label, and served as an important catalyst for Armstrong. Over the next year, from October 1924 to October 1925, Armstrong accompanied a host of blues and novelty singers in the recording studio, whether for the Okeh, the Gennett, or the Columbia label. These included Williams's own wife Eva Taylor, as well as Ma Rainey, Alberta Hunter, and the legendary Bessie Smith. Totally riveting are the two groups called the Red Onion Babies and Clarence Williams's Blue Five, precursors to Armstrong's own Hot Five; these sessions brought Armstrong together with the formidable Sidney Bechet on soprano saxophone. The competitive fire that was lit between Armstrong and Bechet in the two separate sessions featuring "Cake Walking Babies from Home," for example, is unmistakable.[39] By the same token, all of these sessions represent the polar opposite of what was typically required of Armstrong when he was on the bandstand with the Fletcher Henderson Orchestra.

The name of Sidney Bechet raises some sadly ironic issues about the interplay of personality, race, and class. When he recorded those sessions with

Armstrong, Bechet had recently returned to the United States, almost unnoticed by the larger public, after performing to great acclaim in England and France. Here was an indisputably great musician who had clearly acquired "foreign flavor," to borrow Whiteman's term, as well as foreign favor. As a member of Will Marion Cook's Southern Syncopated Orchestra, he had gone to Europe in 1919, playing, among other things, a command performance at Buckingham Palace before George V, father of the prince of Wales, who later became Whiteman's guardian angel during his sojourn there in 1923. It was during the 1919 appearances in London that Cook's orchestra was heard by Swiss conductor Ernest Ansermet, one of the avowed champions of musical modernism. He waxed ecstatic about "the superb taste" and "the astonishing perfection" of the group, singling out for special praise Sidney Bechet, who at the time was still playing only clarinet. Ansermet's piece has proven to be one of the seminal and prophetic early instances of jazz criticism coming from Europe and recognizing jazz as "perhaps the highway the whole world will swing along tomorrow." Writing of the Southern Syncopated Orchestra, he draws attention to "an extraordinary clarinet virtuoso who is, so it seems, the first of his race to have composed perfectly formed blues on his clarinet. . . . I wish to set down the name of this artist of genius; as for myself, I shall never forget it. . . . It is Sidney Bechet."[40]

Selected recordings that Armstrong made with Fletcher Henderson's orchestra provide a valuable sound portrait of the time, helping highlight some of the many ways in which the music was shaped by the changing imperatives of class and race. For example, "Go 'Long, Mule" (October 7, 1924) offers a striking mélange of styles, past, present, and future. Built on an up-tempo tune reminiscent of the then-outdated cakewalk, it is punctuated by "novelty" barnyard breaks recalling the Original Dixieland Jazz Band, supposedly signifying our mule. But there is also a fine balance between Don Redman's contemporary, fully arranged sectional contrasts of reeds and trumpets, and spaces provided for hot improvised solos by Charlie Green on trombone and Armstrong on trumpet. There are also echoes by a trumpet trio of the wah-wah sound popularized by Paul Whiteman's own Henry Busse, who can be heard on Whiteman's recordings beginning in 1920.

This intriguing interplay between black and white bands shows up in so many different ways in this period. "Shanghai Shuffle" (October 10–13, 1924) is a rather provocative takeoff on the hit "Limehouse Blues," as recorded by Paul Whiteman and his Orchestra in January of that year—a number that was an important catalyst in mainstreaming jazz. Especially memorable is the stop-time chorus backing Henderson's Charlie Green in his gutsy trombone solo, not to mention Armstrong's taking a complete chorus leading to his trademark of climactic, repeated, punched single notes. There is a full chorus for Armstrong in the period chestnut "Copenhagen" as well. It forms part of a richly varied arrangement by Don Redman that vividly combines the collective improvisation of early Dixieland with deftly written choruses, contrasting such timbres as clarinet trio, brass and clarinet obbligato, and full ensemble.

The cross-fertilization of Armstrong's King Oliver days with the world of Fletcher Henderson could not be better illustrated than with the recording of "Dippermouth Blues" in its big band incarnation by Don Redman as "Sugar Foot Stomp"—a performance that happily coincides with the introduction of the electrical recording process and much-improved resulting sound quality. Redman expands upon the original sequence of twelve-bar blues choruses to include a perky sixteen-bar clarinet trio. Other enlivening features include the banjo accompaniment to the solo trombone chorus and, the standout, Armstrong's re-creation of the characteristic wah-wah choruses of the original.

In early November 1925 Armstrong finally left Fletcher Henderson to return to Chicago. Within the next four years he was to define the very nature of hot jazz there. The night before his departure a farewell party in his honor was held at Smalls' Paradise up in Harlem. Armstrong recalled:

> After we finished playing we went back to our table and started drinking some more "liquor"—I gotten so "Drunk" until Buster Bailey and I decided to go home. And just as I went to tell Fletcher Henderson Goodbye as I was leaving New York for Chicago the next morning, I said—"Fletcher 'Thanks' for being so kind to me." And-er-wer-er-wer- And before I know it—I had "Vomit" ("Puked") directly into Fletcher's "*Bosom.*" All over his Nice Clean Tuxedo Shirt. Oh—I'd gotten so sick all of a sudden.—I was afraid Fletcher would get sore at me, but all he said—"Aw—that's allright 'Dip'" (my nickname at the time).[41]

Armstrong harbored a sense of resentment that festered for many years. In fact, in December 1970, some forty-five years later, Dan Morgenstern, the renowned jazz critic and director of the Institute of Jazz Studies at Rutgers University, Newark, was told the same story when he visited Armstrong in his home for what would be the last time.[42] Ultimately, differences of personality and class between Armstrong and Henderson were simply not to be reconciled. "Fletcher was so carried away with that society shit and his education he slipped by a small-timer and a young musician-me—who wanted to do everything for him musically. I personally don't think Fletcher cared too much for me anyway."[43]

"That society shit" was something to which Whiteman was also keenly attuned. We know for a fact that Whiteman regularly moved in the kinds of circles suggested by *The Great Gatsby,* from his earliest gigs out on the West Coast for the Hollywood movie set to the upscale clientele at New York's Palais Royal. Even if he was far more genial and had much greater generosity of spirit than F. Scott Fitzgerald's Tom Buchanan, Whiteman was nevertheless keenly aware that whites were "the dominant race." In much of what he did, especially from about 1920 to 1926, he sought to consolidate that position; and in nothing was that clearer than in how he went about validating his ideas of "symphonic jazz" as a synthesis of the new "hot" jazz and European art music. This synthesis was central to his larger purpose in presenting the "Experiment in Modern Music" in 1924, for example, which marked the premiere of the most famous piece of "symphonic jazz" ever written, the specially commissioned *Rhapsody in Blue* of George Gershwin.

In his 1926 book *Jazz,* Whiteman makes a provocative statement about the beginnings of that kind of music, suggesting that it was taken seriously in the United States only after European composers had written jazz-inspired works. As examples he cites Stravinsky's *Ragtime* (1918) and Milhaud's *La Création du monde* (1923), remarking: "Americans were ashamed of the upstart. They kept humming it absent-mindedly, then flushing and apologizing. Nothing so common could be aesthetic, insisted the highbrows. Like everything else that was our own, its merits were, we thought, questionable. So it was left to Europe to discover the possibilities of our creature."[44]

However, the validation of jazz was not limited to Europe's composers. Whiteman crows elsewhere that not only America's social elite, but also visitors of renown from abroad, came to hear him at the Palais Royal. Among foreign dignitaries were Lord and Lady Mountbatten, cousins of the prince of Wales, better known as Edward VIII or the duke of Windsor, who was later to relinquish his throne voluntarily to marry American divorcée Wallis Warfield Simpson. The Mountbattens were avid dancers who began coming often and "got to be friends with every boy in the band." Lord Mountbatten soon began insisting that Whiteman come to London. "The Prince must have a chance to hear the band—that's all there is to it."[45]

A brief word or two about Whiteman's remark that the Mountbattens became friendly "with every boy in the band." Their reaction was fairly typical of Whiteman's dancing patrons and a reflection of his capacity to connect with his public, a tribute to his rare mix of a sense of theatricality and personal qualities of genial expansiveness. He relished the idea of proximity to his dancers and loved being on their level rather than being partially isolated in a "stage box" designed by Norman Bel Geddes. What is more, "he personalized the band by channeling the enthusiasm of the dancers to the players."[46] Included here were such sidemen as Ferde Grofé on piano, Henry Busse on cornet, Mike Pingitore on banjo, and reedplayer Ross Gorman—perhaps best remembered for originating the spectacular opening clarinet glissando in *Rhapsody in Blue*. Buoyed by the encouragement of the Mountbattens, Whiteman risked $18,000 of his own money, sailing with his entourage for Europe on March 3, 1923, eager to acquire "foreign flavor." But upon their arrival they faced problems with the British Ministry of Labour involving work permits, stemming in large part from fear that American jazz, once heard in England, would throw thousands of English musicians out of work; for it was a kind of music the Brits were supposedly unable to play. A compromise was eventually reached which made it possible to proceed as planned. The group played in "Brighter London," a revue at the Hippodrome, followed every evening by an appearance at Grafton Galleries, a chic nightclub. However, a proviso was added—that Whiteman hire for the nightclub performances the same number of English musicians as he had in his band. He was also amused to discover what a celebrity he had become. There were "some sharp little English messenger boys" outside the Hippodrome who kept running over to him for his autograph and would then sell it to a line of people across the street for a penny apiece. Amid all this, Whiteman relished the patronage of the prince of Wales, if the fact that he devotes some five pages of *Jazz* to the many charms of the prince is any indication. He played at a private party given for the prince by Lord Mountbatten; in addition, the prince, a very good dancer, would often grace the proceedings at Grafton Galleries with "no swank and no ostentation."

After five months in England, Whiteman and company returned home, sailing into New York harbor on August 13, 1923, where he was received like a conquering hero—a reception dramatically different from that accorded the itinerant Sidney Bechet just a few years earlier. "Every musician in the city seemed to be waiting to greet Whiteman with a syncopated welcome. Paul looked up from the deck to see a small band playing in an airplane above the ship. From another plane a skywriter had spelled out 'Hello Paul' against the blue sky."[47] A boatload of fans welcomed the incoming ship accompanied by serenading bands, and a plucky contingent of musicians bobbed about in the water wearing life preservers and adding to the delicious din. On shore, political dignitaries waited at Pier 86 at West 46th Street, not to mention representatives from RCA Victor and area theaters.

Climaxing the day's festivities was a gala dinner held at the Waldorf Asto-

2.3 Musicians afloat in New York harbor welcoming the return of Paul Whiteman from his 1923 European tour. Courtesy of Cynthia Magill.

ria with such notables present as George M. Cohan, Irving Berlin, John Philip Sousa, and Victor Herbert. At the end of the evening, following the inevitable toasts and speeches, Whiteman found himself overwhelmed, tears rolling down his cheeks. "For a moment, I forgot any cynicism I had felt about the false value of the European label in America. . . . It seemed to me then that everybody understood me, that my orchestra was a real success, that there was nothing in the future but sunshine and roses. But even at that moment, I didn't forget that we had come home to do bigger things in jazz."[48]

Given the benefit of hindsight, we know that "bigger things in jazz" meant establishing a place for his idea of "symphonic jazz," fusing jazz with classical concert music, and affirming the art of scoring and playing according to the score. It would all soon come together at the historic concert of February 12, 1924. This defining moment in American music was triggered by at least two developments in Whiteman's career. Starting on August 28, 1922, at New York's Globe Theater, Paul Whiteman and his Orchestra had been featured in the revue George White's *Scandals of 1922*—an extravaganza in the Florenz Ziegfeld *Follies* mold, with music by George Gershwin. The revue is best remembered for the song "I'll Build a Stairway to Paradise," the first-act finale in which girls dressed in black patent leather marched up a glittering white staircase. That was how Whiteman and George Gershwin first got to know each other.

An even more compelling and immediate stimulus came in the form of a concert by the mezzo-soprano Eva Gauthier on November 1, 1923, in Aeolian Hall, slightly more than three months before Whiteman's own performance there. Gauthier was joined by George Gershwin himself, who was making his first recital appearance. An ardent champion of contemporary European and American music, Gauthier caused a stir by including on her program American "popular" songs by Irving Berlin, Walter Donaldson, George Gershwin, and Jerome Kern alongside heavier fare by Bartók, Hindemith, Milhaud, and Schoenberg. As an unreformedly highbrow recitalist she was bringing her "artistry" to bear on the performance of popular music. In addition, reports that Vincent Lopez, a rival bandleader, was planning a similar sort of concert apparently got Whiteman's juices flowing. Two days before the Aeolian Hall concert Lopez and his band participated in a lecture-demonstration on the history of jazz given by Harvard professor Edward Burlinghame Hill at the Anderson Art Galleries. The event, which was sponsored by the League of Composers, proved to be a relatively lackluster affair compared with Whiteman's concert the following Tuesday afternoon. Even though Lopez eventually gave his own concert at the Metropolitan Opera House in November

1924, featuring an original composition by W. C. Handy, Whiteman had already effectively stolen his thunder—such was Whiteman's command of the media and the perceived quality of his musical offerings at the time.

In his efforts to legitimatize jazz and prime his public for the big February event, Whiteman mobilized his publicity machine, framing his upcoming concert within the context of a much bigger question—the nature of American music itself. Accordingly, the *New York Tribune* of January 4, 1924, contained a news item headlined WHITEMAN JUDGES NAMED, with the subheadline

> Committee Will Decide "What Is American Music"
> Among the members of the committee of judges who will
> pass on "What Is American Music?" at the Paul Whiteman
> concert to be given at Aeolian Hall, Tuesday afternoon,
> February 12, will be Serge Rachmaninoff, Jascha Heifetz,
> Efrem Zimbalist, and Alma Gluck.

The story claimed that the question "has aroused a tremendous interest in music circles and Mr. Whiteman is receiving every phase of manuscript, from blues to symphonies." But what most sharply defines the underlying thesis of Whiteman's "Experiment in Modern Music" is that it occurred during a decade when "any gangplank interview with European luminaries visiting the United States . . . whether Stravinsky, Bartók, or Ravel, revealed, sometimes painfully, that American jazz, not concert music, was what interested them." This meant that critical frames of reference were apt to meld the jazzy with the modern. There is, for example, a most telling juxtaposition of events—the New York premiere, on January 31, 1924, of Stravinsky's *Rite of Spring*, and Whiteman's concert just two weeks later. The effect was to see *Rhapsody in Blue* "as an example of both symphonic modernism and symphonic jazz." While the critical curmudgeon Daniel Gregory Mason despised both works, dismissing them as "tweedledum and tweedledee," there were many others who saw the Gershwin "as the New World's answer to Stravinsky."[49]

To achieve his purpose, Whiteman sought the help of his manager, Hugh C. Ernst, and the critic Gilbert Seldes. Together they produced a twelve-page program booklet that was absolutely explicit about "the why of the experiment." It was to be "purely educational," demonstrating how the art of "legitimate" scoring or orchestral arranging had transformed "the discordant Jazz" of yesteryear into "the really melodious music of today." The larger goal was to win over those "who ridicule the present so-called Jazz and who refuse to condone it or listen to it seriously." Accordingly, the concert was organized along evolutionary lines into eleven segments:

2.4 The original poster of 1924 announcing "An Experiment in Modern Music" at Aeolian Concert Hall. Note equal billing given to Zez Confrey, master of "novelty piano," and George Gershwin, as well as mention of "new typically American compositions" and product endorsements. Frank Driggs Collection.

1. True Form of Jazz
2. Comedy Selections
3. Contrast—Legitimate scoring vs. jazzing
4. Recent compositions with modern score
5. Zez Confrey
6. Flavoring a selection with borrowed themes
7. Semi-symphonic arrangement of popular melodies
8. Suite of Serenades
9. Adaptation of standard selections to dance rhythm
10. George Gershwin
11. In the field of classics

"Livery Stable Blues," the raucous selection of "hot" jazz associated with the Original Dixieland Jazz Band—"jazz in its true naked form" and the first jazz recording to be commercially released—started the concert. It so happens that this piece was among Armstrong's favorites—together with recordings of opera singers—that he came to own shortly after he acquired his first Victrola around 1917 or 1918. But the condescending Hugh Ernst rated it much lower: "About twelve years ago, five perfectly legitimate instruments of the orchestra—cornet, trombone, clarinet, piano and drum—found themselves in bad company! They were part of the equipment of the first jazz band. The additional instruments consisted of an anvil, sledge, several buckets . . . a lot of similar hardware. Through the efforts of five hard working musicians the worst was gotten out of the instruments and the best from the foundry equipment."

Virtually all of the other items on Whiteman's program were focused on the single goal of demonstrating just how far jazz had evolved from the perceived crudities of the Original Dixieland Jazz Band to embrace the refinements of "legitimate" scoring. The only clear exception was the segment featuring Zez Confrey's solo "novelty piano," a ragtime subgenre, with its "exasperating syncopations." For the rest, excepting Gershwin's *Rhapsody in Blue* and the quasi-recessional *Pomp and Circumstance* march, the program showed, as we shall see, a striking kinship with the Armstrong-Henderson repertoire of the day. Henderson was, we recall, perceived as the "Paul Whiteman of the race," a purveyor of a kind of jazz that was "clean" and "commercial."[50]

This was a time when "jazzing" of the classics was common, typically with a fox-trot beat. Traditional boundaries formerly perceived as separating race, class, and category were now frequently blurred. It was a phenomenon that perhaps reflected something of the angst felt by Tom Buchanan in *The Great Gatsby*, of civilization going to pieces. A couple of vivid cases in point from Whiteman's Aeolian Hall concert are Ferde Grofé's confection "Russian Rose," with elements lifted largely from "Song of the Volga Boatmen," Rachmaninoff's Prelude in C sharp minor, and Rimsky-Korsakov's "Song of India." One could add "Yes, We Have No Bananas," with its appropriations from Handel's *Messiah* and Michael Balfe's opera *The Bohemian Girl*.

A similar process is evident in Armstrong's music making. During his stint with Fletcher Henderson in New York he recorded a selection entitled "Araby," much of which is built on the aria "Avant de quitter ces lieux" from Gounod's *Faust*. And as we have seen, during his early New York career, from 1923 to 1925, Armstrong was highly active in the recording studio, not only working as a member of Fletcher Henderson's orchestra but also backing singers in a variety of separate small-group sessions. On November 11, 1925, for example, he recorded the number "Washwoman Blues" with singer Hociel Thomas, which plunders much of an aria from Bizet's *Carmen*, specifically Don Jose's "Flower Song."

Other cross-influences connect Whiteman and Armstrong. Whiteman's 1920 hit "Whispering," which made bold use of the slide whistle and was included in the Aeolian Hall concert, had a sequel three years later in King Oliver's "Sobbin' Blues," in which Armstrong can be heard playing both slide whistle and cornet. We can also point to Armstrong's 1926 Hot Five recording of the pop song "Who'Sit," which includes a delicious third chorus on slide whistle heard against a gurgling clarinet countermelody. Then again one can point to Whiteman's 1921 traversal of "Mon Homme," popularized by Fanny Brice as "My Man" in the Ziegfeld Follies of the same year, and Fletcher Henderson's "Go 'Long Mule," which was recorded in October 1924, very shortly after Armstrong joined the band. The duet between Whiteman's star trumpet player Henry Busse and reedman Hale Byers is the inspiration for the later pairing of Henderson's Don Redman and Coleman Hawkins; what is more, the performance also includes the characteristic Busse wah-wah imitation. Consider also Whiteman's "Japanese Sandman" (1920), a putative model for Armstrong's "Indian Cradle Song" of ten years later.[51] And we should add that we have not yet even begun to examine the musical interconnections between Whiteman and Armstrong based on a common core repertory of popular favorites—they recorded well over a dozen of the very same standards.

The buzz in the local press after Whiteman's Aeolian Hall concert was hard to ignore. Deems Taylor, a composer and critic writing for *New York World*, said that *Rhapsody in Blue* was "crude, but it hinted at something new, something that has not hitherto been said in music," adding that Gershwin "may yet bring jazz out of the kitchen." Even more important to Whiteman's larger agenda, Taylor sounded a note of hope for the future of symphonic jazz: "This occasion was a concert by Paul Whiteman and his Palais Royal Orchestra. Mr. Whiteman, whose achievements in organizing and conducting contemporary dance orchestras have made him famous even in Europe, has theories regarding the so-called Jazz Band. He feels that the rhythms, melodies and instrumentation of our modern popular music contain the germ of a school of genuine American composition and his concert yesterday was designed not only to exhibit jazz as it is today, but jazz as it was and may become."[52]

Rhapsody in Blue immediately became Whiteman's calling card, living proof for him that there was a bright future for symphonic jazz. Ironically, for his white audiences of the 1920s the work passed for "hot" jazz. Yet signs of change were already in the wind, and Whiteman's programming reflected that. When repeating his program at Aeolian Hall on March 7, he dropped two of the three "recent compositions with modern score," including Jerome Kern's "Raggedy Ann" as well as Zez Confrey's "Nickel in the Slot." And by the time of the Carnegie Hall concert on April 21, a benefit for the American Academy in Rome, all three of Irving Berlin's songs had disappeared as well. It is especially revealing that in this concert "Livery Stable Blues," replete with all its barnyard crudities, was replaced by "Dixieland Jazz One Step." This effectively eliminated any basis for invidious, condescending comparison of jazz "in its true, naked form" with the more "civilized" and "legitimate" scoring for big band. There were changes in instrumentation as well: his violin section was reduced to six players, his saxophones expanded to four—the norm in most later big bands.

By mid-May 1924 Paul Whiteman and his Orchestra had started their first North American tour, on which the Carnegie Hall concert was repeated in all essential details. Their travels took them from Rochester, New York, to Buffalo, Pittsburgh, Indianapolis, St. Louis, Kansas City, Cleveland, Detroit, Toronto, Montreal, and elsewhere. Always image-conscious, Whiteman made his concerts into "productions":

The appearances of the orchestra were carefully staged. First the audience saw a curtain of gold cloth with a silhouette of the Whiteman orchestra; this withdrew to reveal the orchestra dressed in its summer whites and seated on white bentwood chairs on tiers of dove gray trimmed with vermillion. Two white grand pianos flanked the drummer's elaborate traps at the back of the stage, and behind them all was a glittering metallic curtain with huge vermillion floral designs. In front of the orchestra Whiteman conducted from within a curved shell which one critic described as looking like "an ocean liner's smoke stack."[53]

This décor, the creation of one of Florenz Ziegfeld's most gifted designers, has been seen as further proof "that Whiteman was operating in the mixed tradition of the American pops and appreciation concert, rather than the realms of serious music, or jazz, which was often, as at the Cotton Club, far racier."[54] But by the fall of 1924, when he was back in New York, questions were being raised about Whiteman's vision of jazz on the concert stage and the viability of "symphonic jazz." Put in the starkest terms, could there be another *Rhapsody in Blue,* could musical lightning strike more than once? Lackluster compositions by Eastwood Lane, Ferde Grofé, and one Mme. Mana-Zucca simply failed to carry the day at concerts given at Carnegie Hall, Aeolian Hall, the Brooklyn Academy of Music, and the Metropolitan Opera House. To add insult to injury, the performances of Grofé's *Mississippi Suite* and Gershwin's *135th Street* at Whiteman's Second Experiment in Modern American Music at Carnegie Hall on December 29 proved a disappointment, the Gershwin work in particular being dismissed by one critic as "an extremely dreary affair."

Olin Downes of the *New York Times* offered a pointed evaluation of the situation, expressing a guarded optimism about the future of symphonic jazz. While conceding that there was "far more genuine music-making accomplished by the denizens of song factories" than by the professedly "serious" composers, he cautioned that "the jazz composer . . . will not find himself by merely giving concerts, or making symphonic pretensions without substantial material to back them."[55] A critic with impeccable credentials in piano, music history, and theory, Olin Downes was an ardent champion of such composers as Richard Strauss, Prokofiev, Stravinsky, Shostakovich, and Sibelius. In addition, he later became widely known for his quiz programs on Saturday afternoon broadcasts of the Metropolitan Opera. To be fair, given his pedigree, he was not one to approach jazz from the other side of the tracks, from the world of popular music.

That was to be the special contribution of Gilbert Seldes in his 1924 book *The Seven Lively Arts,* which stands as a fascinating artifact of its day. It is the work of a critical visionary who was quick to embrace all popular—that is, "lively"—idioms, whether jazz, dance, the comic strip, the movies, the circus, theater, or journalism. Above all, he wanted all these modes of creative expression to be viewed as "art"; and his essay on jazz specifically, "Toujours Jazz," is a cogent rebuttal of a diatribe entitled "Plus de Jazz" that argues for the death of jazz. Yet for all his enthusiastic embrace of jazz as one of the popular arts, Seldes still unequivocally argues for the superiority of white "civilization." While he admits that James Reese Europe, with his "constructive intelligence," would have surpassed Paul Whiteman as a conductor had he lived longer, and while he does praise the accomplishments of Sissle and Blake in *Shuffle Along,* his racial loyalties clearly lie elsewhere: "I say the negro is not our salvation because with all my feeling for what he instinctively offers, for his desirable indifference to our set of conventions about emotional decency, I am on the side of civilization. . . . Nowhere is the failure of the negro to exploit his gifts more obvious than in the use he has made of the jazz orchestra; for although nearly every negro jazz band is better than nearly every white band, no negro band has yet come up to the level of the best white ones, and the leader of the best of all, by a little joke, is called Whiteman."[56]

Some two years later, Henry O. Osgood, in his 1926 book *So This Is Jazz,* the first major history in the English language devoted entirely to jazz, champions the cause of symphonic jazz in general and Paul Whiteman in particular. Again, the image of jazz as something to be tamed by civilization is inescapable. One of his early chapters, "When Did the Monster First Rear His Head?" leaves little to the imagination. A photograph of Whiteman serves as the frontispiece, and six of the book's twenty chapters are dedicated to various aspects of his work—the jazz orchestra, "anatomy" of jazz orchestration, Ferde Grofé, and so on. In the chapter "The King of Jazz" we find Osgood welcoming Whiteman like royalty. "Paul Whiteman looms large in the history of jazz in more senses than one. (His fighting weight is somewhere around two hundred and eighty.) He has been christened the king of jazz by his publishers. But he deserves it, for if it hadn't been for his ambition and his initiative, jazz would still be the same old tum-tum fox-trot music, with its eternal monotony of *alla breve* and nothing else." In keeping with the general tone of his chapter "Gershwin, the White Hope," we find Osgood being guarded in his hopes for the future; and his assessment of the concert repertoire of jazz is decidedly sober. As he succinctly puts it in his summation: "There were great hopes for the grafting of jazz onto and into legitimate music when Gershwin came along with the remarkable *Rhapsody;* but that was over two years ago, and very little has happened since."[57]

Whiteman's own book, *Jazz,* cowritten with Mary Margaret McBride, appeared very shortly after Osgood's. The fact that it also ran as a three-part series in the *Saturday Evening Post* that year helps explain the unmistakable "fanzine" tone of many of its pages. Besides, his coauthor, a protégé of his press agent, had the distinction of having taken the temperance pledge at the tender age of four; she disapproved of cigarette smoking and later became a fixture on homey network radio programs. In any event, Whiteman unabashedly tells all about his social connections, dwelling on the many charms of the prince of Wales and his acquaintance with the upper crust. As for jazz itself, he does not hesitate to point out that Americans were at one time ashamed of the upstart. As Whiteman saw it, it was only after Stravinsky and Milhaud used jazz motifs in *Ragtime* and *La Création du monde*, respectively, that American musicians began to "look interested." Without this European validation, Whiteman's agenda of making symphonic jazz legitimate would have been that much harder to achieve. Yet he also freely acknowledges the link of early jazz with slavery. "Jazz came to America three hundred years ago in chains. The psalm-singing Dutch traders, sailing in a man-of-war across the ocean in 1619, described their cargo as 'fourteen black African slaves for sale in his Majesty's colonies.' But priceless freight destined three centuries later to set a whole nation dancing went unnoted and unbilled by the stolid, revenue-hungry Dutchmen."[58]

Whiteman goes on to evoke images of the Ku Klux Klan when responding to the barbs of which he has been a target, whether hurled by the Salvation Army, members of the temperance movement, or music critics; and, at the same time, he readily minimizes his role in the larger scheme of jazz history. "It is a relief to be able to prove at last that I did not invent jazz. I took it where I found it and I wish the preachers and club lady uplifters who put on sheets and pillow cases to go jazz-klanning wouldn't concentrate on me. I don't deserve it, really, nor the snorting editorials from Burma to Sydney, either. . . . All I did was to orchestrate jazz. If I had not done it, somebody else would have."[59] The British critic Ernest Newman, an avowed Wagnerian, was among those to savage the efforts of Whiteman. "Your typical jazz composer or jazz enthusiast is merely a musical illiterate who is absurdly pleased with little things because he does not know how little they are. The brains of the whole lot of them would not fill the lining of Johann Strauss's hat. . . . The thing is dead from the neck up."[60]

But Whiteman was apparently undaunted by such views. He responded by waxing patriotic as he articulated his vision for the future of jazz, anticipating the style of much of what Ferde Grofé was later to achieve in such works as his *Grand Canyon Suite* (1931) and *Mississippi Suite* (1933): "I am ambitious for jazz to develop always in an American way. I want to see compositions written around the great natural and geographical features of American life—written in the jazz idiom. I believe this would help Americans to appreciate their own country." Mixed in with this was a little self-styled boosterism and hype, promoting the cause of middle-American capitalism. "It is bulking increasingly large in economics. There are today more than 200,000 men playing it. The number of jazz arrangers is around 30,000. Thus two entirely new industries have grown up in less than ten years. . . . Jazz has made fortunes and bought automobiles, country houses and fur coats for many a player, composer, and publisher."[61]

Yet when all is said and done the books of Whiteman, Seldes, or Osgood seem to have done little to change the minds of the Ernest Newmans of this world. In fact, in March 1927 we find another attack by Newman telling "the jazzhounds to keep their dirty paws off their betters," followed a week later by a vigorous rebuttal by Paul Whiteman.[62] It is significant that, at a time when he was the rising star of hot jazz on the Chicago scene, Armstrong goes unmentioned in the writings of Osgood, Seldes, or Whiteman. And it is equally true that no coat pockets of black musicians were being filled in the manner described by Whiteman. It was only in 1929, when he returned to New York from Chicago, that Armstrong, now the consummate star soloist in a changed political climate, would be poised to become the international lightning rod for jazz, with his first European tours soon to follow. But before then, from about 1925 to 1929, the winds of change were already blowing, driving the debate about jazz in a different direction. And in their distinctive ways Armstrong and Whiteman were each making jazz something hotter.

3 SOME LIKED IT HOT

The *Chicago Defender* of November 14, 1925, left little doubt about what a hot property the city had in its midst. Lil Hardin's band at the Dreamland was featuring "The World's Greatest Cornetist, Louis Armstrong." Armstrong was recently back from his thirteen months in New York with Fletcher Henderson, and Hardin's ambitions for her husband had never burned more intensely. Just as she had initiated Armstrong's break with Joe Oliver, so too did she push for his departure from the Henderson band; and that fire was lit when Armstrong had been with the band for barely a month! As early as November 1924, when she visited Armstrong in New York, staying on through most of December, she made a disturbing discovery: "I joined him after a couple of weeks. I noticed in Fletcher's billing nothing but 'Fletcher Henderson's Orchestra'—nobody else's name."[1]

Going back to Chicago, Hardin worked out a deal at the Dreamland: Armstrong would be paid $75 a week, and his name would be prominently displayed outside. She wrote Armstrong about the job she had lined up for him and pressed him to take it. He was to give Fletcher Henderson two weeks' notice and come back to Chicago. When Armstrong balked, apparently still unsure of his stellar gifts, Hardin issued an ultimatum: show up by a certain date or don't come at all. He came.

The next four-odd years in Chicago were to be a heady time for Armstrong. For most jazz buffs this period is identified with his body of Hot Five and Hot Seven recordings. These groups were actually assembled for recording exclusively, not live performance. Even though these recording sessions—between November 12, 1925, and July 5, 1928—were seminal to the future development of jazz, they give an incomplete picture of the realities of Armstrong's working life. Not only do they represent a mere twenty days of recording activity spread out over some thirty months; they were a small part of a feverishly busy career that included other work in the recording studio, nightclubs, and movie theaters. In the studio alone during this time, Armstrong recorded with such groups as Erskine Tate's Vendome Orchestra, Jimmy Bertrand's Washboard Wizards, vaudeville entertainers Butterbeans and Suzie, and vocalists Hociel Thomas and Sippie Wallace. Most important, within the context of Armstrong's career as a whole, big bands played a far larger role than most people realize; his tour of duty with the Fletcher Henderson Orchestra in 1924–25 was followed in 1929 by a period of some seventeen years when he fronted big bands.

When it came to assembling his Hot Five and Hot Seven groups Armstrong followed a traditional New Orleans formula, filtered and modified through his recent experience of having been a member of Clarence Williams's Blue Five during his Henderson days: a front line of melody instruments consisting of cornet (or trumpet), clarinet, and trombone backed by a rhythm section of piano and banjo. Additional instruments could include guitar, tuba, and drums.[2] Once he had received the go-ahead from the Okeh recording executive E. A. Fearn, Armstrong lost little time hiring his players, mostly tried-and-true colleagues from New Orleans. "I hit the phone and called the Musicians' Union, and asked permission to hire Kid Ory, Johnny St. Cyr and Johnny Dodds (who was already in Chicago, playing at Kelly's Stable). Of course, Lil Hardin joined up with me for my recording dates. . . . After our first date the band impressed the bigwigs of the Okeh Co. so well that they signed us up right away. Then we began to really get into the groove, the New Orleans groove."[3]

The "New Orleans groove" was the kind of hot jazz that was in Armstrong's blood—a mode of music making that stood in sharp contrast to the norm for Paul Whiteman and symphonic jazz. What it meant for Armstrong was "goin' to town . . . cuttin' loose and takin' the music with you, whatever the score may call for . . . [to] break through the set rhythms and melody and toss them around . . . play away from the score."[4] And the collaboration with Lil Hardin helped make Armstrong's brand of hot jazz what it was. "I used to

3.1 Louis Armstrong's Hot Five, 1925. From left, Louis Armstrong (cornet), Johnny St. Cyr (banjo), Johnny Dodds (clarinet), Kid Ory (trombone), Lil Hardin (piano). Institute of Jazz Studies, Rutgers University.

sit on the back steps of Lil's house and write five or six songs a day—just lead sheets—and Lil would put the other parts to them, cornet, clarinet, trombone etc."[5] In the group setting itself decisions were apparently made through an informal and democratic process—something well described by drummer Baby Dodds, a veteran of all of Armstrong's earliest recordings with King Oliver and a constant presence at the 1927 Hot Seven sessions: "With Louis' outfit we used to have rehearsal and anything that we had in mind for any particular number we would work out then. He would tell each of us when to take a solo or when not to, and who would come in at different times. We weren't a bunch of fellows to write down anything. That would have made it too mechanical. We would stop and talk it over more than anything else. If there was any writing involved Lil would write down what the musicians were supposed to do."[6]

This fluid collaborative approach yielded splendid results—a rich stylistic diversity within the larger category of "hot" jazz. Nor did Armstrong forget his audience and the need to "lay it on the public." Even though the Hot Fives and Hot Sevens were groups assembled exclusively for recording purposes, Armstrong was aware early on of his public, his record-buying fans. In his "Gut Bucket Blues," recorded at the first Hot Five session, on November 12, 1925, we hear clear evidence of Armstrong the confident and consummate entertainer, the "actor and musician" as he was to later identify his occupation; he exudes an easy informality that Paul Whiteman was never able to capture on records. Introducing each member of the ensemble is part of Armstrong's routine, and by the third bar of Johnny St. Cyr's opening banjo solo, there is already the unmistakable voice: "Aw, play that thing, Mr. St. Cyr, lawd. You know you can do it. Everybody in New Orleans can really do that thing. Hey, hey." Next up is Lil Hardin with her piano solo. "Oh, whip that thing, Miss Lil, whip it kid! Oh, pick that piano, yeah!" Kid Ory and Johnny Dodds are announced in similar fashion, while in the case of Armstrong himself it is Kid Ory who does the honors.

Hardin's contributions to this phase of Armstrong's career (she did not work professionally with him after December 1927) have all too often been minimized. One fascinating question is the extent of her musical literacy and familiarity with the European repertoire and its influence on her work with Armstrong. Is there possibly a greater early connection between the hot jazz of the time typically associated with Armstrong and a larger European tradition, one which takes in even more than the operatic repertoire of his early record collecting? Consider the intriguing observation of Frank Tirro, which hints at a few of the many factors involved in reassessing Hardin's place: "As a composer, Lil Hardin is an unrecognized master who composed some of the most interesting pieces of this period. When her works and others of the Chicago period are studied, analyzed, and compared, she may well be shown to have invented some of the characteristic Chicago sounds that were distinct from the New Orleans tradition."[7] Hardin herself was sharply critical of the state of musical knowledge on the local Chicago scene when she first began working there with King Oliver's band. As she has recalled: "'Key? We don't know what key. Just when you hear two knocks start playing.' . . . After a second I could feel what they were playing, because at that time I don't think they used over four or five chords. In fact, I'm sure they didn't."[8]

When we reexamine Armstrong's legacy from Hardin's point of view, it becomes much harder to take at face value his own comments about the origins of many pieces of the time for which he is famous. For example, his ebullient comments about how a favorite like "Struttin' with Some Barbecue" was conceived tell us a lot more about his fondness for food than anything else:

This tune was derived and thought of during the days when Zutty Singleton and I were playing at the Savoy Ballroom. . . . And after the dance was over every night, Zutty and I would drive out to 48th and State Street. . . . There was an old man there who made some of the most delicious barbecue that anyone would love to smack their chops on (their lips). . . . One night, while Zutty and I were manipulating those "Chime Bones" (barbecue), a thought came into my head. . . . I said to Zutty—Say, Zoot, as I sit here eating these fine-tasting ribs, it dawned on me that I should write a tune and call it "Struttin' with Some Barbecue." . . . Zutty said, "Dush, that's a real good idea." . . . So then and there, "Struttin' with Some Barbecue" was born.[9]

But the individual musical details of this piece tell another, more complex story. It is certainly hard to ignore such features as the spectacular stop-time chorus in which Armstrong's unaccompanied solo cornet is sharply punctuated by the rhythm section on only "weak" (or "back") beats—that is, on two and four. But what about the nature of the opening melody heard after the introduction, which is built on "an unusual and advanced harmonic idea not stemming from the New Orleans tradition"?[10] This harmonic usage, while quite common in later jazz and pop music from around the 1960s on, is virtually unknown in 1920s jazz; and it is an idea for which Hardin has every reason to claim credit. What is being referred to is a major seventh chord, something that in its simplest form can easily be played on a piano by striking in ascending order the white keys of C, E, G, and B. Most exciting is the way this chord is "barbecued" to produce a rhythmically energized, spicier version of a harmony also heard in a work like Erik Satie's *Trois Gymnopédies* of 1888, with its evocations of the sculpture of Greek antiquity—a "white" sound by a white European.

Pieces like "Struttin' with Some Barbecue" subsequently became the basis for a long-standing copyright feud between Armstrong and Hardin. In a 1967 interview with the British magazine *Melody Maker* she was quite forthright on the subject:

As for the old ones from the Louis days: there's a gang of them. "Struttin' with Some Barbecue," "Got No Blues," "Hotter Than That," "I'm Not Rough," "Perdido Street Blues," "Pencil Papa." When we wrote those tunes, forty years ago and so forth, we didn't think it important to get our songs copyrighted or anything like that. We just put our names on them and thought about the immediate cash. Now I live off them, but it only happened after years. There was a big lawsuit, you know, over "Barbecue." It had Lillian Armstrong's name on it, though [as a result of the settlement], so I got that straight.[11]

Before matters were finally resolved, Hardin's troubles were exacerbated by at least two other events. On September 30, 1938, Armstrong divorced Lil Hardin "after more than fourteen years of marriage, two of which had been more or less conventional, and twelve of which were tormented."[12] In the divorce decree she charged him with having deserted her in 1931, some time after he took up with Alpha Smith, who would become the third of his four wives. But when Joe Glaser became Armstrong's manager for life, in 1935, he really poisoned the relationship by telling Armstrong lies about Hardin. When "Struttin' with Some Barbecue" was finally published, credited solely to Armstrong, Hardin asked for five thousand dollars in exchange for her rights. Glaser told Armstrong that she was demanding one hundred thousand dollars, and Armstrong seems to have believed it without question.[13]

There are other provocative hints of Hardin's hand. For example, the Hot Five's "Skid-Dat-De-Dat" is a tour de force of constantly changing textures that calls to mind the "Whiteman Stomp," commissioned by Whiteman from Fletcher Henderson in a highly energetic arrangement by Don Redman. "Skid-Dat-De-Dat," like the eponymous earlier stomp, approximates Whiteman's goal of "change and novelty" for each half chorus by providing variety "inside the strain." But what makes "Skid-Dat-De-Dat" unique is that it comprises highly contrasted bits and pieces, each no more than four measures in length—whether featuring a bluesy solo break on cornet, clarinet, piano, or trombone, touches of big-band scoring, or interpolations of scat by Armstrong. In terms of structure there is essentially little more to this piece. And for this reason alone it stands out from virtually everything else Armstrong ever performed; for the norm he almost invariably followed was the twelve-bar, blues-based chorus or the thirty-two-bar format associated with the popular song. Yet there is a deeper layer of significance to the repetition of the pervasive four-measure units with the underpinning of four chords in whole notes, one per measure. It is strongly reminiscent of one of the staples of the European symphonic canon, Mozart's "Jupiter" Symphony—specifically, the four whole notes with which its finale opens.

Knowing the extent of Lil Hardin's studies of classical music, the connection with Mozart or Satie is highly plausible. From her earliest days in Chicago at Jones's Music Store on South State Street she was demonstrating music from J. S. Bach to W. C. Handy. She also attended Chicago College of Music, where she was a student of Louis Victor Saar—a revered teacher of piano and composition whose credentials included having worked with Johannes Brahms and Antonín Dvořák—earning the senior diploma there on June 29, 1927, some seven months after "Skid-Dat-De-Dat" was recorded.[14]

Added to this evidence was the announcement in the *Chicago Defender* of May 25, 1929, that Saar was "presenting Mrs. Lillian Armstrong, wife of the noted cornetist, in recital"; she is referred to as "an accomplished pianist" with a repertoire including Mozart, Weber, Chopin, Saar, Debussy, and Scriabin.[15]

Hardin's diploma specifies four areas of study that she completed: pedalogy (pedagogy), musical history, piano harmony (now more commonly called keyboard harmony), and ear training.[16] Turning again to those recurring four whole-note chords in "Skid-Dat-De-Dat," it comes as a revelation to realize that they are all anchored by a pedal point on the pitch of C, the key of Mozart's "Jupiter" Symphony. This kind of harmonic device, virtually unknown in New Orleans Dixieland jazz, provides strong proof of Hardin's familiarity with European practice; it is a tradition harking back to early organ playing and its use of the pedal board, where a tone is sustained in the bass while harmonies above it change.

Now if, as Armstrong claimed earlier, he could smack his "chops" on barbecued ribs, he also had quite an appetite for chop suey—the Hot Five "Cornet Chop Suey," to be exact. And as he once put it: "'Cornet Chop Suey' turned out to be a very popular tune, especially among the musicians & actors and music lovers."[17] Copyrighted on January 18, 1924, as a fox-trot, with the melody by Armstrong and the arrangement by Hardin, "Cornet Chop Suey" is built largely around a format of introduction-verse-chorus.[18] It is a rather dazzling showpiece, a solo virtuoso vehicle for Armstrong, even though Hardin is given solo play in a complete restatement of the thirty-two-bar chorus. The performance swings from start to finish, anticipating the best of big-band phrasing of the following decade.

Closely following the copyright manuscript while listening to the recording of February 26, 1926, one can easily recognize the extent to which there was "a willingness to keep and solidify ideas that worked."[19] The score, in other words, is very largely a "prescriptive" one, approximating a set arrangement of the kind Ferde Grofé or Don Redman might have provided Paul Whiteman. In addition, the fact that the copyright deposit predates the initial recording session by more than two years, coming from a time when Armstrong and Hardin were both still with King Oliver, has given rise to speculation that it would likely have been performed by Armstrong with his mentor's band.[20] But there is a far more plausible explanation that argues for the opposite position. First and foremost, the piece is a solo vehicle; there is no provision for any kind of trumpet or cornet duet of the kind Oliver favored. Then there is the matter of human nature, pure and simple. It was, after all, copyrighted on January 18, at a sweet time for Armstrong and Hardin, shortly before their marriage on February 5; given the unrest at that point in the ranks of the Oliver band as well as Hardin's ambitions for Armstrong, the piece was most likely copyrighted in their joint names as an investment in their future. In any event, insofar as the piece came to be performed as a set arrangement, it clearly links the worlds of Armstrong, Hardin, and Whiteman, the worlds of hot and symphonic jazz.

Speaking of Whiteman and symphonic jazz, there is yet another twist to the story. Armstrong has said that "Cornet Chop Suey," with its ample show of solo virtuosity, "could be played as a trumpet solo, or with a symphony orchestra."[21] A sense of the excitement this might have generated is suggested by a report of an event at Chicago's 1,500-seat Vendome Theater, which was primarily a movie theater. Armstrong had just played there as a member of Erskine Tate's Vendome Orchestra, often advertised as the "Little Symphony." In the course of his regular column for the *Chicago Defender,* "The Musical Bunch," Dave Peyton, otherwise a champion of Paul Whiteman and symphonic jazz, writes with obvious pleasure about a performance earlier in the week at which the symphonic and hot styles had melded: "This week the Vendome Orchestra put over a unique novelty presentation that won instant favor with the large audience. It was somewhat of a departure from the general style of orchestral entertainment. Director Tate took Clarence Williams' 'Royal Garden Blues,' partitioned it for each section of the orchestra, who were hid in different parts of the house. Each unit had its solo part. The drum gave the old familiar minstrel roll off and then the march to the pit by these music masters, ending the scene with hot jazz—a very good musical treat."[22]

Performing with Tate and his "Little Symphony" at a movie theater before the advent of sound demanded considerable versatility on Armstrong's part, requiring him to play such classics as the "Intermezzo" from Mascagni's *Cavalleria Rusticana* and the *William Tell* and *Poet and Peasant* overtures of Rossini and Suppé, as well as hot numbers on the order of "Static Strut" and "Stomp Off, Let's Go." One of the big moments for Armstrong was his solo in the final "red hot number," coming during the break in the movie when reels were changed. In certain unmistakable ways the whole Vendome experience encouraged a significant expansion of Armstrong's repertoire, building on the operatic music he had come to know and love when he first began collecting records around 1917–18. Armstrong had already deeply internalized much of that music, incorporating operatic sound bites in his improvisations, further blurring the distinction between jazz and the European classics in his own mind.[23] As for working at the Vendome, he recalled: "We played some difficult shows with that orchestra, good for reading; you'd suddenly get the call to turn back five pages in the overture or something like that. . . . I learned a lot playing under Erskine Tate; we played all kinds of music. . . . We played the scores for the silent movies, and a big overture when the curtain would rise at the end of the film. I got a solo on stage, and my big thing was Cavalleria Rusticana."[24]

The larger message of "good for reading" carries over into the later incarnation of the Hot Five, the group with which Armstrong was to record six months after his last session with Lil Hardin in December 1927. There are admittedly some quaint old-time routines, as when he engages in delightful banter with Earl Hines, arguably the greatest pianist with whom he ever worked. Some scintillating stride piano introduces "A Monday Date," a Hines number, leading to the following exchange. Armstrong is indulging here in a form of "signifying," commenting in effect on the Afro-American tradition of the minstrel show and echoing his earlier Hot Five routine. While he also includes the usage "Pops," an affectionate nickname for both himself and Whiteman, he is clearly expressing here not so much a sense of affection for a father figure as a feeling of comfortable familiarity as he addresses Earl Hines and his drummer Zutty Singleton:

A: Hey, say, Earl Hines, why don't you let us in on some of that good music, Pops?

H: Well, come on, let's get together then.

A: Okay, tune up boys [sounding of pitch of A]. Hi, is that alright, is that alright?

H: That sounds pretty good.

A: Yes, "That sounds pretty good" (somewhat sarcastically). I'll bet that if you had half a pint of Mississippi gin you wouldn't say "That sounds pretty good." Well anyhow we're gonna play anyway. Say, come on Zutty, whip those cymbals, Pops.

The reconstituted group, with Fred Robinson on trombone, Jimmy Strong on clarinet, and Earl Hines on piano, had sidemen who could read well and quickly master sophisticated arranged passages as needed and also strike fire by playing hot—that is, "playing away from the score." It certainly helps one to more fully appreciate the transcendent quality achieved in most of these final sessions. Armstrong, Hines, and other members of the new Hot Five captured for posterity at least one performance on disc that is without peer. In his seminal 1968 book *Early Jazz* Gunther Schuller opens his third chapter, "The First Great Soloist," by speaking of "West End Blues" as a defining moment in the history of jazz:

When on June 28, 1928, Louis Armstrong unleashed the spectacular cascading phrases of the introduction to "West End Blues," he established the general stylistic direction of jazz for several decades to come. Beyond that, this performance also made quite clear that jazz could never again revert to being solely an entertainment or folk music. The clarion call of "West End Blues" served notice that jazz had the potential capacity to compete with the highest order of previously known musical expression.[25]

What is remarkable about Armstrong's introduction is that it was hardly a divinely conceived spontaneous creation, unique to the 1928 session. In fact, its genealogy went back almost four years—a lineage of "licks," breaks, and gestures inspired by operatic bravura and such. There are some six sound bites from recordings predating the historic 1928 session which help highlight the complex gestation of Armstrong's creative process and how much the intricate details of his whole mode of music making still elude us.

A discussion of the introduction to "West End Blues" also invites us to reexamine the very idea of improvisation.[26] At the very least, the nonsensical notion that improvisation is all about making things up as you go along can be laid to rest. To really appreciate the process behind the creation of the introduction, the most pertinent recordings to listen to include "Cake Walking Babies from Home" (with Sidney Bechet and Clarence Williams's Blue Five); bravura pieces by two of Armstrong's favorite operatic divas, Luisa Tetrazzini and Amelita Galli-Curci; "High Society" (with King Oliver's Creole Jazz Band); and a number called "Changeable Daddy of Mine," in which Armstrong plays cornet behind the vocal of Margaret Johnson. Equally relevant is an Armstrong session of 1931 of "Blue Again," which begins with an elaborate solo conceived in the manner of an accompanied recitative, with an allusion to "West End Blues," not to mention echoes of such operas as Wagner's *Tristan und Isolde* and Ponchielli's *La Gioconda*.

Looking beyond the "West End Blues" introduction itself, one has to marvel at the exquisite balance among its five component choruses and at the way they build on the original blues—a joint effort attributed to King Oliver and Clarence Williams. The collaborative process of playing small-group hot jazz, of "goin' to town . . . cuttin' loose and takin' the music with you . . . play[ing] away from the score," as Armstrong once put it, is superbly realized. The result is a performance remarkable for "ideas of phrasing and melodic rhythm that would lie neglected until the arrival of Charlie Parker," as well as for the continuum achieved between its opening and closing choruses, "in which shining virtuosity and grandiose simplicity are in perfect balance."[27]

One of the happiest marriages of the arranged and the hot can be heard in the group's performance of the number "Beau Koo Jack"—a collaboration of composer-arranger Alex Hill and Louis Armstrong. The piece, which combines in its title the phonetic equivalent of the French "beaucoup," meaning "very much," with "jack," slang for money, is remarkable for several things. A vivid, clear, relaxed sound is communicated through tight ensemble, variety is achieved "inside the strain," and the dramatic juxtaposition of ensemble and solo passages as "twos" (two-phrase units) are traded only adds to the excitement. Among the most memorable moments are the solos of Don Redman on alto saxophone and Armstrong on trumpet. Redman, Armstrong's former colleague in the Fletcher Henderson Orchestra, and sought after as an arranger by both Henderson and Whiteman, contributes sixteen measures that are so brisk as to momentarily disorient Earl Hines in his segue. As for Armstrong himself, his solo has been described as one of his most perfect, "economically structured and superbly executed despite the bright tempo."[28]

Returning for the moment to Armstrong's middlebrow world of performing popular operatic classics from written scores, with hot numbers mixed in to provide spice as needed—as was the case during his stint with Erskine Tate—one recognizes certain similarities to the kind of fare that Paul Whiteman offered early and late in his career. And like both Erskine Tate and Carroll Dickerson, with whom Armstrong was to work slightly later in the decade, Whiteman was a classically trained violinist-turned-bandleader. Operatic chestnuts figured rather prominently in what he served up to his clientele, starting in 1919 at Santa Barbara's Belvedere and continuing the following year at Atlantic City's Ambassador Hotel. Excerpts from Verdi's *Aida*, Donizetti's *Lucia di Lammermoor*, Ponchielli's *La Gioconda*, and Saint-Saëns's *Samson et Delila* were among his staples. One could also add Whiteman's fox-trot rendition of "Meditation" from Massenet's *Thaïs*. Then by the early to mid-1930s Whiteman could be heard on network radio, such as Kraft Music Hall, conducting programs that included actual operatic arias from works like *Manon* or Puccini's *Madama Butterfly*. Nor should one forget that his character as a middlebrow musician was limned very much by his identification with George Gershwin, as he made *Rhapsody in Blue* his signature piece—for him the epitome of symphonic jazz—and also rather often programmed Gershwin's Concerto in F, *American in Paris*, or excerpts from *Porgy and Bess*.

Yet as early as the fall of 1924, a little more than six months after his historic Aeolian Hall concert that included the world premiere of *Rhapsody in Blue*, Whiteman was beginning to sense the limitations of symphonic jazz, realizing that he had to do more than depend on the arrangements of a Ferde

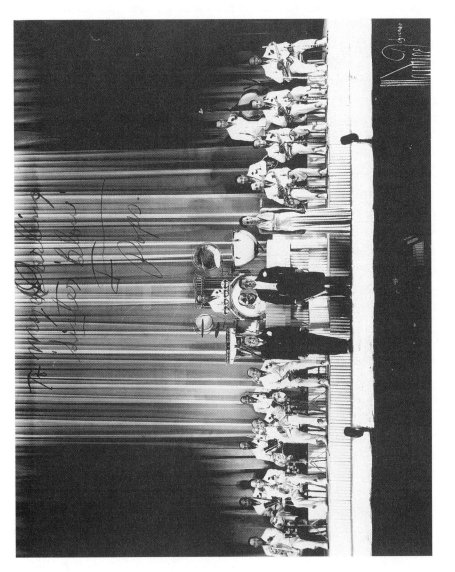

3.2 A 1937 publicity shot of Armstrong as a mainstream popular entertainer leading the Luis Russell Orchestra at Chicago's Regal Theatre. Frank Driggs Collection.

Grofé or a Don Redman. And the point was driven home by such critics as Olin Downes to the effect that "the jazz composer . . . will not find himself by merely giving concerts, or making symphonic pretensions without substantial material to back them."[29] In the course of the next three years Whiteman was to gradually turn up the heat of his music making, first hiring Bing Crosby in September 1926. By the end of the summer of 1927 the arranger Bill Challis had joined his ranks, to be followed in late October by Bix Beiderbecke and Frank Trumbauer on cornet and saxophone. And thanks to these developments, the worlds of Paul Whiteman and Louis Armstrong were to be brought closer together than ever before.

Beiderbecke first caught Whiteman's ear on September 12, 1924—seven months to the day since the Aeolian Hall concert—when he went to hear Beiderbecke and the Wolverines open at New York's Cinderella Ballroom. Located at 48th Street and Broadway, just three blocks south of the Roseland, where Louis Armstrong was to begin his engagement with Fletcher Henderson some three weeks later, the Cinderella must have packed plenty of excitement that evening. We know from Richardson ("Dick") Turner, a trumpet-playing Yale undergraduate who showed up with a party of ten Ivy League friends a few nights later, that people were going wild. This was something much more than seeing and hearing someone play a hot solo "inside the strain," within the chorus, as prescribed in the arrangements of the Henderson band. What was happening was completely off the charts in every way— a full eight-piece white band playing hot without depending at all on any written dance band arrangement. The group even looked different, especially Bix Beiderbecke. As Turner put it: "[Bix] played in an unorthodox way. He shook the horn with all fingers up, and played leaning over at the floor at about a 45° angle. They'd take about ten 'last' choruses on each tune, standing around the drummer and playing at him. It was frantic."[30]

The trade press was equally enthusiastic. Writing in *Variety,* Abel Green proclaimed: "As a torrid unit it need doff the mythical chapeau to no one. Their sense of rhythm and tempo is ultra for this type of dance music, and their unquestionable favor with the dance fans speaks for itself. . . . The band has struck favor from the start! Out west they recorded for the Gennett disks, but although less than a week on Broadway they have had 'dates' with a number of minor companies, with the Brunswick also interested."[31] Green's mention of Gennett discs brings to mind the first of several links drawing Beiderbecke and Armstrong together. When Bix Beiderbecke and the Wolverines showed up for their first recording session at the Starr Piano Company's Gennett Studios in Richmond, Indiana, on February 18, 1924, they found themselves in the very spot where King Oliver and his Creole Jazz Band, with his New Orleans protégé on second cornet, had made history only ten months earlier. This occasion, however, was a little different in that Beiderbecke was fronting his own ensemble, something that was not to happen for Armstrong until November 1925, with the premiere recording of the Hot Five. Even more touching was the warm personal relationship between the two, sporadic though their contacts were. Its origins date back to August 1919, some three years before Armstrong made his historic move to Chicago to join King Oliver, at a point when he was playing aboard the Mississippi riverboats of the Streckfus Line. That summer the sixteen-year-old Bix Beiderbecke came down to the levee of his hometown of Davenport, Iowa, eager to make the acquaintance of Armstrong, who recalled: "He was a cute little boy. He'd come down to hear the bands, and then go home and practice what he heard. He and I became friends the first time we met—he was the type of youngster I admired all the way. No matter how good the solo was that he played, he wasn't very much satisfied with it. He never seemed satisfied with his efforts; this was true in later years too, even while he was driving all the cats wild."[32]

Around February 1927, with Armstrong now firmly ensconced in Chicago and fronting Carroll Dickerson's band at the Sunset Café, Beiderbecke and his friends were all eyes and ears in front of the bandstand. They were awed by his ability to play chorus after chorus, building the solo organically; it all seemed so effortless. As Armstrong characteristically put it: "Well, I tell you . . . the first chorus I plays the melody. The second chorus I plays the melody round the melody, and third chorus I routines."[33] But in truth Beiderbecke himself was no slouch at this stage. He had assiduously studied many of Armstrong's solos, beginning with such numbers as "Go 'Long Mule," to develop the "correlated chorus" with its gradually unfolding phrases to shape a form of utterance distinctively his own.

Armstrong was to return the compliment on July 2, 1928, when he came to the Chicago Theater to hear Beiderbecke, now a member of the Paul Whiteman Orchestra. Armstrong recalls hearing them in an arrangement of Tchaikovsky's *1812 Overture*, in particular: Whiteman "had those trumpets way up into the air, just blowing like mad, and my man Bix was . . . blowing beautifully, and just before the end, they started to shooting cannons, ringing bells, sirens were howling like mad, but you could still hear Bix. The reason why I saw through all those different effects that were going on at the ending—well, you take a man with a pure tone like Bix's and no matter how loud the other fellows may be blowing, that pure . . . tone will cut through it all."[34]

When Armstrong went backstage to see Beiderbecke after the performance, they "hugged and kissed something wonderful." And their mutual admiration was altogether special; for on that night and on several subsequent nights it appears that Beiderbecke rushed to the South Side where Armstrong was playing to patiently wait until 4 A.M., when the last customers left. "Then," according to Armstrong, "we would lock the doors. Now you talking about jam sessions, huh, those were the things, with everyone feeling each other's note or chord, and blending with each other instead of trying to cut each other. We tried to see how good we could make music sound."[35]

Unlike Armstrong, however, Beiderbecke concentrated on the midrange of the cornet to communicate a more intimate, restrained, and introspective sound with minimal vibrato—something distinctly different from the more flamboyant brilliance of Armstrong's trumpet. At the same time, he was a hot player, "playing way from the score" to produce deeply memorable solos that commanded the attention of fellow musicians. Even though he failed auditions several times in an effort to get his union card, and never became the most fluent of readers, his fabulous ear more than compensated for his not ranking with the best of the legitimately trained musicians.

In cultivating his brand of hot jazz and tapping the talents of Bing Crosby, Whiteman was adding to his roster a musician "in the know"—or, as they said in the 1920s, someone who was "hep to the jive." As the clarinetist and bandleader Artie Shaw once put it: "The thing you have to understand about Bing Crosby is that he was the first hip white person born in the United States."[36] The BBC commentator Alistair Cooke later put it even more pointedly: "Word ran through the English underground that a genuine jazz singer—and a white man!—had appeared in the unlikeliest place: breezing along on the ocean of Paul Whiteman's lush 'symphonic sound.'"[37] Whiteman's manager, Jimmy Gillespie, was therefore understandably excited, and raved about the routine of Bing Crosby and his sidekick Al Rinker, "the hot piano-singing novelty duo" that he had seen at Los Angeles's Metropolitan sometime in late September 1926. Bing Crosby and Al Rinker were soon to add a third partner, Harry Barris, to form the Rhythm Boys, who became part of Whiteman's act. The flair with which this trio incorporated instrumental influences, especially from the drum set, was irresistible. What is more, in his arrangements Bill Challis would sometimes have them provide a backing for an instrumental soloist such as Bix Beiderbecke.[38]

But for the time being, Whiteman and his band were in town busily enjoying a run at the city's sumptuous Million Dollar Theater; and he was not sure that he had any real use for Crosby and Rinker. But Gillespie persisted: "You've got to hear these two guys," which brought the retort, "If you think they're the bee's knees, bring 'em to me."[39] At the same time, Whiteman was not one to take Gillespie at his word and promptly dispatched two of his trusted musicians to check out the pair. One of them was the violinist, arranger, and songwriter Matty Malneck, a former student of Wilberforce Whiteman and also a champion of hot jazz; he was highly enthusiastic—it was "like hearing a great jazz player for the first time."[40] More important, here was a singer who could contribute a black sense of phrasing, swinging, enunciation, and black vowel coloration to Whiteman's sound palette during a period of segregation when the sight of black performers joining whites on the same bandstand was taboo.

Crosby's memory of his first meeting with Whiteman recalls the axiom that perception sometimes equals reality. He described Whiteman, with his ample girth, sitting on a bed "looking like a giant Buddha, and he had a pound of caviar in his lap and a bottle of champagne on his breakfast table . . . the ultimate in attainment."[41] According to the biographer Gary Giddins, Crosby's depiction of Whiteman's "habiliments of success" echoes the aspirations of a piece of Crosby juvenilia—a poem entitled "A King," with the image of a monarch "in robes of white / With vassals kneeling left and right."[42] Even though witnesses like Al Rinker remembered Whiteman sitting in his dressing gown drinking beer, no one apparently would ever contradict Crosby's often repeated version while he and Whiteman were alive. At the same time, Crosby was perhaps unwittingly helping burnish the image of Whiteman as King of Jazz—an icon soon to be projected in the 1930 movie of the same title, as boundaries between jazz and popular music became increasingly blurred.

Because of prior commitments, Crosby did not actually join the Whiteman organization until early December 1926, in the course of a Chicago run. Almost every musician in town, it seemed, was going gaga over one of the latest recordings of Louis Armstrong—"Heebie Jeebies," part of the same Okeh session of February 26, 1926, that produced "Cornet Chop Suey." "Heebie Jeebies" created a sensation, selling some forty thousand copies thanks to the rhythmic thrust and melodic ingenuity of its scat chorus—a torrent of improvised nonsense syllables: "Say I've got the Heebies, I mean the Jeebies. . . . Talkin' about, the dazza heebie-jeebies. . . . Poppa's got to do the heebie-jeebie's dance." Armstrong once explained that he dropped the paper with the lyrics during the recording session and, not wanting to "spoil the record which was moving along so wonderfully," began scatting there and then. Yet contrary to popular myth, he did not "invent" scat at this session, he simply drew upon an old routine dating back to his days as a street singer in New Orleans.

As the clarinetist Mezz Mezzrow remembered it: "You would hear cats greeting each other with Louis's riffs when they met you around town. . . . 'I got the Heebies,' one would yell out, and the other would answer, 'I got the Jeebies,' and the next minute they were scatting in each other's face." Mezzrow also recalled that the young Bix Beiderbecke "kept chuckling as the record played over and over. . . . Soon as it was over he tore out of the house to wake up everybody he knew . . . and make them listen to it."[43] As for Bing Crosby himself, he had some time before been primed by Al Rinker's big sister, Mildred Bailey—she herself soon to become a headliner with Paul Whiteman and to be identified with a black southern sound—to check out all of the recordings of Armstrong. And once he was in Chicago, Paul Whiteman lost little time in rushing Crosby and Rinker over to the Sunset Café, where Armstrong was appearing with Earl Hines. It was a revelation. In later years Crosby was to recall how he was bowled over by Armstrong's many routines—in particular, one in which he put on a frock coat and dark glasses as he began preaching as the Reverend Satchelmouth. "I'm proud to acknowledge my debt to the Reverend Satchelmouth. He is the beginning and the end of music in America. And long may he reign," Crosby said. He hastened to add: "I got a lot out of Bix Beiderbecke when we were both beating around the country with the Whiteman band. And just as Bix himself found inspiration in Louis Armstrong out on the South Side in the late 20s, so did I."[44]

Southern themes figure prominently in the Crosby canon of solo recordings with Whiteman, starting with the mighty Mississippi. One of the earliest instances is his "Muddy Water" of March 7, 1927—an interracial evocation of Dixie by the white composer Peter De Rose and the black lyricist Jo Trent. After opening with a promising trombone solo and some brass and string exchanges, most of the straight instrumental part of the piece plods along with little to commend it. Or are the thick doublings of strings and brass, not to mention the heavy-footed beat, perhaps intended as metaphors for mud? In any event, Matty Malneck's arrangement does provide Crosby with his first complete recorded chorus—a total of thirty-two measures—that is notable for its swinging rhythm and its "down-home" rendition of such phrases as "Muddy water in my shoes / rockin' through those low-down blues." The accompanying blues fiddle adds just the right touch.

"Mississippi Mud" is filled with the spirit of black minstrelsy and vaudeville. It is reportedly the first song to have been put together by the vocal trio the Rhythm Boys, though much of the credit goes to Harry Barris, the last to join the group. Barris, "a wildly kinetic singer, pianist, and tunesmith," had actually spent his high school years in Denver, where he had studied under

Wilberforce Whiteman; now in New York, he was the "quintessence of Jazz Age show business." Scat vocals, slamming the piano lid, and Barris's making a cymbal sound with his mouth were all part of the trio's act. When they sang "Mississippi Mud" for Matty Malneck, he was bowled over, telling them: "If Whiteman doesn't flip over you three guys, he's gotta be nuts."[45] Whiteman did indeed flip, which partially explains why the piece became a hit on tour; it got a further boost when Crosby recorded it three times between June 1927 and the following February, though only the first of these recordings was with the Rhythm Boys. An Okeh session of January 20, 1928, recorded under the name of Frank Trumbauer and his Orchestra, is notable for featuring a cohort of sidemen from the Paul Whiteman Orchestra, among them Bix Beiderbecke, Matty Malneck, and Jimmy Dorsey; and most striking is the blackface routine between Trumbauer and Crosby.

Among the most vivid and deftly scored numbers Crosby recorded with Whiteman is "'Tain't So, Honey, 'Tain't So" (June 10, 1928). One of the best-known pieces of the white composer, bandleader, and singer Willard Robison, the song evokes images of a rural South conveying an underlying gospel message of homespun religion. Indeed, so "impatient" is Bing Crosby to spread the good news of the opening verse, that he starts a fraction of a second before everyone else:

> Hey people, you should come to Arkansas
> Meet a friend of mine old Aunt Phoebe Law
> She's known to everyone from miles around
> She will help you when friends forsake you and when troubles wear you
>   down.

According to rumor, the studio session did not go smoothly for Crosby, who failed to get his initial pitch correct until the tenth take, when Challis reportedly intervened with a pitch pipe—an ironic case of patience being needed to properly project impatience. But Challis himself has suggested otherwise. "I wanted to start off with a vocal, just a prank sort of, so I gave him the note he starts on. I think Paul beat off, or I did, well, anyway, he came right in and sang it. No problems or anything."[46] In any event, the catchy swing of the vocal is matched by Crosby's homey vowel coloration of the opening phrase of the chorus: "'Tain't so, honey, 'tain't so / Spoke to the Lawd, the Lawd said no." Last but not least, there are the memorable hot solos of Beiderbecke and Trumbauer. Beiderbecke's solo in particular has been cited as a quintessential example of how he played his cornet without using the "approved" fingerings of schooled brass players to operate the instrument's valves; he would resort instead to a more instinctive approach, depending on the mood and key of the piece at hand.[47] And Trumbauer, for his part, comes in with a raucous passage played in the earthy bottom register of the bassoon.

One of the most dramatic examples of the transformation of Whiteman's sound into something hot can be heard in the selection "Changes" (November 23, 1927). The title of the piece can be thought of as a double entendre: the "changes" alluded to in this song by Walter Donaldson are changes of key, but Whiteman's recording session illustrates the major changes brought about by his newly acquired arranger Bill Challis, the Rhythm Boys, and Bix Beiderbecke.[48] In addition, writers like Gary Giddins have associated "Changes" with such contemporaneous events in American history as Lindbergh's flight, Sacco and Vanzetti's execution, Babe Ruth's sixty home runs, and the appearance of *The Jazz Singer,* the first sound motion picture.[49]

Running slightly less than three minutes, the arrangement packs plenty of energy and variety "inside the strain" to produce a performance of great polish as the large forces of nineteen instrumentalists, the three Rhythm Boys, and three additional "sweet" vocalists are marshaled with great skill and imagination. Every detail has a point to make right from the beginning. So what we hear in the introduction is a clever manipulation of a whirling three-note chromatic figure that anticipates the motif of the tune coming in the opening chorus. This opening chorus—it evokes the Charleston—in turn provides ample contrast of timbre and texture as the melody of the saxophones is greeted by snappy, syncopated muted trumpets, to be followed by interpolations for strings and open trumpets. The "sweet" vocal trio, backed by a vibrant rhythm section, sings of "Beautiful changes in different keys / Beautiful changes and harmonies," followed by some scat by the Rhythm Boys, and Crosby's rapid-fire solo: "first he changes into B, changes into C, changes into D, changes into E as easy as the weatherman. . . . He's been the talk of Dixieland." This launches Beiderbecke's exquisite sixteen-bar hot solo played against a cushion of vocal harmony and the underpinning of a rhythm section pulsing with energy. The rich sonority of the full ensemble carries us through the out chorus.

A memorable feature of this hot phase of Whiteman's career is a riveting routine of Beiderbecke and Trumbauer. On the Bill Challis arrangement of "Borneo" (April 10, 1928), for example—the original music is again by Walter Donaldson—we are treated to not only an outstanding first chorus by Beiderbecke and a vocal by Scrappy Lambert lampooning the Tin Pan Alley song; there is also a signature chase chorus by Beiderbecke and Trumbauer. Two measures on the cornet will be answered by two on the saxophone, and so on through the whole chorus. "They keep the melodic line going in one continuous improvisation, and when Bix mousetraps the last eight bars of the chorus with a pregnant little silence, Tram does it too when it's his turn."[50]

This particular session was recorded under the name of Frank Trumbauer and his Orchestra, even though ten of the eleven musicians involved were fairly regular sidemen in the Paul Whiteman Orchestra. Musicians could drift in and out, depending on the gig or recording session—as was the case for Armstrong when he was with Fletcher Henderson in New York or squeezing in his work with Erskine Tate at the Vendome in Chicago or backing singers in the recording studio while also performing at the Dreamland or leading the Hot Five or Hot Seven. At the same time, the fact that band members were typically paid every week provided a degree of flexibility.

Paul Whiteman had the capacity to chase after the hottest talent. His acquisition of musicians of the stature of Bill Challis, Frank Trumbauer, and Bix Beiderbecke, not to mention the fiddler Joe Venuti and Tommy and Jimmy Dorsey, was an early example of corporate raiding; all had been members of the Detroit-based orchestra of the pianist, bandleader, and entrepreneur Jean Goldkette, who had fallen on bad times. Jimmy Dorsey, among the first of this group to sign on with Whiteman, kept reminding Whiteman of the imminent collapse of Goldkette's enterprise. And it was at Dorsey's behest that Whiteman went to hear the group in Detroit and subsequently in Atlantic City. Some measure of the financial resources Whiteman commanded at this point is indicated by his $7,440.00 payroll for the week ending January 20, 1928. Thirty-six people are on salary: thirty-three musicians, Whiteman's manager Jimmy Gillespie, a valet, and a stagehand. Loyalty and ability are clearly rewarded. Long-standing members, like Henry Busse on trumpet and Chester Hazlett on saxophone, are paid $350 each, Mike Pingitore on banjo $300. Relative newcomers, like Bix Beiderbecke and Frank Trumbauer, earned $200 each, Bing Crosby $150. Dramatizing the extreme difference between the old and the new are the salaries for that week for Ferde Grofé and Bill Challis: $375 and $175, respectively.

Whiteman's respect for Beiderbecke's ability and fondness for him as a person are evident from the fact that Whiteman maintained his star hot cornetist on full salary after Beiderbecke succumbed to alcoholism and pneumonia and had to cut short his career in the band. This prodigiously gifted player, so much admired by fellow musicians, including Louis Armstrong, actually played with Whiteman slightly less than two years, from October 27, 1927, to September 13, 1929. A few weeks later came Black Friday, October 29, 1929. The Depression was on. Recording would soon go into a slump, dance halls

1928 JANUARY 20 SALARIES. — PAYROLL 3
PAUL WHITEMAN ORCHESTRA
WEEK ENDING JAN. JAN. 20.28
MOSQUE THEATRE— NEWARK N.J.

MAYER, RED	sax	"	175
BARRIS, HARRY	piano	"	150
BIEDERBECKE, BIX	trumpet	"	200
BOUMAN, J.	violin	"	185
BROWN, S.	bass	"	175
BUSSE, HENRY	trumpet	"	350
CROSBY, BING	vocal	"	150
CULLEN, B.	trombone	"	150
DIETERLE, K.	violin	"	175
DORSEY, JIMMY	sax	"	200
FULTON, J.	trombone	"	200
GAYLORD, C.	violin	"	200
HALL, WILBUR	trombone	"	350
HAZLETT, C.	sax	"	350
CROZIER, R.	sax	"	175
McDONALD, N.	drums	"	175
McLEAN, HAL	sax	"	200
MALNECK, MATTY	violin	"	150
MAYHEW BROS.	sax	"	350
PERRELLA, N.	piano	"	300
PERRY, MARIO	accordian	"	180
PINGITORE, MIKE	banjo	"	300
RINKER, AL	piano	"	150
RUSSELL, M.	violin	"	150
SATTERFIELD, TOM	piano	"	150
STRICKFADEN, C.	sax	"	200
TRAFFICANTE, MIKE	bass-tuba	"	175
YOUNG, A.	banjo-vocal	"	200
MARGULIS, C.	trumpet	"	175
GILLESPIE, J.F.	manager	"	350
GROFE, FERDE	arranger	"	575
CHALLIS, G.	arranger	"	175
LORENZEN, M.	stage	"	110
BLACK, W.	valet		50
TRUMBAUER, FRANK	sax	"	200
RANK, W.	trombone	"	200	7440

3.3 Whiteman payroll ledger sheet for the week ending January 20, 1928. Jack Bradley Collection.

would close. The growing emphasis, with radio becoming more and more important, was on set, standardized arrangements—anathema to a hot player and an original like Beiderbecke. He met his untimely death August 6, 1931.

Beiderbecke's final months with the band brought heat from another quarter—the tobacco industry. Two corporate giants of the day, American Tobacco and the Lorillard Company, were seeking to aggressively promote their respective cigarettes, Lucky Strike and Old Gold, using the newly emerging medium of network radio; what ensued was a supreme battle of the bands borne on the smoking airwaves. So it was that *R. A. Rolfe and the Lucky Strike Dance Orchestra* debuted September 15, 1928, on NBC, to be followed on February 5, 1929, by the *Old Gold–Paul Whiteman Hour* on CBS.

Eager to increase its market share and drawing upon resources of some $30 million, Lorillard touted the slogan "Not a cough in carload." Flaunting the claim of immunity from the affliction of smoker's cough, together with images of flapper girls and the music of Paul Whiteman, proved to be a winning combination for that season. Nothing remotely similar in terms of exposure on a national radio network was to come Armstrong's way until 1937, when he began hosting the weekly *Fleischmann's Yeast Hour* on NBC.

Whiteman's 1929 debut on CBS coincided with the dawning of a new age for the network. The previous September an ambitious twenty-seven-year-old William S. Paley, using funds from his father's cigar company shares, had purchased working control of a floundering organization he was eventually to develop into a world-class communications empire. This "20th-century visionary with the ambitions of a 19th-century robber baron," as the *New York Times* once described him, was from the start a savvy matchmaker, in this case bringing together sponsor and Whiteman-as-commodity as he expanded his stations into a national network. In next to no time Paul Whiteman and his Orchestra were to be heard in places spanning the length and breadth of the country, from New York and Boston to San Francisco and Spokane, and from Minneapolis and Chicago to Birmingham and New Orleans. Adding to the sense of excitement was the network's transmission of Whiteman's programs from locations as he and his band traveled to the West Coast, where they would soon make history in the movie *King of Jazz*.

For its time, the movie represents a high degree of photographic sophistication in its use of animation, matting, and double exposure. For example, very shortly after the opening credits we see Paul Whiteman arriving with a portable bandstand. Momentarily Lilliputian band members using ladders climb out of a box and take their places on stage. We are also soon treated to some compelling introductory snippets as some of Whiteman's star players

3.4 Publicity still of the *Rhapsody in Blue* sequence from *King of Jazz,* showing the Paul Whiteman Orchestra performing on a forty-foot piano. Joshua Berrett, personal collection.

strut their stuff: the duo of Joe Venuti and Eddie Lang on violin and guitar, Harry Goldfield on trumpet, and Mike Pingitore on banjo. Released in 1930, *King of Jazz* was Universal's first all-Technicolor feature-length musical film. Loosely modeled after such extravaganzas as George White's *Scandals* and Florenz Ziegfeld's *Follies,* it consists of seven revue numbers conceived on a grand scale, as well as a series of comedy routines, blackout sketches, and individual song, dance, and novelty numbers. As such it encompasses 1920s jazz at its most inclusive, harking back to the position taken by Louis Armstrong himself that "anything you can express to the public is jazz." Jazz is presented as having charms like all other music. The point is made by Bing Crosby as he sings his breezy vocal during the opening credits.

> Music hath charms that nothing else has,
> Music hath charms, though it's classy or jazz.
> A symphony grand by Schubert or Brahms,
> A popular band or a uke needs a palm.

Yet there is hardly a black presence to speak of in the entire movie. It is thus hardly surprising that blacks are conspicuously absent from the film's climactic final number, where a huge boiling cauldron fills the center of the stage to drive home the compelling message of the quintessential metaphor of the day: "America is a melting pot of music where the melodies of all nations are fused into one great new rhythm—Jazz!"

If anything, *King of Jazz* makes a rather astonishing statement in sheer denial and irony, while at the same time effectively turning down the heat of jazz. In the words of Krin Gabbard: "A more elaborate, more thorough denial of the African American role in jazz is difficult to imagine. Not surprisingly, the repression of blackness leaves its mark all over the film: there are constant allusions to African Americans, and much of the film explicitly evokes minstrelsy, the film's grand predecessor in the ambivalent appropriation of blackness by whites."[51]

In fact, no sooner do the opening credits end than we find ourselves "in darkest Africa" learning how Whiteman was crowned "King of Jazz." It is a seemingly innocuous story of colonial domination told with an animated cartoon created by a young Walter Lantz, years before Woody Woodpecker became his inimitable signature. A comic-book Whiteman, pursued by a lion, fires his musket at the animal. Meanwhile, there are various snatches of atmospheric music, among them a biblical-spiritual allusion ("My Lord delivered Daniel, why can't he deliver me?") and an excerpt from "Hoochy Koochy." After stripping off his skin, the lion allows the bullet to play on his ribs, like a mallet striking the bars on a xylophone. With the firing of a second round the lion's teeth have become piano keys. These the lion removes and begins stropping on his elongated tongue as if preparing to eat Whiteman. But as Whiteman plays his violin, the savage beast is promptly tamed, falling to his knees and crying out "Mammy!"—a reference to Al Jolson's hit. Rather than hunting in Africa for something like musical inspiration, is Whiteman perhaps bringing the light of his music to the Dark Continent?

Equally telling is the sequence featuring the white "prop man" Jack White in the role of "Old Black Joe"—a throwback to the minstrel show tradition and a routine reminiscent of some of what we saw with Armstrong earlier. Like the clever fool central to this tradition, White delivers a crazy "stump speech," an exercise in "nonlogical modes of thinking and speaking" as he careens from an account of a boxing match between a tuna and a bass in a fish store—"Oh, how I'd like to own a fish store, that's what I wish for"—to waving the flag of freedom as he goes into battle; and all the while members of the band, seated like the minstrel show endmen in a semicircle, not only deride him but also make animal sounds on their instruments.

If blacks are present at all, they are "comfortably infantilized," as when Whiteman is shown with a smiling little black girl on his lap, who pinches his cheek as he winks at her. Similarly, the introduction of the production number so closely identified with Whiteman, Gershwin's *Rhapsody in Blue*, includes the image of a "coal-black, muscular body with a voodoo headdress dancing on a large drum with an animal hide stretched tightly over it," in effect removing "any sexual threat of the black male body." At the same time, we are told that "the most primitive and the most modern musical elements are combined in this rhapsody, for jazz was born in the African jungle to the beating of the voodoo drum."[52]

The segment with the Rhythm Boys offers a southern take on blackness. Initially seen as black silhouettes, the trio sing "Happy as a cow, chewing on a cud, / When the darkies beat their feet on the Mississippi Mud." Harry Barris then urges a loftier tone to the proceedings as they segue into song about cooperation, "So the Bluebirds and the Blackbirds Got Together":

First the bluebird said: "We've got to have sunny weather."
So the bluebirds and the blackbirds got together.
Then the blackbird said: "We're birds of a different feather."
So the bluebirds and the blackbirds got together.

Viewers of the day watching this number would surely not have missed the connection with the very popular theme song of Florence Mills, "I'm a Little Blackbird Looking for a Bluebird." Originally introduced by her and Shelton Brooks as part of the show *Dixie to Broadway* during the 1924–25 season, it quickly became recognized as a protest song delivering the message that all people, regardless of color or creed, have the right to search for "the bluebird of happiness." There were soon several sequels, including another starring vehicle for Mills, *Blackbirds of 1926*, which opened at Harlem's Alhambra and had subsequent highly acclaimed performances in England and

France.[53] And during the Paris run in July 1926 Mills shared billing with the Paul Whiteman Orchestra. Yet it is sadly ironic that less than three weeks after the untimely death of Florence Mills in 1927 (November 1), we find Paul Whiteman having to defend himself against "fictitious and harmful stories" in the foremost black newspaper of the day, the *Chicago Defender:*

> When Miss Florence Mills first came to London she met with many obstacles. I accompanied S. J. Kaufman, representative of Miss Mills' manager, Sam Salvin, on numerous trips to newspapers of London, urging them to give Miss Mills the same opportunity that they gave white artists of similar ability.
>
> Were Miss Mills alive, she would resent, as much as I, the falsehood which links me with prejudice and snobbery.[54]

"I'm a Little Blackbird Looking for a Bluebird" figured in Armstrong's early career as well, very close to the time of its premiere. It was on December 17, 1924, during his Fletcher Henderson days in New York, that he recorded it for Okeh as a member of Clarence Williams's Blue Five, with the legendary Sidney Bechet on soprano saxophone sharing the honors in the front line. Eva Taylor, recently married to Clarence Williams, can be heard performing the vocals and underscoring the political message of the lyrics with the phrase "building fairy castles same as all the white folks do."

King of Jazz ultimately serves as a stunning demonstration of how much the technology of the movie soundtrack had developed within the span of only three years. In 1927, with the release by Warner Brothers of *The Jazz Singer,* audiences first saw a kindred feature, with its segments of blackface with spoken dialogue by Al Jolson, who plays the aspiring jazz singer son of an orthodox Jewish cantor. Indeed, *The Jazz Singer* included what are possibly the most prophetic words in the history of film: "Wait a minute, you ain't heard nothing yet."

Whiteman is given credit for helping originate, during the making of *King of Jazz,* an innovation in the recording of music for talking pictures—actually prerecording the band and singers so as to achieve the proper balance. And so it was that, as circumstances dictated, soundtracks came to be made independently of the actual filming of a given scene or song.

Improvements in microphone design in the late 1920s also helped transform radio and recording. As early as 1926, when Bing Crosby began recording with Paul Whiteman, he was using the newly improved condenser microphone that, by being held close to the mouth, made possible the crooner sound; the same equipment was used in the first generation of "talkies." By 1929 Paul Whiteman was required by Lorillard to have the Rhythm Boys on every program; for in the minds of the advertisers the warm resonance of the trio would be able to lure young smokers, the flappers, and the collegians. And Bing Crosby, with his alluring baritone, was fast becoming the vocalist of choice, communicating an intimate message to a mass audience. At the same time that movie actors like Francis X. Bushman, John Gilbert, and the dapper, handsome Charlie Farrell, with his "high and heavy Cape Cod twang," failed to successfully make the transition from the silent screen to sound, the new condenser microphone was Crosby's "ultimate ally, perfectly suited to his way with dynamics and nuance and timbre. As he explored gradations in projection, Bing collaborated with the electric current as if he were romancing a woman."[55] Starting in March 1929 Louis Armstrong, too, was recast in a new image, thanks in no small way to the microphone. He effectively blurred the distinction between jazz and popular music, recording in his inimitably subtle high baritone renditions of "I Can't Give You Anything But Love, Baby," and two numbers from *Hot Chocolates*, "What Did I Do to Be So Black and Blue?" and "Ain't Misbehavin'."

Before making it back to New York, Armstrong was a whirlwind of activity in the Windy City. His final Hot Five sessions in Chicago in June and July 1928 marked the culmination of an historic series of recordings in the jazz canon, but the sheer range of his day-to-day activity helped hone his image as a pop icon. The members of his reconstituted Hot Five—Fred Robinson on trombone, Jimmy Strong on clarinet, Earl Hines on piano, and Zutty Singleton on drums—were drawn from the ensemble with which he was regularly performing. This was the Savoy Ballroom Orchestra led by Carroll Dickerson who, like Paul Whiteman, was a classically trained violinist bandleader. Even more important, the opening of the Savoy Ballroom, located at South Parkway Boulevard and East 47th Street, signaled a shift downtown of Chicago's center of black entertainment and commerce from the area around 35th and State; and radio broadcasts from the Savoy brought that sound to an ever-widening audience. Then there were developments that had far-reaching implications for Armstrong's public persona and style—developments that were to align him more than ever before with popular music and the world of Paul Whiteman.

Rarely given the attention it deserves was Armstrong's growing attraction to the sweet big band sound of Guy Lombardo and his Royal Canadians—as their slogan had it, "the sweetest music this side of heaven." A defining moment came on September 21, 1928, when Armstrong and Zutty Singleton visited Lombardo at the whites-only Granada Café. It must have been quite an event, as the pair were "wined and dined until the wee hours of the morning."[56] Armstrong valued what Lombardo's ensemble could do to make jazz both relaxed and soothing, qualities he soon emulated with his recordings of "What Did I Do to Be So Black and Blue?," "Ain't Misbehavin'," and many more. As he once put it: "That band plays the tune, they put the melody there and it's beautiful. You can't find another band that can play a straight lead and make it sound that good."[57] Drawing attention to the "spellbinding effectiveness" of Armstrong's recordings at the end of the 1920s and in the early 1930s, Richard Sudhalter has said it more pointedly: "Armstrong's Lombardo-style supporting bands, their stodgy rhythm sections and mooing saxophones so often decried by jazz commentators, provide a context within which Louis, both singing and playing, comes across vividly and forcefully. It is an infallible way of highlighting a soloist's work, comparable to the role of mat and frame in displaying a great painting."[58]

As for Paul Whiteman, there was a long-standing, cordial relationship with Guy Lombardo extending over forty years, from 1927 until Whiteman's death in 1967. It all began when Whiteman recommended Lombardo to take over for him at his failing Club Whiteman in New York, only to discover that Lombardo had already been lured away to Chicago's Granada Café. But there were many subsequent Lombardo-Whiteman endeavors, whether on the Committee of Five for the Betterment of Radio, in joint publishing ventures, recording for Decca, or performing on the Blue Network (precursor of ABC radio) under Whiteman's aegis as music director.

Meanwhile, life for Armstrong at Chicago's Savoy Ballroom came to have its ups and downs. "They'd always have a basketball game first, then the dance would start." Stripped down to his bathing suit, the 230-pound Armstrong and his teammates would drive the crowd into hysterics. "I put it [the ball] under my arm and started running like mad with it. And the people laughed an' roared thunderously. I ran almost to the basket, took a good aim at the basket, threw it up there. Then I missed it. Both of our teams were so weak from laughing at me. Oh, what fun we had."[59]

But soon there was a slowdown in business at the Savoy; the owner began to lay a hard luck story on the musicians week after week. Armstrong was still signed with the Okeh Record Company, even though the handling of his contract had been transferred to Tommy Rockwell, a hard-drinking Irishman who reportedly "couldn't carry two notes of a melody—completely tone deaf." Based in New York, Rockwell was to become one of Armstrong's managers before Joe Glaser; he redirected Armstrong's career, positioning him for his success on Broadway—most notably in *Hot Chocolates*—and helped him diversify his repertoire with more pop-song material.

Rockwell put his money where his mouth was. A telegram and an advance from him was all Armstrong needed to make his way to New York by early March 1929. It was then that he recorded such titles as "Knockin' a Jug," "Mahogany Hall Stomp," and his first mainstream pop tune, "I Can't Give You Anything But Love"—a remarkable instrumental and vocal rendition, and one profoundly prescient in that Black Friday was in the near future. Equally notable was Armstrong's working with one of the very first interracial ensembles; for among his sidemen were the banjo player Eddie Condon and two musicians who at different times played in the Paul Whiteman Orchestra—the guitarist Eddie Lang (1929–30), and the trombonist Jack Teagarden (1933–38). Eddie Lang, in fact, was almost concurrently featured in *King of Jazz*, together with his partner, the violinist Joe Venuti. Armstrong later worked intensively with Teagarden in the first Louis Armstrong All Stars from 1947 to 1951; in addition, there were other special occasions when they would "groove" together.

No doubt buoyed by his success, Armstrong returned to Chicago to coax fellow band members from the Savoy Ballroom to whom he had become especially attached—Carroll Dickerson, Zutty Singleton, and a few others—to drive back with him to New York. Besides, he had been invited to try out for a new Vincent Youmans musical, *Great Day*. After a mishap or two the motley group finally made it to Harlem, and Armstrong lost little time in heading to Rockwell's downtown office. Even though Rockwell hit the ceiling upon learning that Armstrong had brought his band with him, he apparently soon calmed down. As Armstrong later recalled: "Just the same, Mr. Rockwell, we're here now. I just couldn't leave my boys, that's all. I know you can book us some place."[60] Indeed, within two weeks the group had a job at one of Harlem's hottest clubs, Connie's Inn at 131st Street and Seventh Avenue, second only to the legendary Cotton Club. It was June 24, 1929. As fate would have it, the Youmans musical flopped, but Armstrong was to put his indelible stamp on another show.

The Harlem Renaissance was at its zenith. In its October 18, 1929, issue the *New York Herald Tribune* editorialized: "Negro dancing and music are, with the exception of Christian Science, the only American *articles d'export* which have really swept the world." The *Herald* writer continued: "When Broadway sets its sign and seal upon a movement, it is made. . . . The Negro, not merely as a vaudeville joke, and not merely as a highbrow cult, has arrived." Much of the excitement had been aroused by the show *Hot Chocolates*, which had moved from Connie's Inn in Harlem and opened on Broadway at the Hudson Theater on June 20, 1929. This all-black revue written by Thomas "Fats"

Waller, Andy Razaf, and Harry Brooks was replete with skits of black life in Harlem. In keeping with the title, women in the chorus were listed as "Hot Chocolate Drops," the men as "Bon Bon Buddies." But what it came to be remembered for were the two hit songs: "Ain't Misbehavin'" and "What Did I Do to Be So Black and Blue?" Even though Armstrong entered the show after the premiere and was therefore not mentioned in reviews covering the opening, his performance of these two songs, especially "Ain't Misbehavin'," was so sensational that he soon found himself moving from the orchestra pit to center stage. After the show he would taxi up to Harlem to join his band at Connie's Inn. As he later recalled: "Had to get my sleep coming through the park in a cab. Didn't exactly feel I had the world at my feet, but it was nice that everyone was picking up on the things I was doing."[61] These were indeed heady times.

Armstrong's renditions of "Ain't Misbehavin'" and "What Did I Do to Be So Black and Blue?" were recorded almost immediately—on July 19 and 22, 1929—and took on lives of their own. This was especially true of "Black and Blue," which was elevated by the power of Armstrong's horn and vocal into a poignant, profoundly moving statement about the brutality of racism—a message that later inspired Ralph Ellison in his 1952 novel *Invisible Man*. This excerpt speaks for itself.

> I'm white inside,
> It don't help my case,
> 'Cause I can't hide what is on my face.
> How will it end?
> Ain't got a friend.
> My only sin is in my skin.
> What did I do to be so black and blue?

Robert G. O'Meally has written eloquently about the song's larger message: "This song served as a vehicle of remorse by a brown-skinned female character who regretted that all boys seemed to prefer light-skinned girls. Trumpeter and vocalist Louis Armstrong . . . elevates it to a level of a racial protest piece and generalized plaint against life's undeserved brutalizing aspects. . . . A history of a people, may be discerned between the blue beams of sound in this mighty song."[62]

Armstrong was now poised to become an international star, but as we shall soon see, it was a process undertaken in the face of a unique mix of racism and adulation. At the same time, the vicissitudes of political change, both in the United States and on the other side of the world in Russia, were to cause a fundamental change in the perception of jazz; the focus on blackness and the plight of the underdog was about to redefine the historiography of jazz and its aesthetic. Meanwhile, during the period from 1929 to about 1933 Paul Whiteman was to vigorously pursue his own agenda, continuing to incorporate elements into his sound that were hot and black-tinged. Thanks to the prompting of Al Rinker, Bing Crosby's sidekick of Rhythm Boys fame, Whiteman hired Rinker's sister, Mildred Bailey—a harbinger of female jazz band vocalists in general. She was the first major singer of her sex to record Hoagy Carmichael's "Rockin' Chair" with Paul Whiteman in 1932, and she became so identified with the song that she came to be dubbed the Rockin' Chair Lady and formed an integral part of this standard's discographic history. It was a history initiated by Armstrong in 1929, when he joined forces with Hoagy Carmichael himself; it would later become the calling card of the interracial duo of Louis Armstrong and Jack Teagarden. And even more telling is that Mildred Bailey looked to two black singers as role models: Ethel Waters, so vital to Fletcher Henderson's early career, as we have already seen, and Bessie Smith. Then again, Whiteman was to collaborate with Al Jolson of blackface and *The Jazz Singer* fame when the *Kraft Music Hall* radio series was launched on NBC in 1933. That same year the African-American composer William Grant Still, one of his most valued arrangers, was to figure prominently in Whiteman's Sixth Experiment in Modern Music.

4 UNEASY LIES THE HEAD

King of Jazz was a landmark, but it also left Whiteman open to charges of turning down the heat of jazz, diluting its African (and African-American) blood. Even more critical, around the time of the movie's release, changes were already under way challenging the supremacy of the "King of Jazz." One especially vivid manifestation of such change was a poll conducted in December 1931 by one of the nation's preeminent black newspapers. The *Pittsburgh Courier* had this to say: "Crowned 'King of Jazz' last week in the National 'Most Popular Orchestra' Contest conducted by the *Pittsburgh Courier,* reigning supreme and having polled 50,000 votes, the largest amount, competing with over 50 orchestras and bands all over the United States, Duke Ellington has proved that he is the most popular orchestra leader today."[1] Whiteman was dethroned in the eyes of a major mainstream publication in 1949, when *Time,* in its issue of February 21, portrayed Armstrong on its front cover as the "King of Jazz," wearing a crown of gold trumpets. And in essence this chapter tells the story of how and why the immortal line of Shakespeare—"Uneasy lies the head that wears a crown"—speaks so directly to what transpired in the respective careers of Armstrong and Whiteman between about 1930 and 1949.

Two defining issues of the 1930s—the Great Depression and segregation—are addressed in two poignantly prescient 1929 recordings by Armstrong, "I Can't Give You Anything But Love" and "What Did I Do to Be So Black and Blue?" His "I Can't Give You Anything But Love," anticipating the stock market crash of October 29, 1929, by some eight months, is remarkable for such features as its dark reedy timbre and the halting fragility of the vocal in the second chorus. As for "What Did I Do to Be So Black and Blue?" we hear in it a set of lyrics that was never more movingly sung than by Armstrong—one of the most touching statements about the injustices of racial inequality:

> How will it end?
> Ain't got a friend
> My only sin is in my skin
> What did I do to be so black and blue?

Sentiments such as these set a tone in the 1930s, at a time when the Great Depression and issues of racial segregation resonated in the course of the sometimes diverging, sometimes converging careers of Louis Armstrong and Paul Whiteman. But even more important, the process of how Armstrong came to be written into jazz history as one of its very greatest icons and a symbol of a proletarian "people's" music, even as Whiteman was relegated to the sidelines, is very much part of our story. Whiteman was a casualty of a socialist agenda coupled with the heightened black consciousness emerging during and directly after World War II. And it was a political process which effectively denied or ignored much of what he had achieved to foster the careers of such African-American musicians as Don Redman, Earl Hines, William Grant Still, Duke Ellington, and others.

Much of this process was driven by issues of labor. In fact, certain historians have gone so far as to speak of the "laboring of American culture," using the phrase to encapsulate several overlapping arguments that drove so much of the ideological debate of the decade of the 1930s and beyond. First, the rhetoric of "labor," associated with the "labor movement" and the Labor Party, came to be identified with "the proletariat" in the minds of Communist Party members and their fellow travelers, whether in the United States or in the Soviet Union. Second, labor evokes the growing creative influence of working-class Americans on, and their participation in, the cultural life of the nation—in short, the growth of mass culture, through radio and film, for example. Third, artists, musicians, writers, and many more creative workers were organizing into unions and defining a new relationship with management, thus giving greater visibility to a "labor of cultural production." And fourth, a "social democratic culture" was arising, bringing, by the time of World War II, significant efforts to achieve racial equality.[2]

The connection of Armstrong and Whiteman with the "laboring of American culture" and the international crises with which it was aligned cannot be fully appreciated without briefly going back to 1917; for it was then that two antipodal, seemingly unrelated, events occurred within a few days of each other. On March 7, 1917, the Victor Talking Machine Company released the first recordings ever of jazz, featuring the Original Dixieland Jazz Band, the five-piece band that had created a sensation at New York's Reisenweber's the previous month. Three days later, on the other side of the world, Russian troops mutinied in St. Petersburg following two days of strikes and rioting. Within a matter of days more than three centuries of Romanov rule abruptly ended, and by mid-April, with the arrival of Vladimir Ilyich Lenin, the Bolshevik Revolution was in full cry. What is more, American popular music and jazz figured prominently both during the death throes of the Romanov dynasty and in the early years of the Soviet Union, starting in the early to mid-1920s—testimony to the impact of modern recording and the impressions left by visiting American musicians. It is not so much that the tsar's own regiment had thrilled the public with its recording of "At a Georgia Camp Meeting," with other two-steps and cakewalks, or that the mad monk Rasputin had been fatally poisoned to the accompaniment of "Yankee Doodle."[3] In 1926 appearances there by bands led by Sam Wooding and Benny Peyton had created a stir. Sam Wooding, in particular, a classically trained bandleader from Philadelphia, was an early champion of Paul Whiteman and promoted the cause of symphonic jazz. Close on the heels of the Wooding visit that year, the Russian pianist Leopold Teplitsky arrived in the United States. Heading straight for Philadelphia, he was intent on following the directive from the Commissariat of Public Enlightenment to "master the techniques of American jazz, buy up stock arrangements and all the necessary musical instruments, and then put all to use in a new jazz orchestra for the city of Lenin's Revolution." When he returned home the following year, he was carrying with him several crates of jazz recordings, some twenty Paul Whiteman arrangements, and more than double that number of instruments.[4]

For Whiteman himself, 1926 proved to be a decisive year as well, particularly after he raised the heat of his music making by hiring Bing Crosby in September. As we have seen, that process continued for well over a year as he added the arranger Bill Challis, Bix Beiderbecke, and Frank Trumbauer to his roster. But during the spring and summer of 1926—from early April to late July—other developments were under way as he and his entourage made their second trip to Great Britain and the Continent. Times had changed since their first appearances in England in 1923. He now had the added attraction of offering *Rhapsody in Blue* as his signature piece wherever he went, and capacity audiences greeted the orchestra at London's Royal Albert Hall as well as at venues in Liverpool, Manchester, Edinburgh, Vienna, and Berlin. But widespread labor unrest and growing economic austerity were also in evidence—conditions that presaged so much of what was to soon hit hard in the United States.

The advertising copy for Whiteman's concert in the Royal Albert Hall on April 25, 1926, has certain shock value as we look back to this time of unrest with the benefit of hindsight. It is not so much the claim that "20,000 people came on Sunday April 11 last" or that "10,000 people failed to gain admission" as the sense of the vast crowds that Whiteman could command, something which would seem to have prompted such "fascist" billing as "The Mussolini of Ragtime." Six years later, when Armstrong first appeared in Italy, he was to relish "seeing his own picture blown up to the same size as Mussolini's, hanging on the opposite side of the theater doorway ('Mussolini was big stuff in those days')."[5]

It was a time when Whiteman had to contend with a protest from the British musicians' union, up in arms over the fact that the regular orchestra at London's Tivoli Theater would be denied work. Matters were eventually resolved, but not without negotiations between theater management and the Ministry of Labour. Not so amicably settled, however, was the general strike that effectively crippled the nation, as members of the Trade Union Congress rallied to the slogan "Not a penny off the pay; not a minute of the day." Coal miners, railway men, printing trade workers, truck drivers, dockworkers, and many others walked off their jobs, forcing the Whiteman musicians to borrow bicycles to pedal to work hither and yon.

The general strike caused the cancellation of several concerts, freeing up an extra week or two in the schedule. In June, Whiteman and company crossed over the Channel to the Continent to be warmly received in such cities as Vienna and Berlin. The Vienna visit, in particular, was memorable, in part for the reception given by famous operetta composer Franz Lehar, but even more because Whiteman was befriended by a brash young reporter who was then eking out a living on a tabloid—Billy Wilder. The tenor of the times affected what Wilder was to later do in film. Wilder went on to direct films of stinging satire, often exposing social inequities, with such classics to his credit as *Double Indemnity, The Lost Weekend, Sunset Boulevard,* and, most pertinent here, *Some Like It Hot,* that great American farce of jazz musicians from the

ROYAL ALBERT HALL

Acting Manager   REGINALD ASKEW

Sunday Afternoon, APRIL 25 at 3

20,000 PEOPLE

Came on Sunday April 11 last to the ROYAL ALBERT HALL to hear

"THE MUSSOLINI OF THE RAGTIME WORLD." *Daily Express*

PAUL

WHITEMAN

AND HIS BAND

10,000 PEOPLE

FAILED TO GAIN ADMISSION

SECURE YOUR SEATS NOW FOR APRIL 25

POPULAR PRICES   (Including Tax)—Reserved: Stalls 7/6   Arena 7/6, 5/9   Balcony 4/9
Unreserved: Balcony 3/6   Orchestra 3/-   Gallery 2/4   Admission Free

MAY BE OBTAINED AT THE BOX OFFICE, ROYAL ALBERT HALL, LIBRARIES, USUAL AGENTS and of

LIONEL POWELL & HOLT, 161-2, New Bond Street, London, W.   Booking Telephone: REGENT 1204 (Private Branch Exchange)

Booking Office open 10 to 5.   Saturday 10 to 12.
A stamped addressed envelope must accompany all applications for tickets by post.

Vail & Co. Printers, London, W.

4.1 Poster announcing Whiteman concert of April 25, 1926, in London's Royal Albert Hall and hailing him as "The Mussolini of the Ragtime World." Williams College Archives and Special Collections.

Chicago of the Depression era, finding work by dressing as women and eluding gangsters in the process.

Many years later Wilder was to recall his first meeting with Whiteman, hinting at how the meeting changed the course of his life:

> Then Whiteman came to Vienna on a visit. He did not know Europe, so he went to see Vienna. He gave concerts, in London, in Paris, and in Amsterdam. I made an interview with him. In Vienna, in the hotel where I made the interview, he had a black man who he only used to wind up the Victrola. In my broken English I told him I was anxious to see him perform. And Whiteman told me: "If you're eager to hear me, to hear the big band, you can come with me to Berlin . . ." He paid for my trip, for a week there or something. And I accepted it. And I packed up my things, and I never went back to Vienna. I wrote the piece about Whiteman for the paper in Vienna. And then I was a newspaperman for a paper in Berlin.[6]

It was Wilder, Whiteman's German-speaking guide, who brought to his attention a haunting ballad, "Madonna, du bist schöner als der Sonnenschein," with music and lyrics by German dentist-composer Robert Katscher. First recorded by Whiteman in June 1927, it became far better known by its English version, "When Day Is Done," with lyrics by Buddy DeSylva—a song of romantic reverie when the day's labors are over: "When day is done and shadows fall, I dream of you." It soon became a favorite of Whiteman's, and was even performed at his funeral, when his own life's work was done.

The Berlin stay in early July 1926 was highlighted by a series of five concerts within four days in the city's biggest auditorium, the Grosses Schauspielhaus. Critics and composers of note, like Arnold Schoenberg and Franz Schreker, sat in on rehearsals intent on comprehending the "new" Whiteman phenomenon. While his orchestration and the virtuosity of his players earned high marks, the music itself was damned with faint praise. In the words of one newspaper: "We Germans heard jazz yesterday for the first time. It will not become popular in Germany, for it does not suit the folk character, but it is a magic note from another world and cannot be dismissed contemptuously as 'negro music.'"[7]

The reference to "folk character" touches on a general theme which is central to much of the thinking about jazz and its cultural ownership during the late 1920s and much of the 1930s. For now it suffices to note that Whiteman's Berlin concerts took place against a backdrop of growing economic austerity. The value of the German mark had plummeted to the point where banknotes bundled into billions were carted in laundry baskets or used as toys by children. Nor can one ignore the ominous shadows of isolationism as the country lurched from crisis to crisis, a harbinger of what was to come with the appointment of Adolf Hitler as Chancellor of the Reich.

It was during these dark days that Kurt Weill and Bertolt Brecht created their preeminent masterpiece of social consciousness, that revolutionary call to arms, *The Threepenny Opera*. In writing his score Weill saw the jazz idiom as a means of reaching a mass public, creating a work striking for its instrumentation no less than its use of the tango, fox-trot, and blues. His generalizations of 1926 about the place of jazz in the music of his day are telling: "The Americanization of our whole external life, which is happening slowly but surely, finds its most peculiar outcome here. Unlike art music, dance music does not reflect the sense of towering personalities who stand above time, but rather it reflects the instinct of the masses. And a glance into the dance halls of all continents demonstrates that jazz is just as precisely the outward expression of our time as the waltz was of the outgoing nineteenth century."[8]

The Threepenny Opera was later to have enormous impact on Louis Armstrong, particularly the showstopper "Mack the Knife," the ballad of the notorious cutthroat leader of a gang of thieves. This was a song with which Armstrong could closely identify; it was not simply about the exploits of Macheath but also harked to his own early days of hardship in New Orleans. Starting in 1955, following the enormous popular success of Marc Blitzstein's English translation of the previous year, Armstrong recorded the song a total of forty-two times! Even "Hello, Dolly!" came in a distant second, with a tally of half that number. But already in the mid-1920s, a hot musical property in Chicago, Armstrong was never too far from the underworld. In the city where Al Capone had recently taken over as boss of bootlegging, gambling, prostitution, and dance hall business, Armstrong struck up a lasting friendship with Joe Glaser, who in 1935 became his manager for life.

Armstrong first got to know Glaser in 1926, when Glaser was managing the Sunset Café, a black-and-tan at 35th Street and Calumet, on Chicago's South Side. In the early 1940s he reminisced about their earliest times together.

I finally left the Vendome and settled down . . . at the Sunset. I liked the setup there better, with Earl Hines at the piano, Tubby Hall on drums, Darnell Howard, sax and clarinet, and down the line of the good ol' times. Joe Glaser was the boss of the place. I always admired Mr. Glaser from the first day I started working for him. He just impressed me different than the other bosses I've worked for. He seemed to understand colored people so much. And he was wonderful to his whole show and band, would give us nice presents. . . . And don't you think for once that Mr. Glaser didn't pitch a bitch when things aren't jumping right. I did not know about managers, etc. like they have nowadays. I don't think Mr. Glaser was thinking about it either, or else he wouldn't have signed me up then.[9]

Committing these recollections to paper some twenty years after the fact, Armstrong certainly had a basis for comparing Glaser's treatment with that accorded him by such managers as Tommy Rockwell, Connie Immerman, Johnny Collins, and N. J. Canetti. At the same time, however, he never forgot the advice given him back in New Orleans by his muscleman, drummer, and protector Black Benny Williams; for, with an absentee father and a motley succession of surrogates and stepfathers, Armstrong learned early on the necessity of depending for his survival on the power and protection of men in whom he could place his trust: "Dipper," Williams had told him, "as long as you live, no matter where you may be, always have a white man [who] can and will put his hand on your shoulder and say 'This is my nigger,' and can't anybody harm ya."

Armstrong's deep-seated need for such protection was understandably driven by his drive to succeed in a segregated, racist society, whether in New Orleans or elsewhere. Certainly social conditions were exacerbated before his historic move in 1922 from his hometown to Chicago, when during 1919–20 much of the United States was consumed by the hysteria of the Red Scare. The situation was exploited to the full by Attorney General A. Mitchell Palmer and his twenty-four-year-old protégé J. Edgar Hoover, as lowly Italian, Jewish, or Slavic immigrants—and especially suspected communist radicals in the labor movement—became the targets of a purge, the notorious Palmer Raids. Ultimate responsibility for the wave of radicalism sweeping the country was pinned squarely on the Communist International (Comintern). But in 1928 the Comintern, in concert with developments in the United States, began to rewrite jazz history.

The Comintern of 1928, perhaps more than any other prior congress, addressed itself both to the "Negro question" in the United States and to various liberation movements around the world, including in its resolution a number of critical theses and a call to revolution:

The emigration of the negroes to the North continues at an ever-increasing rate, where the huge majority of the negroes become unskilled laborers. The growth of the negro proletariat is the most important phenomenon of recent years. . . . One of the most important tasks of the Communist Party consists in the struggle for a complete and real equality of the negroes, for the abolition of all kinds of racial, social, and political inequalities. . . . Only the victorious proletarian revolution will completely and permanently solve the agrarian and national questions of the Southern United States in the interests of the overwhelming majority of the negro population of the country. . . . American imperialism utilizes every possible form of slave exploitation . . . for the purpose of extracting super-profits. On the basis of these slave remnants, there has grown up a superstructure of social and political inequality that expresses itself in lynching, segregation, Jim Crowism. . . . The negro race everywhere is an oppressed race. . . . A common tie of interest is established for the revolutionary struggle of race and national liberation from imperialist domination of the Negroes in various parts of the world.[10]

The Resolution of 1928 first appeared in the *Daily Worker,* "Organ of the Communist Party U.S.A.," in February 1929. Vigorous discussion of proletarian music and jazz followed soon in the newspaper's columns; Charles Edward Smith's "Class Content of Jazz Music," published some four years later, was a quintessential example of agitprop journalism.[11] The piece combines three overlapping themes: Negro oppression, jazz as folk art, and the idea of hot jazz as the only genuine article:

Jazz has its roots in the oppressive measures of southern plantation owners against the Negro masses. . . . What was the music of the serf (sharecropper) and worker? . . . The spirituals. Next the work songs, the first songs in America to have a proletarian content, expressing clearly and with profound sincerity the state of oppression of the American Negro. . . . Hardly were the blues introduced . . . than their spontaneous folk quality became designated in the realm of jazz by the term hot. . . . Hot is the music having the folk quality. . . . The hot element in jazz . . . has its basis in the class struggle. Hot jazz aims to be genuinely the folk expression of a people.

Drugged with the poison of popular music and with the virulent poison of the capitalist propaganda machine, prejudices are imposed upon the masses. . . . That which is in reality shallow, cheap and sensational—symphonic jazz, so-called semi-classical music—is often-times mistaken for the real thing.

While Smith concedes that hot jazz continued to flourish and that at least some of those producing it were awakening to its class content, he deplores the "impurities" introduced into hot jazz through popular music; they are a symptom of a corrupting "bourgeois-capitalist world," which has stifled the expression of "the creative and emotional depths of the people." For him this is why jazz very seldom can claim equality with the folk music of the African Negro, the Spanish gypsy, or the singers of Bali. And hence his rallying cry: "The revolution must be fought out on every front, cultural as well as economic." Yet conspicuous by its absence from Smith's column is any mention of how, some seven years earlier, both Kurt Weill and Paul Whiteman, despite sharply contrasting political agendas, could think of jazz as a form of folk music. Weill, we will remember, generalized in 1926 about "the Americanization of our whole external life" through dance music and observed that it "reflects the instinct of the masses"; this was shortly before he completed his proletarian masterpiece, *The Threepenny Opera,* with Bertolt Brecht. And Paul Whiteman came to be identified with a bylined feature in the *New York Times Magazine,* where he spoke of jazz as "the folk music of the machine age."[12]

For many champions of the cause there came to be a simple formula: white meant sweet and part of the status quo, while black was hot and dynamic, representing so much of what many intellectuals and radicals associated with the struggle to liberate an oppressed race. There were, of course, the inevitable derisive comments. The British composer and writer Spike Hughes bluntly said that such "purists . . . are most dreadful snobs; to them only the illiterate have any aesthetic standing."[13] Meanwhile, driven by the spirit of idealism, some within the communist movement had a vision of interracial understanding and were eager to attract black people to their ranks. In their enthusiasm for jazz and black artistic achievement they published news and reviews, also "featuring jazz musicians at gatherings, rallies, parties, and at a summer resort, Camp Unity, some seventy-five miles north of New York City. A number of musicians accepted such invitations as pleasant jobs during hard times."[14] But this idealistic sentiment was embraced far more by whites within the movement than by any blacks. Most important, it came to profoundly shape their writing of jazz history in the 1930s and 1940s and the perception of such figures as Armstrong and Whiteman.

Events in Scottsboro, Alabama, in 1931 served as a true lightning rod for the international Communist movement and a host of fellow travelers, among them the future record producer John Hammond. The gross miscarriage of justice as nine black defendants were forced to endure sixteen trials, including the declaration of a mistrial by the U.S. Supreme Court, proved to be a harrowing experience in American jurisprudence spanning some seventeen years; most of the youths would remain damaged for life. These developments helped validate the black cultural ownership of jazz and perception of the form as the music of an oppressed race.

The chain of events began on March 25, 1931, when nine black teenagers, dirt poor and barely literate, stole a ride on a freight train bound for Memphis, only to get into a fight with a group of white youths. Just north of Scottsboro, a white boy accompanied by four or five others had just made his way back across the top of the car only to then suddenly double back, this time stepping on the hand of a black youth hanging on to the side of the Southern Railroad tank car. Like their black counterparts, these were hoboes who "had taken to the rails in search of a shorter breadline, a warmer place to sleep, and, if they got lucky, a few days' work."[15] The train periodically stopped or slowed down, the boys hopping off and on again, regrouping or scattering along the length of the train, with the white boys at least at one point pelting their opposite numbers with stones. Tensions escalated and a fight broke out in which the whites were bested by the blacks. Word about the commotion somehow spread, and by the time the train had stopped at Paint Rock, Alabama, there was an armed posse waiting, ready to charge the black youths with "assault and attempt to murder." Most damning was that the youths were falsely accused of raping two white girls; no matter that they had actually never seen them before the arrival in Paint Rock, let alone touched them. As it later transpired, these were impoverished mill workers who had a record of trading sex for money and had served time for vagrancy and adultery.

Sensational coverage was given to the subsequent trials, with the NAACP and the Communist Party taking the lead in defense of the Scottsboro Nine. Around the time of the trial of June 1933, for example, columnists in the *Daily Worker* and the *Communist* lambasted the judge, who had become, "unwittingly or not, part and parcel of the lynching machinery which gapes for the bodies of the nine Scottsboro boys," a man who had become the "official lyncher for the Scottsboro bourbons, dressed in sheep's clothing to hide the fangs of lynch justice."[16] Without a doubt, "radicalization of the masses" was in the air.

A key player in the drama of "radicalization of the masses" who came to chart the future direction of so much jazz recording was John Hammond. Better known for his later work as a producer for Columbia Records who championed the careers of such musicians as Billie Holiday, Fletcher Henderson, Bessie Smith, Count Basie, Teddy Wilson, his brother-in-law Benny Goodman, Bob Dylan, and Bruce Springsteen, Hammond was a unique figure straddling the worlds of privilege and privation. He was born in 1910 in a mansion on Manhattan's Upper East Side, on 91st Street, just off Central Park, "a late and welcome surprise" in a family of four daughters. His mother's pedigree was one of high status; she was a descendant of both Cornelius Vanderbilt, the railroad tycoon, and William Douglas Sloane, one of the founders of W. & J. Sloane. But Hammond's heritage was less prophetic of his future than was his pricking up his ears at a young age when hearing the music played on a Columbia Grafanola by the servants in the rear of the mansion; Paul Whiteman and the Original Dixieland Jazz Band were among his early favorites. The upscale Victrola and Red Seal Victor records of opera and classical music in the front parlor, of which his mother was so fond, held relatively little interest for him. A few years later, quite predictably, life at the Hotchkiss School and at Yale turned out to be not for him; he was simply not destined to follow the career paths for which he was being groomed, those of business or law. In fact, by the middle of his sophomore year he had dropped out of Yale, never to return. Hammond, a self-described "New York social dissident," marked his twenty-first birthday—it was 1931, the year of Scottsboro—by moving out of the family mansion to a modest apartment in Greenwich Village, where he found a neighborhood of political activists, artists, and writers. It was, as he once said, quoting Lincoln Steffens, "as pleasant to change one's mind as it was to change one's clothes." But what drove him more than anything else was his passion for jazz. "The strongest motivation for my dissent was jazz. I heard no color line in the music. While my early favorites were white players, the recorded and live performances of Negroes excited me more. The fact that the best jazz players barely made a living, were barred from all well-paying jobs in radio and in most nightclubs, enraged me. . . . To bring recognition to the Negro's supremacy in jazz was the most effective and constructive form of social protest I could think of."[17]

Living on an ample income from family trust funds, Hammond, to a large extent, was able to put his money where his mouth was. By 1935 he could point to having produced some forty records on both sides of the Atlantic, featuring a roster of predominantly black artists, among them Fletcher Henderson, Benny Carter, Coleman Hawkins, Bessie Smith, and Teddy Wilson. And as we shall see, during Armstrong's second voyage to England in July 1933, Hammond delivered a well-placed punch to the jaw of Armstrong's abusive manager of the time, Johnny Collins. There was a special force behind that punch. Hammond had very recently made his mark as a columnist for the *Nation,* reporting on a new trial in Alabama for the Scottsboro boys and also arranging a benefit for the International Labor Defense (ILD) of the Communist

Party—they had sent representatives to Alabama to designate them as counsel—in support of the Scottsboro Defense Committee. The ILD had successfully petitioned the U.S. Supreme Court for a hearing and had persuasively argued that the judgment of the Alabama Supreme Court should be reversed and a new trial ordered. Hammond did not mince words in recalling the episode years later: "Whatever the South's outrage, this cruel and hasty Justice—and the stench of frame-up—caused an uproar elsewhere in the country. The NAACP reacted cautiously. . . . The Communist Party was less reticent. . . . The ILD's aggressive and emotional efforts on behalf of the Scottsboro boys appealed strongly to blacks in the various Negro enclaves of America, while the temporizing of the NAACP earned it contempt. . . . I was exasperated by the NAACP's whole performance."[18]

Hammond's downward mobility to champion black music and related causes was symptomatic of a period when by default, little by little, a figure such as Paul Whiteman was being relegated to the sidelines. This was true even though Whiteman actually had both black and white talent on his payroll, and worked to promote the growth of an inclusive jazz style. At the same time, a close look at the careers of both Armstrong and Whiteman against the background of proletarian ideology of the 1930s reveals a great deal about the relationship between management and labor—particularly in the case of Armstrong—as well as about the promotion of a mass musical culture.

During the time of the Great Depression and proletarian activism of the early 1930s, Armstrong's 1929 recording of a popular song such as "I Can't Give You Anything But Love" spoke to the anxieties of a whole period, with masses of people standing in breadlines hoping for a handout. And it was surpassed in impact by the release in 1932 of "Brother, Can You Spare a Dime?" as sung by Paul Whiteman's recently departed protégé, Bing Crosby. But while untold masses were huddled on breadlines, both Armstrong and Whiteman were able to cut figures of considerable girth, obsessing about diet in the process.

In the invaluable memoir of his early years, *Satchmo: My Life in New Orleans*, Armstrong tells the cautionary tale of what transpired one summer when he was playing in Fate Marable's band aboard one of the Mississippi side-wheelers. In many essential details it is a dark precursor of what was to happen to so many with the coming of the great crash of 1929. A member of the band had starved himself all summer—he would eat an apple rather than a good hot meal—in order to save his earnings and send "all his money to a farm down South where employees and relatives were raising cotton for him." Unfortunately, there was no one there to safeguard his interests and to monitor how the money was actually being used. Far worse, the boll weevils ate all of his cotton before the end of the season. The young Armstrong, sensing a potential suicide in his fellow band member, would warn Fate Marable: "Fate, keep an eye on David Jones. He's liable to jump in the water most any minute." Armstrong goes on to say: "This incident taught me never to deprive my stomach. . . . I'll probably never be rich, but I will be a fat man. I never deprived myself of things I thought absolutely necessary."[19]

In matters of the stomach Armstrong's mother Mayann taught her son something else early on—the importance of taking a laxative or cathartic. "You are still young, son, and have a long ways to go. Always remember when you're sick nobody ain't going to give you nothing. So try to stay healthy. Even without money your health is the best thing. I want you to promise me you will take a physic at least once a week as long as you live."[20]

An obsession with the regularity of bowel function led Armstrong to later promote the wonders of the herbal remedy Swiss Kriss and tout its benefits to anyone within earshot. His stationery, in fact, gave a keyhole view of him grinning on the toilet, accompanied by the caption: "Satchmo says: Leave it all behind ya!" A closely related passion of Armstrong's, one that was traceable to a vital piece of folk wisdom Mayann had taught her son for fighting illness by drinking boiled herbs, was his love of marijuana, which he smoked heavily throughout his life, starting around the early 1920s. For Armstrong this was not dope at all: "My mother and her church sisters used to go out by the railroad track and pick baskets full of pepper grass, dandelions, and lots of weeds similar to gage, and they would bring it to their homes, get a big fat slice of meat, and make one most deelicious [*sic*] pot of greens anyone would want to smack their lips on—physics you too."[21]

John Hammond, among others, deplored the habit, remarking of Armstrong: "He considered alcohol evil and marijuana virtuous, and he smoked it constantly, to my horror. It never led him to try anything stronger, however, but in my opinion it did hurt him, for it enabled him to become the exhibitionist he became to the detriment of his genius." Armstrong saw it differently, averring that "it makes you feel good, makes you feel wanted," helping you forget "all the bad things that happen to a Negro."[22]

All of which brings us to developments in late March 1931, when Armstrong ran afoul of the law in Los Angeles and had to mark prison time, precisely when the Scottsboro Nine were given their first taste of southern justice. His problems developed during a run while fronting the resident band at Frank Sebastian's Cotton Club in Culver City. It was a heady time for him in the fullest sense of the word. For one thing, he was delighted with the quality of the band: "These boys had something on the ball musically that I had not witnessed."[23] And at the first rehearsal he had made two big discoveries—the immense gifts of Lawrence Brown on trombone and of Lionel Hampton on drums. For another, he landed his first role in a full-length feature movie, *Ex-Flame* (1931), a production of the MGM studio just next door. Last, but not least, there was the matter of marijuana.

The young Buck Clayton, eager to learn the secret of creating a glissando on the horn, remembers seeking out his hero backstage at the Cotton Club. Armstrong, in a mellow mood, proceeded to show him how to create the special effect by pushing the valves way down and tightening the lips. But Armstrong's "mellow mood" came at a price, because it was around that time that he and drummer Vic Berton got busted by "two big healthy dicks [who] came from behind a car" out in the parking lot of the Cotton Club. This, however, did not faze Armstrong in the least; if anything, he relished his time behind bars as he rubbed shoulders with kindred spirits and enjoyed the growing admiration of his fans:

> When we reached the police headquarters there were several officers . . . sitting around. And the minute we came through the door they all recognized me right away. They too had been diggin' my music nightly over the radio. Oh boy, were those guys glad to see me. . . . I spent nine days in the Downtown Los Angeles City jail, in a cell with two guys who were already sentenced to forty or forty-five years for something else. . . . The most important thing was we were so very glad to see each other. Because it was a week ago I was blowing some good shuzzit with both of those characters.[24]

Armstrong's absolute faith in marijuana and how it "makes you feel good, makes you feel wanted," gives weight to his firm decision to always be a fat man. At bottom, it is all about his commitment to connect with his vast public. A master showman known to millions around the world, Armstrong never lost sight of that goal: "I never tried to prove nothing, just always wanted to give a good show. My life has been my music; it's always come first; but the music ain't worth nothing if you can't lay it on the public. The main thing is to live for that audience, 'cause what you're there for is to please the people."[25]

Armstrong clearly saw jazz as a totally inclusive music and himself as a vital force in the cause of a mass populism promoting a "social democratic culture." In an interview with Richard Hadlock, Armstrong says, "Anything you can express to the public is jazz." It is a deep-seated conviction stemming from his self-image, and was never more true than in the period starting in the late

1920s. It was then that Armstrong began fronting big bands, something he continued doing through 1946, and effectively crossed the imagined line separating jazz and popular music. When he applied for a passport in anticipation of his first European tour in 1932, Armstrong identified himself as "actor and musician." Dichotomies superimposed by misguided or ill-informed critics lose any solid basis. It is, in other words, patently absurd to separate "art" from "entertainment," "high" art from "low," or jazz from popular music when considering Armstrong's total output and how he perceived his role as a creative performer. Here was an entertainer in the best sense. During 1930 alone he melded jazz and widely diverse popular styles in such numbers as "Blue Yodel No. 9" (recorded with country music singer Jimmie Rodgers), the rumba hit "The Peanut Vendor" ("El Manisero"), and "Song of the Islands," a Hawaiian tribute in which "blues goes hula."

As for Paul Whiteman, his girth became the stuff of popular lore early on. In 1924, for example, *Vanity Fair* published the following alphabet rhyme:

> J is for JAZZ by our plump Prince of Whales,
> Whiteman, who staggers the musical scales.[26]

But by 1931 Whiteman's weight had become a liability in the courtship of the woman who was to be his fourth and last wife, the film actress Margaret Livingston. Dieting became serious business, as Whiteman—Hollywood wisecrackers called him The Covered Wagon—"labored" to give a more appealing shape to his popular image. In fact, in 1933, two years after their marriage, Margaret Livingston published *Whiteman's Burden,* billed as an "intimate, humorous record of a famous courtship and marriage, full of Hollywood gossip and lively anecdotes." All of this serves as a parallel to what would happen after Armstrong made Lucille Wilson his wife, his fourth and last as well, in 1942. The two of them cowrote *Lose Weight the Satchmo Way,* offering a rather idiosyncratic diet regimen to the world, with heavy doses of the herbal laxative Swiss Kriss, and Bisma Rex to cut gas. There is much wit and charm to the account by Margaret Livingston of their courtship and marriage, and what transpired after Whiteman first met the red-headed actress on the Universal lot during the filming of *King of Jazz:*

> Paul Whiteman, King of Jazz, was FAT—so fat that he couldn't get life insurance—so fat that the girl he loved wouldn't marry him. "Not," she said, "until I can put my arms around you." But she made him a sporting proposition—she would help him to shed the awful avoirdupois. She consulted specialists, worked out daily menus, and concocted tempting recipes which made reduc-

THE PEANUT VENDOR!

The
Big Hit
Played by
**Louis Armstrong's
Sebastian New
Cotton Club
Orchestra**

DANCE....

41474 10 in. .75	**AND THEN YOUR LIPS MET MINE**—Fox Trot; Refrain **BLUE AGAIN**—Fox Trot; Refrain Both played by **The Yale Collegians** (Director—Robert Bruce)
41475 10 in. .75	**YOU'RE DRIVING ME CRAZY!** (What Did I Do?)—Fox Trot; Refrain **HURT**—Fox Trot; Refrain Both played by **Ray Seeley and His Orchestra**
41478 10 in. .75	**THE PEANUT VENDOR**—Fox Trot; Refrain **YOU'RE DRIVING ME CRAZY!** (What Did I Do?)—Fox Trot; Refrain Both played by **Louis Armstrong and His Sebastian New Cotton Club Orchestra**

4.2 A 1930 advertisement of Okeh Records showing Armstrong's cross-racial appeal, featuring "The Peanut Vendor" alongside a performance by The Yale Collegians. Frank Driggs Collection.

ing a pleasure. He began at 303 pounds, a sick and unhappy fat man. Now he weighs a modest 190, looks and feels like a young athlete, is an A-1 risk for life insurance, and is married to Margaret Livingston, the girl of his dreams and the mentor who brought about his transformation.[27]

Despite his earlier avoirdupois, Whiteman was able, in effect, to put his arms around those who were less privileged and help transform their lives. His inclusiveness could extend to members of his band as well, becoming the stuff of sweet memory and touching anecdote. In 1980 the tenor saxophone player Buddy Tate recalled how in early November 1928, as an eager thirteen-year-old black youth from Sherman in north Texas, he had come to Dallas to hear, or perhaps overhear, the Paul Whiteman Orchestra. They were on a two-month fall tour, sweeping through states from New York and Virginia to Mississippi and Louisiana. Under segregation Tate usually had to resign himself to standing and listening in an alley behind the Sherman movie theater when a visiting jazz band was on hand. He expected the same in Dallas. Still, he recalled hoping, "If we could just get in and hear the Paul Whiteman band. I know there's going to be some beautiful music played . . . [but] you couldn't have bought a ticket for a thousand dollars, because it was segregated." Frankie Trumbauer, however, the C-melody saxophone star of the Whiteman band, was one of Tate's early idols and proved to be a guardian angel, even though the details of what exactly he did remain murky. In any event, the young Tate was about to have the biggest surprise of his life. "He just tells them—and they just run the place—well, man, you can hear Paul Whiteman. Hell, don't worry about that. We'll see that you hear Paul Whiteman. . . . We'll get you in, don't worry about it. Just come on and see me. So you know where I ended up? On the band stand. I had a better seat."[28]

Revealing too is the sworn affidavit in support of Armstrong that Whiteman wrote in 1931. But to put it all in context, one has to begin with the sequel to the marijuana arrest in Culver City, California—specifically the role of organized crime in getting Armstrong out of jail and securing for him a suspended sentence. Johnny Collins, a fixer, manager, and one-time errand boy of Tommy Rockwell, was delegated to do just that. Tommy Rockwell, as we have seen, was the executive with the Okeh Record Company who had positioned Armstrong for his success on Broadway—in *Hot Chocolates*, in particular—and had him performing a more diverse repertoire that came to include more pop song material.

For now, all the notoriety surrounding Armstrong's arrest, imprisonment, and trial had boosted his popularity a few notches. And at the end of March

1931, with the gig winding down at Sebastian's Cotton Club, he was off to Chicago accompanied by Collins, only to discover all too soon that he was caught in the crossfire of two feuding managers—Tommy Rockwell and Johnny Collins. Armstrong was into his second week of a six-week run as orchestra leader at the Chicago club Show Boat—it was around April 11, 1931—when he and Johnny Collins were allegedly confronted by Rockwell himself, now in the company of eight thugs, among them known hoodlums from Chicago's West Side. There were attempts at extortion and various threats; one tough suggested burning off Collins's moustache, for example. Only when Collins's wife called the police did the confrontation end. But there were more strong-arm tactics a week later when Armstrong, this time reportedly at gunpoint, was forced into a telephone booth to speak to Connie Immerman. Immerman, who with his brother George operated Connie's Inn in Harlem, demanded that Armstrong send a telegram guaranteeing that he would leave Chicago by airplane for New York that night. Armstrong would have none of that. He later put it this way: "All I know is, whoever was the gang in New York sent gangsters to Chicago where I was working and tried to frighten me into quitting the job and coming to New York to open up back at Connie's Inn again. And I felt that, as dirty as Connie fired me and my band [in December 1929], I did not want any part of those people ever again."[29]

In an effort to defuse the crisis, Collins sent Armstrong and the band on the road. The troupers crisscrossed the country, from Milwaukee to New Orleans, to Boston and New York. Some engagements lasted a week, but for much of the tour they had to contend with exhausting one-night stands. But the harassment continued, with the president of the American Federation of Musicians, now at the behest of the Immermans and Tommy Rockwell, using his muscle to force Armstrong to honor his alleged contract to appear at Connie's Inn and threatening to place his AFM membership in jeopardy—something which would effectively cut off virtually all major sources of income. As it turned out, not only had Armstrong canceled his original contract with Rockwell in September 1930; a handwriting expert in June 1931 had determined that the "new" contract the Immermans were holding over his head was not legally binding at all because signatures had been affixed only a few days before—not, as they claimed, some ten months earlier. To say the least, Rockwell and the Immermans had not been operating in good faith.

Armstrong filed a deposition with the United States District Court, Southern District of New York, in late June 1931, claiming "irreparable injury" and seeking an order which would restrain the defendants from "molesting and excluding the plaintiff from exercising his rights and privileges as a member of the American Federation of Musicians."[30] On July 9 the court ruled in Armstrong's favor. Yet this order was not enough to make Rockwell and the Immermans cease and desist; they persisted in their claim into the early months of 1932. Still, by the fall of 1931 the truth was out. Writing in the *Evening Graphic* of October 9, Ed Sullivan, then working as a young reporter, wrote about "the affidavits that backfired."[31] There was a supremely ironic twist in this dark story as plaintiff Rockwell and company had sought to establish by a series of affidavits from the likes of Paul Whiteman and others that Armstrong's services were of a unique order, and that they were the ones who had been caused harm. Rockwell's petition was denied.

The affidavits to which Ed Sullivan referred had been filed in late September—depositions not only from Paul Whiteman but also from Jack Kapp of Brunswick Records, Ralph Wonders of CBS Artists Bureau, and Irving Mills, Duke Ellington's booker and publisher. Yet none equaled Whiteman's in the enthusiasm of his support. "I have intimately been connected with music for the past twelve years, have come in contact with thousands of musicians, and Louis Armstrong is outstanding. He is a creator, his style of phrasing unique, and he is the one and only exponent of that type of phrasing. It is entirely original, individualistic, and impossible of duplication. His services are most definitely and decidedly extraordinary. I know of no colored performer who could replace him."[32]

Despite Whiteman's assessment of Armstrong as a "colored performer," not as simply a jazz musician, and what that says about the ongoing segregation in the music world of 1931, the warmth of his endorsement is evident. Then again, it is of a piece with his earlier fascination with Armstrong in the Chicago of 1922, when he went "slumming" after his Trianon Ballroom performances to hear Armstrong at Lincoln Gardens. We recall too how tight the subsequent Beiderbecke-Armstrong bond was and what it did to help bring the Armstrong and Whiteman domains closer together. Telling also is that in 1936, some five years after his showdown with Rockwell and company, Armstrong published his *Swing That Music*, which contains a touching inscription. It begins as follows: "To the memory of the original 'Dixieland Five,' to 'King' Oliver, to 'Bix' Beiderbecke and Eddie Lang, now gone, and those other pioneers of a century past." Two years later, in 1938, for Whiteman's Eighth (and last) Experiment in Modern Music, he shared the Carnegie Hall stage with Armstrong.

During these years of grueling schedules, crisscrossing the country and suffering the slights of racism and managerial abuse, Armstrong was able to work his unique mix of brashness and charm on his audience; and it subsequently extended to his public in England and on the Continent as well. A defining vehicle for him at the time was the number "I'll Be Glad When You're Dead, You Rascal You." He could humor King George V with the remark, "This one's for you, Rex," while also winning over the larger public wherever he went. Here was a piece charged for him with racial dynamite and one that could shatter virtually all norms for an African-American performer in a segregated society.

The tour which Armstrong and his band undertook during the second half of 1931, under the management of Johnny Collins, carried him in frenzied fashion from Illinois, Ohio, and Kentucky to Tennessee, Louisiana, and Texas. Included was a residency at New Orleans's Suburban Gardens, where, under Jim Crow, some ten thousand blacks were excluded. The venue had its own radio program which would broadcast only white bands. When it came time to introduce Armstrong, the announcer balked, protesting: "I can't announce that nigger." As was so often the case, Armstrong was seemingly unfazed. "I turned to the boys on the bandstand and said, 'Give me a chord.' I got an earsplitting chord and announced the show myself. It was the first time a Negro *spoke* on the radio down there."[33]

A subsequent incident aboard a Greyhound bus in Memphis, Tennessee, led to a confrontation with local police that culminated a few days later with an ironic turn of events which only someone like Armstrong could pull off. It all began with the police crowding around the bus "goggle-eyed, staring at the well-dressed coloured boys . . . and especially at the one coloured boy up front who was, God forbid, sitting there actually talking to a white woman cool as pie, just like he was human. They couldn't let that go down."[34] A police order was fast in coming. "All right you niggers, get out here. You're in Memphis now, and we need some cotton pickers too."[35] But after being hauled off to jail, where they were kept for a day or two, Armstrong and company were bailed out by the management of the local Palace Theater, where they were due to appear, with the proviso that they make a live radio broadcast on the morning following their gig at the theater. They were pleased to oblige.

But in his inimitable style, Armstrong leaned into the microphone and blithely announced: "Ladies and gentlemen, I'm now going to dedicate this song to the Memphis Police Force." They all then swung directly into "I'll Be Glad When You're Dead, You Rascal You." Even more bizarre was the reported reaction of the cops who had been milling around the premises, only to rush over after the broadcast with beaming faces, absolutely delighted. "You're the first band that ever dedicated a tune to the Memphis Police Force."[36]

One final "Rascal" riff: an eponymous 1932 Betty Boop animated cartoon created by Max Fleischer. In a stroke of cultural juxtaposition, before the actual animation begins, we see footage of Armstrong and his band playing "High Society Rag," followed by scenes of the travails of Betty Boop in the jungles of Africa and her subsequent rescue. She is borne on a litter by the dog Bimbo and the clown Koko, only to be captured by Africans. Eventually she is rescued by the trusty pair, who themselves have barely escaped with their lives from a boiling cauldron surrounded by Africans. Images of this big pot and drumming rhythms help foster the perception of Africa as a savage and primitive place—an important parallel to much of what was suggested earlier in Whiteman's *King of Jazz*. But in the Betty Boop cartoon there is an additional overlay of cultural and racial irony. We see Bimbo and Koko escaping a couple of Armstrong-voiced crocodiles and fleeing their pursuers onto a volcano, which erupts and miraculously carries away only the Africans.

Racism continued to bedevil Armstrong when he arrived in England in 1932 at the start of his first tour of Europe. Johnny Collins proved himself to be something of a troglodyte, bigot, and incompetent. The entourage had apparently come ashore without any permits. "Collins said he just talked them in." Just as serious, the group, surrounded by many pieces of luggage, had nowhere to stay. Thanks to the intervention of Dan Ingman of the *Melody Maker* magazine, accommodations were eventually found off the Strand, but it was no easy matter: "So there was work to be done; accommodations to be found in the early hours of the morning for five travelers, most of them flamboyantly dressed and some of them black. Ingman started telephoning the London hotels. He began with the most famous—Savoy, Dorchester, Mayfair, and so on—and, having no luck, worked his way through the second-rankers. Sometimes there was simply no room for five guests. When he found acceptance he thought it wise to mention that some of the party were blacks. At that, a total close-down."[37]

The relationship between Armstrong and Collins completely unraveled the following summer when the musician returned for a more extended stay in Great Britain and on the Continent. What transpired in the course of Armstrong's voyage to Europe in late July 1933 makes quite a story, as we learn from a rap session that took place some twenty years later, between Armstrong and the veteran producer George Avakian. More striking than Armstrong's use of profanity is his ability to contain his justifiable rage in the face of racist behavior:

> Called me a nigger in the middle of the ocean. When that motherfucker called me a nigger for no reason at all, he's my manager and he's never done it be-

fore. . . . Now, I could bash his fucking brains out. See what I mean. But, it's a different story. It's a white man. So I don't fuck with Johnny. . . . He swung at John Hammond. Missed—[Hammond] gave him a short, hard jab in his fucking chops. Zoom! And I'm standing right behind him, seeing he's falling. All I can do is just catch him with a finger. But I said: "I'll get this motherfucker myself." But, I still let him fall and bash his fucking brains out. Boom! Let him make an ass of himself. And he did. All I did was step aside. And then it was the same as though I had hit him with a fucking right myself.[38]

Dan Ingman tells of an incident one evening during this particular tour at a "Midland palais," just as Armstrong was poised to go out on stage. Once again, of all the principals involved, given his acute awareness of his place in the social hierarchy, he was the best behaved. And it came as no big surprise to those in the know when the *Melody Maker,* in its issue of August 19, 1933, headlined a story "Armstrong and His Manager to Part":

The band was ready—there had been no rehearsal—and he was about to perform. Then Collins suddenly said: "Where's the dough? If I don't get the dough, Louis don't play." The promoter had a huge crowd and there was no problem. He offered a cheque, but Collins was adamant—no cash, no Louis. It must have been humiliating for Louis, though he showed no sign of it. . . . He seemed utterly detached as this pasty-faced man with the cigar in his mouth demanded the money. . . . I estimate they had some two thousand people in there, and the promoter went to his box office and came back with several bags of half-crowns, of silver anyway, and put them down in front of Collins. "There's your money" he told Collins, and I remember thinking: he doesn't know how to count it.[39]

Speaking of hierarchy and money, it is revealing how Armstrong's earnings at about this time compared with those of Whiteman. *Variety,* reporting in late 1932, quoted weekly salaries paid dance orchestras. Whiteman's ensemble was at the top, receiving £1,700 (about $500), while Armstrong, ranking twelfth in a group of thirteen, earned only £500 ($150).[40] All of which helps pinpoint the two very different sets of priorities that defined much of their respective lives; and it was not simply a matter of race. For Armstrong his life was his horn and his music. Whiteman, by contrast, was primarily a businessman, an entrepreneur. We have seen that from his earliest years in New Orleans, working for the Karnofsky family or during his detention in the Colored Waif's Home, Armstrong's instrument was his talisman. Thanks to a loan from the Karnofskys on his salary, he was able to save fifty cents a week and eventually buy "the horn, all dirty. But it was soon pretty to me." One of his shining moments came when he was asked by Peter Davis in the reformatory to become leader of the band. "I jumped straight into the air." He goes on to talk about how he began to shine up the instrument—"the brass was dirty and green"—and how the kids around him gave him a big hand when they saw "the gleaming bright instrument instead of the old filthy green one." So strong was Armstrong's work ethic that in March 1971, during what was to be his last gig, at the Waldorf Astoria's Empire Room, he was not deterred by his suffering from congestive heart failure, shortness of breath, and the risk of dying onstage. His personal physician, Dr. Gary Zucker, who attended him in his hotel suite, has recalled feeling a chill go up and down his spine as Armstrong, assuming the position of holding the horn, looked up at the ceiling and confessed how his whole life and soul were committed to blowing the horn, and that it was impossible for him to let his public down.[41] What is more, Armstrong's passion for his instrument and his public was such that leading a band ranked rather low in his scheme of things: "I never cared to become a band leader; there was too much quarreling over petty money matters. I just wanted to blow my horn peacefully as I am doing now. I have always noticed that the band leader not only had to satisfy the crowd but that he also had to worry about the box office."[42]

Whiteman showed no such bonding with his violin or viola, as the instrument-smashing episode during his early teens in his mother's sewing room in Denver makes plain. Instead, he felt a sense of liberation when he discovered jazz along San Francisco's Barbary Coast and realized how much more economically rewarding it might be leading a dance band than sawing away at the back of a symphony orchestra's string section. In fact, his prowess as bandleader and entrepreneur was such that by the fall of 1921, flush with his successes at Atlantic City and the sales of his first Victor recordings, Whiteman formed the company Paul Whiteman, Inc., for the purpose of developing and supplying satellite dance bands performing under his banner at clubs, in cabarets, and even aboard luxury liners. By October 1922 he reportedly had some twenty orchestras working out of his office. But this was only the beginning: his satellite bands proliferated during the 1920s under such names as Barney Rapp and his Boardwalk Orchestra, the Carlton Terrace Orchestra, the New Ocean House Orchestra, Paul Whiteman's Collegians, or the Whiteman Saxophone Sextette. The extent of his empire was such that it took in cities ranging from Cleveland and Cincinnati to Swampscott, Massachusetts, not to mention ships bound for Havana or Kingston, Jamaica.[43] By 1939, however, the party was over and Whiteman was forced to report: "A few years ago I had fifty-eight Paul Whiteman bands scattered all over the country. . . . I thought I was getting rich. So what happened? At the end of the year when I checked up I found that although the bands had grossed a little better than five hundred thousand dollars, I had lost fifty thousand dollars on the deal. . . . So I had to . . . learn about overhead and gate receipts and gross and net returns."[44]

Whiteman's coronation as King of Jazz can be dated from August 13, 1923. It was then that he and his orchestra returned to New York as conquering heroes from their first tour of England, to be met dockside by representatives of the music industry and other dignitaries. The literal crowning event of the reception was orchestrated by the Buescher Band Instrument Company of Elkhart, Indiana, whose products Whiteman had recently started endorsing. The golden Buescher crown bore replicas of the company's instruments, including their popular saxophone, as well as the following inscription: "To Paul Whiteman in appreciation of his art and artistry and his aid to self-determination in the music of the nation."[45] Whiteman's regal title was something he came to protect rather jealously, at least into the early 1930s. In 1934, for example, the *New York Times* carried news of a judgment in Whiteman's favor against a bandleader in Albany, New York, who had used Whiteman's name and photographs in his own publicity. Whiteman was awarded $10,056 in damages, and the offending bandleader was enjoined against further use of the title King of Jazz.

Whiteman's 1923 coronation and the associated product endorsements have their counterpart in an Armstrong event occurring nine years later and separated by the expanse of the Atlantic Ocean. In 1932, on the occasion of his first tour of Great Britain, Armstrong offered some reflections on the significance of his voyage. His piece "Greetings to Britain!" is resonant with meaning, recalling for him a defining journey of ten years earlier. And in basic ways, the transatlantic voyages of Whiteman and Armstrong, respectively westbound and eastbound, serve as a variation on a theme introduced in a previous chapter. There each was seen making a move critical to his career, together defining trajectories within the United States, west to east and south to north. "When I boarded the steamer, I thought of another journey I made exactly ten years ago this month [August]. I was a young man, and I packed my precious cornet in New Orleans, along with my other belongings, which didn't make more than a trunkful. I was leaving the city in which I had spent my entire life and where I had all my friends. I was leaving the city for lands I did not know and for people who did not know me."[46]

There was considerable fanfare to celebrate Armstrong's arrival in En-

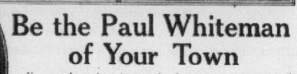

4.3 Buescher Band Instrument advertisement (1923) with Paul Whiteman endorsement. Joshua Berrett, personal collection.

gland. The firm of Henri Selmer advertised the appearance of its new Selmer Challenger Trumpet and the Louis Armstrong Special. Some of their copy reads as follows: "Louis 'Satchel-mouth' Armstrong is going strong with his new Selmer 'Challenger' Trumpet which he acquired on his arrival in London, and with which he was so delighted that he was constrained to pay it an entirely spontaneous tribute during his performances at the London Palladium. . . . [The] 'Louis Armstrong Special' is an entirely new model to the original 'Challenger,' and is supplied, if desired, with a replica of the mouthpiece used by Louis himself."[47]

Armstrong was clearly taken with Selmer's instruments and was featured repeatedly in the company's advertising. In fact, over the next thirty-odd years he owned at least eight of them, including one presented to him in 1934 by King George V. Dan Ingman, writing in the August 1932 issue of the *Melody Maker*, hailed Armstrong as "King of the Trumpet," and perhaps more important, he clarified something that to this day is misunderstood—the actual meaning of the moniker "Satchmo." Fulsome in his praise of Armstrong, Ingman wrote: "His technique, tone and mastery over his instrument (which he calls 'Satchmo,' a contraction, I am told, of 'Satchelmouth') is uncanny."[48] So rather than a nickname for Louis Armstrong himself, it was his way of addressing his trumpet, as one can hear in his banter in "You're Driving Me Crazy" of 1930, when he says "Watch it, Satchelmouth!" Along similar lines there are period cartoons in which Armstrong speaks to his trumpet—recalling what was said earlier about his trumpet as talisman—treating it as though it had a life of its own: "Speak to 'em, Satch'mouth." In addition, Selmer's advertising copy made the connection clear as it touted "Satch-mo as a Selmer Challenger Trumpet."

Amid the critical frenzy greeting him, the reception of Armstrong sometimes took on a blatantly racist tone. A week after his debut at the London Palladium on July 18, 1932, a columnist in the *Daily Herald* spewed these words of venom: "Armstrong is the ugliest man I have seen on the music-hall stage. He looks, and behaves, like an untrained gorilla. He might have come straight from some African jungle and then, after being taken to a slop tailor's for a ready-made dress-suit, been put straight on the stage and told to sing."[49] But for the most part Armstrong was welcomed with a mix of wonder and adulation, and with his unique stage persona and stylistic voice he became the quintessential embodiment of hot jazz. It was a development that took shape in the course of his more extended stay in England and on the Continent, from July 1933 through December of the following year. The writing of jazz history would never be the same.

No writers have better captured the role of Armstrong in the jazz milieu on the Continent in the early 1930s than Robert Goffin and Hugues Panassié. Goffin, a prominent Belgian criminal lawyer who was once dubbed "the world's most versatile jitterbug," wrote books on topics ranging from finance to spiders and rats to jazz history. One of his most representative pieces is his essay "Hot Jazz," which originally appeared in 1934 in a limited edition of a monumental compendium, Nancy Cunard's *Negro: An Anthology*, alongside pieces by Langston Hughes, W. E. B. Du Bois, Zora Neale Hurston, and many others. The headstrong Nancy Cunard's career paralleled in a number of ways that of John Hammond. She was born into the wealth of the ship-owning Cunard family but turned her back on their values, flirted with communism, and took the black lover Henry Crowder, whom she paraded in white society, among other transgressions against the code of her family's class.

Naïve and tendentious, and based on a limited number of musical examples, Goffin's essay is nevertheless a valuable period piece, immensely helpful in any effort to place Armstrong, "the supreme genius of jazz," in the context of hot jazz and how it was perceived at the time. According to Goffin, to appreciate what is "hot," the raison d'être of jazz, requires that we recognize what the slaves transported "from their scorching Africa": "that prodigious sense of rhythm which their traditional dances and their tom-toms beating in the equatorial night had made so ineradicably part of them. Instinctive and unhappy, highly endowed with the most complete, because the most simple, poetical faculties, they soon began to express their emotions in song." He does, however, deplore those with "the commercial instinct" who "transposed jazz airs in a way quite foreign to the Negro tradition." Included here are musicians like Paul Whiteman, "who industrialized jazz to such an extent that nothing remained but a weak dilution devoid of all real musical character."[50]

It was, however, Hugues Panassié, who, more than anyone else on the Continent at the time, championed the cause of Armstrong and hot jazz. One of the founders of the Hot Club of France in 1932, as well as Quintette du Hot Club de France two years later—an ensemble identified with Stephane Grappelli and Django Reinhardt—Panassié became a lifelong friend of Armstrong's, producing records and writing one of the first biographies and discographies of him. Armstrong himself was honorary president of the Hot Club from 1936 until his death. Panassié's essay "Louis Armstrong at the Salle Pleyel" superbly captures the excitement generated by his concerts at that venue in early November 1934, when Darius Milhaud, composer in 1923 of the celebrated jazz-inflected, Afrocentric ballet score *La Création du monde*, was among the notables on opening night. While Panassié was a literate musician—he had studied saxophone in his youth—he was, like Goffin, a product of a time when French passions for hot jazz had been aroused by Sidney Bechet and Josephine Baker in such musicals as *La Revue Nègre,* not to mention the concerts of Duke Ellington. This was a world in which conditions were markedly more hospitable for blacks than in the United States, shrouded as France was in a certain myth of primitive African innocence.

The memory of that Armstrong night stayed with Panassié for many years to come. "When I entered Salle Pleyel the evening of November 9 I had promised myself a wonderful evening. The entrance of Louis on stage was something unforgettable: as the first measures of his band resounded he made his appearance running like a brilliant meteor, flourishing his trumpet." Panassié adds some astute observations about Armstrong and the newly improved condenser microphone. Gary Giddins's vivid characterization of Bing Crosby's singing style—"He collaborated with the electric current as if he were romancing a woman"—can be applied in equal measure to Armstrong's rendition of such numbers as "I Can't Give You Anything But Love, Baby" or "Ain't Misbehavin'." Musing about Armstrong and the microphone at the concert itself, Panassié has this to say: "When Louis sang, he seemed to address himself to the microphone, to caress it or contrarily to attack it; his eyes gleaming, he gave himself up to series of mimicries that were stupefying in their mobility. Louis is not able to sing, in a large hall at least, without the help of a microphone because, contrary to what one would be led to believe from records, his voice is very feeble in spite of the beauty of its timbre." Perhaps most compelling of all is the larger context within which Panassié places his hero: "To understand a genius as exceptional as Louis Armstrong, one has to abandon all preconceived ideas, the prejudices learned in the course of a musical education that has its good aspects certainly, but which cannot be much help when it comes to judging musicians of another race whose art is developed on the fringes of such an education."[51]

Panassié's implication of a black African essence to Armstrong's music making finds a parallel in the continuing efforts of Whiteman, from 1929 to 1933, to cultivate a hotter African-American sound. His most valuable asset for all to see and hear during this period was his headline vocalist Mildred Bailey. Bailey is recognized as the first female singer to be featured with a jazz band and served as a vital link helping determine the direction of several interconnected careers. Arguably one of the first white vocalists to capture the nuances of hot jazz, Bailey found her role models in Ethel Waters, so pivotal in Fletcher Henderson's early career, and in the "Empress of the Blues" Bessie

Smith. Bailey's story, however, was not simply that of a white artist soaking up black influences but that of mentor, at times straddling the racial divide to shape the careers of nonwhites. Born in Tekoa, Washington, and part Coeur d'Alene Indian, she was the older sister of Al Rinker of Rhythm Boys fame (the surname of Bailey was retained from a brief early marriage). She guided the early careers of her brother and Bing Crosby, encouraging them to make the move from Spokane, Washington, to Los Angeles to try their luck in show business, where she was performing in vaudeville, on the radio, and as a song demonstrator. As Crosby often told interviewers later in life, "Mildred got us started." And it was she who insisted that he check out all available recordings of Louis Armstrong. The Rhythm Boys later returned the favor. Shortly after landing their contract with Paul Whiteman, they had Bailey throw a party for the orchestra. It was a ruse for an audition, with calls for her to "give us a song" when Paul Whiteman had knocked back some of her homemade beer.[52] Finally, Bailey led John Hammond to a nightclub to hear Billie Holiday, whom he then plucked out of obscurity. And it is no accident that in phrasing, vocal timbre, and repertoire, let alone many of the musicians with whom they worked, there is so much in common between Mildred Bailey and Billie Holiday.

Another Whiteman property of the day, crucial to his African-American agenda though conspicuous by his absence from the bandstand, was William Grant Still, widely recognized in the 1930s and 1940s as "the dean of Afro-American composers." But Still's role as arranger was in effect that of a compromise candidate, for Paul Whiteman initially had an altogether different strategy in mind. Seeking to add more spice to his sound, Whiteman was thinking of hiring Eubie Blake, Duke Ellington, or Fletcher Henderson, and some of their sidemen, only to have his managers and advisers balk at the idea; they were nervous about what a racially mixed ensemble could mean in terms of box office, let alone travel arrangements.

Still began working for Whiteman in February 1929, continuing under contract until the end of May of the following year. It was a period spent mainly in California while *King of Jazz* was being filmed, when Still's primary job was to provide arrangements for the weekly, one-hour Old Gold broadcasts. Still relished the experience because he could promptly hear the results of a broad range of his orchestral effects; better still, he was paid in timely fashion and well. The prolific Still provided fresh orchestrations of such standards as W. C. Handy's "St. Louis Blues," including a special part written for Bix Beiderbecke. While in California, Still completed some 118 of his 127 arrangements that have been preserved in the Paul Whiteman Collection.[53]

Then, about three years after expiration of Still's contract, Whiteman commissioned several additional pieces from him. One of them, "Land of Superstition," is actually a reorchestration of a movement from his suite *Africa,* with parts designated for such Whiteman reed players as Charles Strickfaden, Frankie Trumbauer, and Fud Livingston, who also earned his own stripes as a Whiteman arranger.[54]

In his somewhat murky commentary written for *Africa,* Still speaks of "an American Negro [who] has formed a concept of the land of his ancestors, based largely on its folklore, and influenced by his contact with American civilization." We are told that what happens in the third and final movement, "Land of Superstition," is that "contact with American civilization has not enabled him to completely overcome his inherent superstitious nature. It is *that heritage* of his forbears binding him irrevocably to the past, and making it possible for him to form the most accurate concept of Africa."[55]

Distilled here is one of the quintessential elements defining Still as the "dean of Afro-American composers," as a bridge across both a racial and cultural divide. More than that, he embodies the worlds of high and low, the sophistication of the cultivated composer and the earthier qualities of the jazzy and the popular. How many others, after all, had gone on the road with W. C. Handy, served as recording director of his Black Swan Phonograph Company, played in the orchestra during the opening run of Eubie Blake and Noble Sissle's *Shuffle Along,* attended Wilberforce University and Oberlin Conservatory, taken private lessons in composition with George Chadwick and Edgard Varèse, written copious arrangements for Whiteman's weekly radio broadcasts, composed original works commissioned by Whiteman for the concert hall, and worked with him at the Ziegfeld Follies? In fact, Still was among several celebrities adding his autograph to a gold oval on Whiteman's dressing room door at the Follies. Here was a consummate craftsman of immense versatility who once prompted Gunther Schuller to remark that Still was one of the three "greatest arrangers that ever worked in the field of popular music" and a creator of some of the most original sounds heard in that area. Artie Shaw, for whom Still wrote arrangements in the 1940s, was highly complimentary as well. "Bill had a rare thing: a sense of musicality or savvy. He invariably did the right thing musically."[56]

The relative frequency with which Whiteman programmed "Land of Superstition" and a number of other commissioned Still works during the 1930s is telling. The third movement from *Africa,* for example, was not only played by Whiteman at his Fifth Experiment in Modern Music in Carnegie Hall, January 25, 1933; it was also repeated at New York's Lewisohn Stadium that summer and featured two summers later as part of a blockbuster event in a Philadelphia amphitheater, reportedly before an audience of 9,100 who heard a Whiteman program of twenty-six selections plus an encore.[57] *A Deserted Plantation,* a richly reedy evocative work of the old South inspired by a Paul Laurence Dunbar poem—it includes five saxophone parts—was premiered at Whiteman's Sixth Experiment in Modern Music at New York's Metropolitan Opera House on December 15, 1933. Other Still works dating from this general period include *Ebon Chronicle, Down Yonder, Three Portraits,* and *Jungle Episode: The Origin of Jazz.* They include the characteristic twang of the banjo, that quintessential traditional African-American signifier among instruments, as well as parts specified for Whiteman players.

Whiteman was thus advancing his agenda for a broad-based symphonic jazz, one of mass appeal harking back to the defining work of his own early career and that of American music, Gershwin's *Rhapsody in Blue.* And with his consummate skill at evoking a sense of collective racial memory through orchestrations awash in blues, spirituals, syncopation, the timbres of saxophones, the percussion section, and the banjo, Still was immensely successful. He earned the admiration not only of Paul Whiteman or conductors like Leopold Stokowski and Howard Hanson but also of critical movers and shakers within the black community, like Alain Locke. As one of the most erudite and articulate voices of the Harlem Renaissance, Locke argued for a jazz style that would rid itself of "shoddy superficiality and . . . repetitive vulgar gymnastics," a music performed by academically trained musicians who preserve the African-American folk idiom.[58] For Locke, only William Grant Still and Duke Ellington were equal to the challenge of creating works worthy of the genre of symphonic jazz. At the same time, Whiteman himself was treated kindly in the black press, as when the *New York Amsterdam News* ran a piece on September 13, 1933, in anticipation of the orchestra's appearance at Harlem's Savoy Ballroom: "Whiteman long ago established an *entente cordiale* between himself and Negro orchestra leaders, when he unhesitatingly paid tribute to the Harlem boys."

While Paul Whiteman's movie *King of Jazz* offers a world in which "the repression of blackness leaves its mark all over the film," his programs on NBC radio's *Kraft Music Hall* present something quite different; that series was launched in late June 1933 with Al Jolson as cohost. Jolson appeared with Paul Whiteman and his Orchestra in a total of twenty-eight shows, from June 26, 1933, through August 16 of the following year; and there was no mistaking the presence of the star who was so identified with *The Jazz Singer* and his signature song "My Mammy":

Mammy, Mammy
My heart strings are tangled around Alabamy
I'se a-comin', sorry that I made you wait
I'se a-comin', hope and pray I'm not too late
Mammy, Mammy
I'd walk a million miles for one of your smiles
My Mammy

Captured here is the essence of Jolson's personality, an entertainer inspired by "the traditions of burnt cork . . . and the black mask." As Gary Giddins puts it: "He is never more electrifying or natural than when playing black."[59]

The Jolson-Whiteman programming choices made for these Kraft shows abundantly prove the point made by Giddins. While there are the mainstream pop standards like "California, Here I Come," "Blue Skies," "Always," and "Night and Day," most of the musical fare vividly dramatizes the conviction of a performer "genuinely inspired by the black mask." Examples include "Call of the South," "Sonny Boy," "My Old Kentucky Home," "Ol' Man River," and one of the signature pieces of Paul Robeson, "Water Boy," a number closely based on a Southern chain gang work song. Jolson would also play the role of Uncle Zeke in a sketch entitled "Goin' to Heaven on a Mule," where, with the backing of Whiteman's music, he would utter such lines as: "Look . . . who dat feller in de purple night shirt and de long white whiskers? . . . Why it's ole St. Peter hisself." And one could add to the list such numbers as "Run Little Chillun'," which Jolson performed with the Hall Johnson Choir.[60]

As for Armstrong, it was unheard of in the world of the 1930s for someone of his race to host a radio show. But in 1937, in the course of his second year as Armstrong's manager, Joe Glaser changed all of that. Starting on Friday, April 9, and continuing into early June of that year, Armstrong substituted for Rudy Vallee on the weekly Fleischmann's Yeast Program on WJZ, the key station of NBC's Blue Network and a precursor of ABC. Listeners were brought "another half-hour of high-stepping hilarity and harmony": a variety show with Armstrong appearing in the triple capacity of emcee, vocalist, and trumpet player fronting a big band of some sixteen pieces. Musical selections by Armstrong himself could include "Rockin' Chair," "I'll Be Glad When You're Dead, You Rascal You," "On the Sunny Side of the Street," "Memories of You," "Washington and Lee Swing," "Chinatown, My Chinatown," or "Tiger Rag," while others could be heard doing a stride piano number in the style of Fats Waller or singing a song like "I'm Going to Get Even With You." Further variety could be provided by special appearances of vocal groups like the Four Vagabonds or the more famous African-American foursome of the day, the Mills Brothers. A staple of the show was the comedy duo of vaude-villian Eddie Green—he was a veteran of such major 1920s shows as *Shuffle Along* and *Hot Chocolates*—and his sidekick, Gigi James. In a throwback to minstrel show routines, they would regale their audience with such repartee as the following, and with the appropriate infusion of plantation dialect and malapropisms:

GREEN: No wonder you're so full of avoirdupois.

JAMES: Is you incinerating that I'se plump.

GREEN: Honey, if you had one more curve, you could pass for the Lincoln High-way.

Juxtaposed with all of this black-tinged fare was the refrain of commercials aimed at the white middle class for Fleischmann's Yeast, guaranteed to "clear away skin eruptions . . . and make skin smooth and clear." This would come with an invitation to send in eighty-one labels from Fleischmann's Yeast cakes, which would earn the faithful a "free" copy of Arthur Murray's ballroom dancing book, replete with diagrams on how to dance the tango, rumba, shag, waltz, fox-trot, and more.

The following year, 1938, marked both a twilight for Paul Whiteman and the dawning of a new era for Armstrong. The shift was defined by two contrasting events, both taking place in Carnegie Hall in December, within two days of each other. In fact, jazz history had already been made in that legendary hall on January 16 of that year, when Benny Goodman introduced jazz to what was, and still is, generally perceived as the shrine of classical music. Jazz, it would seem, was now being raised to the same social status. But the juxtaposition of John Hammond's "From Spirituals to Swing" concert of December 23 with Whiteman's Eighth Experiment in Modern Music on Christmas night—it was to be his last in the series—foretold even more important things to come.

Hammond's intentions in presenting his concert were crystal clear. "For several years I had wanted to present a concert which would bring together for the first time, before a musically sophisticated audience, Negro music from its raw beginnings to the latest jazz. The concert should include, I thought, both primitive and sophisticated performers, as well as the music of the blacks in which jazz is rooted."[61] In the process, what he accomplished was to lay out an agenda not only for his concert but also for the course of jazz historiography for many years to come. Two crucial points were made: (1) the positing of a linear evolution of the music from "its raw beginnings to the latest jazz" and (2) the music as essentially "Negro music" and one rooted in the black experience. As the program notes asserted: "Most of the people you will hear are absurdly poor." In addition, not only did radio stations barring Negro performers come under attack, but so did "Jim Crow unions and unscrupulous nightclub operators."[62]

Superficially, the first item on the program was not all that different from the avowed purpose of Paul Whiteman at the First Experiment in Modern Music of 1924. But the political climate had undergone radical change since then and was due for further shocks as World War II approached; besides, Whiteman's ideas of symphonic jazz were not exactly au courant at this juncture. Fervently pursuing his goals, Hammond traveled far and wide seeking out singers of gospel music—notably Sister Rosetta Tharpe, a precursor of Mahalia Jackson—blues singers and shouters, singing laborers from the backwoods, blind harmonica players, boogie-woogie pianists. The resulting program presented an Afrocentric, more or less chronological evolution, from the introductory "scientific recordings" of West African tribal music through a series of seven sets as follows:

1. Spirituals and Holy Roller Hymns
2. Soft Swing
3. Harmonica Playing
4. Blues
5. Boogie-Woogie Piano Playing
6. Early New Orleans Jazz (Sidney Bechet and his New Orleans Feet Warmers)
7. Swing (Count Basie and his Orchestra, Basie's Blue Five, the Kansas City Six)

All of this came with a price tag, and the story of how the concert came to be funded in the first place harks back to an issue discussed early in this chapter: the role of labor and what historian Michael Denning has referred to as the "laboring of American culture." Hammond was repeatedly frustrated in his efforts to find a sponsor to underwrite the costs of his production. He was rebuffed by the NAACP because "jazz and, particularly primitive black music were too unfamiliar to the middle-class leaders . . . to be anything they could take pride in."[63] The International Ladies Garment Workers Union gave him much the same treatment. He finally found the support he needed, for both the initial talent search and the subsequent Carnegie Hall performance, from the leading leftist monthly magazine of the day, *New Masses*. Somewhat skittish about the source of his dollars, Hammond insisted that there be no obvious involvement on the part of *New Masses* and its communist activists, and that this concert, with its integrated audience, be treated simply as a musical event. For perhaps similar reasons, one can parenthetically speculate that Joe Glaser was against having his most valuable property, Louis Armstrong, participate in this event, even though Hammond credits Glaser with making possible the reunion of trumpeter and singer Hot Lips Page with the Basie orchestra. Then again, there was no mistaking in the printed program either who the sponsor was or what the racial focus of the event was to be. Three telling lines appear at the top:

NEW MASSES presents

FROM SPIRITUALS

TO SWING AN EVENING OF AMERICAN NEGRO MUSIC

By contrast, Whiteman's Christmas night concert two days later, though uneven in quality, offered a racially inclusive program. Included among the guest artists, and appearing all too briefly with Paul Whiteman in public on the same stage, was Louis Armstrong, who was heard singing two numbers with the backing of the Lyn Murray Singers: the traditional "Going to Shout All Over God's Heaven" and Robert MacGimsey's "Shadrack." His modest contribution seemed like little more than a prelude to the signature final offering of Whiteman, Gershwin's *Rhapsody in Blue*. But earlier in the evening the cause of interracial jazz was better served with a six-movement suite of short pieces ostensibly inspired by bells, with each movement assigned by Whiteman to a different composer. Duke Ellington's particular contribution, "The Belles of Harlem," stood out from lesser efforts by Morton Gould, Roy Bargy, Fred Van Epps, and others. It also came with a wry comment in the program booklet: "Judging from the general tenor of this work by one of our most popular composers and band-leaders, he obviously thought the spelling was 'belles.' They are undeniably blue, but not too much so." Separate solo turns by Artie Shaw and Jack Teagarden elsewhere on the program helped relieve the tedium of what critics otherwise found to be a rather humdrum affair. The composer and critic Deems Taylor—he had been in Whiteman's corner from the time of the historic First Experiment in 1924—was guarded in his program notes to the Eighth Experiment. "Their sponsor's purpose in presenting them . . . is trying to offer a medium of expression . . . a market for composers who are writing in what we know, loosely, as the 'jazz' idiom: something that will give them their say in rather more ambitious terms than those of a song-hit or dance number. . . . As to their permanent value in the literature of music—that is up to you and that vague audience known somewhat apprehensively as posterity."[64]

The Carnegie Hall concerts of John Hammond and Paul Whiteman that

Christmas weekend both had their statements to make, their marks to leave. But they could not quite match in historic impact and symbolism what was to happen on Easter Sunday morning, April 9, 1939. Although this was clearly not a jazz event, it nevertheless represented a major breach in the wall of racial segregation, giving dramatic visibility to African-Americans and their claims for equal rights. It was on that day that the contralto Marian Anderson sang at the Lincoln Memorial, drawing an audience of some seventy-five thousand people. After the Daughters of the American Revolution had denied her permission to use Constitution Hall in Washington, D.C., prominent Americans, among them first lady Eleanor Roosevelt, had rallied to her cause.

The same year saw the publication of a landmark book in jazz historiography: *Jazzmen,* an anthology edited by Frederic Ramsey, Jr., and Charles Edward Smith. The choice of title was inspired by a free verse poem by Carl Sandburg, "Jazz Fantasia," part of a 1920 collection entitled *Smoke and Steel.* Sandburg's poem contains the first known use of the word *jazzmen;* the energy of Dixieland jazz is palpable in the following characteristic lines:

Drum on your drums, batter on your banjoes,
sob on the long cool winding saxophones.
Go to it, O jazzmen.[65]

What Ramsey, Smith, and company present is essentially a heroic jazz epic centering on "the relatively small company that made hot spots hotter in New Orleans of the late nineteenth century." The story is then carried forward to include a second group "who have carried on the traditions of the pioneers and continued to play jazz at its best" in Chicago and New York.[66] Lineage is key and is embodied in the montage on the book's cover showing a trinity of cornet- or trumpet-toting musicians, as we see a youthful Armstrong clutching photographs of the New Orleans pioneer Bunk Johnson and Bix Beiderbecke. The book is racially inclusive—there are warm appreciations of Beiderbecke and Jack Teagarden, for example, not to mention perceptive observations about earlier 1920s jazz commentary by, among others, Paul Whiteman, Henry Osgood, and Gilbert Seldes. Yet one cannot overlook the condescending sneer in the remarks made about Whiteman from the perspective of the late 1930s. He is condemned as a self-serving showman, selling cheap imitations of the genuine article while he rode on the crest of a commercial recording wave.

Whiteman took his new way of doing old things into a hotel job at Atlantic City that began pulling crowds. . . . The phonograph companies . . . that were destined to stay right on the ground floor, heard about this fat man . . . and fell over each other signing him up. . . . Now what happens in an Atlantic City hotel is nothing I as an average citizen want any part of. . . . But . . . something on a new phonograph record is a different thing. It's national, it's everywhere, it's the kind of fame you can ride on. . . . Even Joe Dope and Suzie Cutie in their thousands of home towns all over the country might have found this music strictly pseudo alongside what was going on at the Friar's Inn, the Sunset Café, the Lincoln Gardens. . . .

He was a showman twenty-four hours a day and forty-eight on Sundays . . . but the opening wedge and the hammer behind it was the really "new" thing: the publicity and multiple coverage of modern reproduction. And that, boys and girls, is the whole campus of the New York school of jazz.[67]

The bombing of Pearl Harbor and the entry of the United States into World War II in 1941 brought a whole raft of changes for African-Americans. President Roosevelt banned racial discrimination in defense industries in 1941 and issued Executive Order 8802 in 1942, which created the Fair Employment Practices Committee for war industries. The Congress of Racial Equality (CORE) was founded in 1942 and soon began to conduct sit-ins to protest discrimination in restaurants; much of CORE's activism took place within the context of pervasive rioting in 1943. But this was also a time when Paul Robeson reached Broadway in the role of Othello and Adam Clayton Powell became the first black congressman from an eastern state. In 1945 *Ebony* magazine began publication, while in 1947, as every baseball fan knows, Jackie Robinson joined the Brooklyn Dodgers as the first black on a modern major-league team; and it was also the year when John Hope Franklin published the first edition of his major study *From Slavery to Freedom: A History of Negro Americans.*

While much of the war effort in the 1940s focused on the Pacific theater, so too did decisive events in the careers of both Paul Whiteman and Louis Armstrong play out in the recording and movie studios in the Los Angeles area; and what was happening in that area in terms of war mobilization had enormous implications for the production and marketing of recordings and movies. In 1941 President Roosevelt had urged conversion of the United States into "an arsenal of democracy," and under the Lend-Lease Act of the same year had authorized the "manufacture in arsenals, factories, and shipyards . . . [of] any defense article for the government of any country whose defense the President deems vital to the defense of the United States."[68] The manufacture of warplanes became a major industry in southern California, with companies like Northrop, Lockheed, and Douglas dominating the scene. By the time of Pearl Harbor the industry was employing more than 34 percent of factory workers in the Los Angeles area, and soon after it was producing more than a third of the nation's aircraft for the war effort.[69] During the 1940s national defense appropriations came to be institutionalized, as tax resources were shifted from elsewhere in the country "to irrigate the Los Angeles area's aircraft plants and military bases."[70]

With defense industry plants operating around the clock there was an influx of thousands of black migrant workers from the Southwest. Among them were a number of blues musicians from Texas, Oklahoma, Kansas, and Louisiana. It was from them that the leading exponents of the rhythm and blues sound in the city later in the decade were to emerge and help spawn the growth of new and independent studios. Along sections of Los Angeles like Central Avenue one could find "an elongated Harlem set down by the Pacific."[71] Nightspots like Club Alabam or the Downbeat were really jumping, and it was at venues such as these that "swing shift" dances were set up for late-night workers, with bands playing until dawn.

It is within this context that one can properly appreciate the founding in Los Angeles in 1942 of Capitol Records by two old colleagues of Paul Whiteman, Johnny Mercer and Buddy de Sylva. Jazz represented the core of the label's catalogue from the very beginning, with notable recordings by Nat "King" Cole, Stan Kenton, and Benny Goodman produced in the early years. As for Paul Whiteman, we find him in the studios of Capitol in June 1942, performing on the company's first releases—it was barely two months old at the time. In many ways this was Whiteman's twilight, with his lineup on that occasion consisting of the last of his own bands. At the same time, it was an event bringing him back full circle to a place where he had seen some of his first successes before heading east to greater triumphs in Atlantic City and New York.

Actually none of Whiteman's Capitol recordings sold well, except for the exquisitely crafted ballad "Trav'lin' Light," which dates from the session of June 12 and features Billie Holiday doing the vocal. It was originally an instrumental piece, a joint effort of the trombonist Trummy Young—for many years a staple in Louis Armstrong's All Stars—and the saxophonist-arranger Jimmy Mundy. Johnny Mercer later added lyrics, and "when he had studied the song, Pops asked that Billie record the tune."[72] And what this meant for Whiteman was his first interracial studio date. The languorous legato sound of muted trombone—it evokes some of the spirit of Tommy Dorsey—frames Billie's solo thirty-two-bar chorus, which itself is embedded in a richly scored mainstream swing arrangement replete with strings, low reeds, muted brass, and a vibrant rhythmic underpinning. Adding to the overall effect is the fact that the piece seamlessly juxtaposes three progressively higher keys, for the opening trombone solo, Holiday's chorus, and the out chorus, respectively—a touching metaphor for the title of a song whose lyrics express the changed fortunes of a woman now that her lover has left her.

In early September 1942 Armstrong too came to Los Angeles, to record his portion of the soundtrack to the MGM movie *Cabin in the Sky.* The movie, with its all-black cast, including Ethel Waters and Lena Horne as the female leads, represented a breakthrough for a major studio; it also marked the directorial debut of Vincente Minnelli. Playing the role of Georgia Brown, Horne is a symbol of black sexuality, the young temptress luring Little Joe (Eddie "Rochester" Anderson) in an allegory about the forces of good and evil. Much of the action unfolds during a dream sequence while Little Joe is recovering from a wound received in a knife fight. He struggles to break his gambling habit and remain faithful to his God-fearing wife, Petunia (Waters), who does "some powerful praying." He is given six months "to whitewash his soul"; otherwise, Lucifer "gets permanent control." Armstrong himself makes only a cameo appearance as The Trumpeter, one of the key members of the Idea Department in Hotel Hades. Yet his role serves as a dramatic fulcrum in that he persuades Lucius/Lucifer, Jr., that they should fix the Irish sweepstakes so that Little Joe wins. And in the climactic scene at Jim Henry's Paradise—Duke Ellington and his Orchestra provide the musical focus—there are at least three thought-provoking allusions to earlier movies, two of them crossing racial boundaries. When John "Bubbles" Sublett as Domino Johnson does his song-and-dance version of "Shine," he represents the city dandy, the urban counterpart to Armstrong's earlier image in the 1932 *Rhapsody in Black and Blue;* in that film Armstrong had appeared in leopard skin at the court of the "King of Jazzmania" performing "Shine" on a set awash in soap bubbles. At the same time, the cross-racial influence of Fred Astaire on Sublett's dance routine is unmistakable. Finally, as Jim Henry's Paradise is destroyed, the tornado shown is footage left over from the twister scene in *The Wizard of Oz* (1939).[73]

These activities of Whiteman and Armstrong in the Los Angeles of the early 1940s represent, of course, only part of the picture of what they stood for on the international scene of the day; and knowing something of how both served as sources of inspiration in Europe and the USSR during the war years adds immeasurably to our appreciation of their rich legacy. Louis Bannet—sometimes called "the Dutch Louis Armstrong"—is a case in point. Bannet was a gifted Jewish trumpeter from Amsterdam whom Armstrong met in 1934. One of the tragic ironies of his life is that in 1942 he found himself in the concentration camp at Auschwitz after being betrayed by a fan who happened to be a Gestapo agent. But fate intervened to save his life. Bannet learned that the camp was auditioning a handful of prisoners for the camp orchestra. Taken to a room where instruments were lying around, he met two other prisoners who, like him, were blue from frostbite. The leader of the music detail then gave the signal for the proceedings to begin. The first two musicians struggled to make a sound on trombone and saxophone, only to be led away. Then it was Bannet's turn. "I was standing toward the back of the room and noticed a small stove in a corner. . . . I inched toward the stove and placed my hands on top. My lips were frozen, so I started rubbing to warm them. As my friend placed a trumpet in my hand . . . and I'll never forget this . . . he said: 'Louis, you must play for your life.'"[74] At first there was only a faint sound; then after trying again he was able to manage a few sputtering notes. Finally, with the guards walking toward him, he was able to burst out with the strains of W. C. Handy's "St. Louis Blues." Bannet had saved himself from certain death, and he continued to play in the camp orchestra until his liberation.

Meanwhile, on the eastern front there was the "white Louis Armstrong," Eddie Rosner, the foremost jazzman in the Soviet Union from 1939 until 1946, when he was arrested by Stalin's henchmen. Audiences thrilled to the sound of full-blooded brass and saxophone sections of his band, and to the power of his own horn. Born in Berlin, the son of a Polish-Jewish shoemaker, Rosner was a musical prodigy who was bitten by the jazz bug while in his late teens at the Berlin Conservatory. By the time Hitler came to power in 1933, he was touring with various bands, making appearances in other countries. In Italy in 1934 he met Louis Armstrong, with whom he engaged in a "cutting contest"—the jazzman's competitive showdown. Armstrong won the event but was sufficiently impressed by Rosner's abilities to give him a photograph of himself, signed and dedicated "to the white Louis Armstrong." In a reciprocal gesture, Rosner reportedly gave Armstrong a photograph inscribed to "the black Eddie Rosner." Rosner hewed closely to the standard international repertoire of the time, including a number of Armstrong staples such as "All of Me," "On the Sunny Side of the Street," and "I Can't Give You Anything But Love."[75]

Whiteman apparently had his wartime Soviet admirers as well. One of Stalin's aides, first secretary of the Moscow Party Committee and "purger of the Soviet railways," one Lazar Kaganovich, considered jazz to be a highly effective "musical organizer of our high-spirited youth." Taking Paul Whiteman as his ideal, Kaganovich in 1939 published a widely distributed brochure entitled *How to Organize Railway Ensembles of Song and Dance and Jazz Orchestras.* His grand ambition was to establish ensembles at every railroad station in the USSR to ensure that the local citizenry was entertained and general enthusiasm kept high; and he had his functionaries in many areas of the Soviet Union, all of them exerting their regional powers to promote jazz at every opportunity.[76] But how successful or long-lasting such ventures were is a matter of conjecture, especially given the nature of Soviet propaganda and the murky secrecy of Stalin's regime.

Back in New York, 1942 was a banner year for adult education; a course of lectures on jazz open to the general public was initiated at New York's New School for Social Research.[77] Created in 1918 in an effort to develop an American equivalent of the London School of Economics, the New School from its inception placed top priority on its programs in economics, philosophy, and the social sciences. Some of its characteristic institutional thinking was shaped early on by such founding members as the social critic and economist Thorstein Veblen, best known for his book *The Theory of the Leisure Class,* in which he coined the phrase "conspicuous consumption." And as the dark clouds of imminent war gathered over Europe, many of the Continent's intellectual elite came to the United States to join the New School faculty, constituting a university in exile at a preponderantly leftist institution. The Dramatic Workshop was established in the 1940s by Erwin Piscator, a disciple of Bertolt Brecht's theater in Berlin and mentor to such students as Marlon Brando, Shelley Winters, Harry Belafonte, and Elaine Stritch. Among the other luminaries was Claude Lévi-Strauss from France, the father of structural anthropology and author of such works as *The Raw and the Cooked* and *The Savage Mind,* in which he argued for the equality of the savage and the civilized minds.

Also working in this heady atmosphere was the Belgian Robert Goffin, who with Hugues Panassié in the early 1930s had been among the first to champion hot jazz, Afrocentrism, and the music of Louis Armstrong on the Continent. During the period of 1941 to 1945, when Goffin was in New York, much of his energy was devoted to organizing "a full, officially sponsored course on the history of jazz at the New School for Social Research." He was joined in this effort by Leonard Feather, himself a fairly recent émigré from England, who was exerting his growing influence as arranger, writer, and producer on the American scene. Feather charmingly put their collaboration this way: "Because he still spoke a somewhat hilarious fractured English (friends imitated his standard greeting, 'Ow you feel?'), and because of my fluency in French, he suggested that I collaborate with him, translating his scripts and giving separate lectures."[78]

The fifteen-lecture series itself—set to begin in early February 1942—was defined by a very clear point of view. An undeniable Afrocentric slant was coupled with a sense of lineage. Feather tells us that the "African Student Group from Columbia University arranged to send Liberian musicians to demonstrate the origins of rhythmic concepts that were said to have laid the foundations for jazz."[79] Some of the lecture topics included:

Before jazz in New Orleans;
First period of Negro jazz;
From New Orleans to Chicago—King Oliver;
Louis Armstrong;
From Fletcher Henderson to Duke Ellington;
Outdated and small Negro bands;
Big Negro bands.

Interspersed were such "guest speaker-performers" as Louis Armstrong, Sidney Bechet, and Benny Carter. Feather writes also about the relative paucity of jazz surveys, mentioning books by Goffin and Panassié ("already somewhat outdated"), Armstrong's largely ghosted *Swing That Music,* and what was then the very new Ramsey-Smith *Jazzmen.* Conspicuous by their absence from his short list are the books on jazz from the 1920s written by Paul Whiteman, Henry Osgood, and Gilbert Seldes. In all fairness, there were lectures covering such topics as "white pioneers" and "big white bands," but the centrality enjoyed by Whiteman earlier was now clearly a thing of the past.

There was one other aspect to the endeavors of Goffin and Feather, and it meant something unprecedented—giving jazz "continuous, serious exposure" in a national magazine. This would be achieved by having a jazz poll, printing the results in the magazine, and running a series of related articles. Their guardian angel proved to be Arnold Gingrich, editor of *Esquire,* whose great enthusiasm for jazz was matched by his passion for such modern writers as Ernest Hemingway, John Dos Passos, and Ring Lardner. The publisher of the magazine, David Smart, not only gave the enterprise his strong support but took matters a step further by suggesting that they not simply announce poll winners but present them in concert. And so it was that Esquire All Stars was born, the name given to recording and concert groups drawn from winners of the magazine's annual critics' poll. On January 18, 1944, history was made when the First Esquire All American Jazz Concert was presented at

THE NEW SCHOOL
FOR SOCIAL RESEARCH
66 W TWELFTH ST   NEW YORK

SWING MUSIC

15 weeks. Tuesdays, 8:20-10 P.M. $12.50.   **Robert Goffin** and **Leonard Feather**

Beginning September 29. The course deals with the background and development of jazz, musically and historically. The lectures are illustrated by recordings and by musical demonstrations in the form of weekly "jam sessions," featuring outstanding white and Negro musicians from the leading swing bands.

Sept. 29   Before jazz in New Orleans
Oct. 6   Ragtime and the pioneers
Oct. 13   First period of Negro jazz
Oct. 20   From New Orleans to Chicago—King Oliver
Oct. 27   Jazz from America to Europe
Nov. 3   Original Dixieland
Nov. 10   White pioneers
Nov. 17   Louis Armstrong
Nov. 24   From Fletcher Henderson to Duke Ellington
Dec. 1   Chicago style
Dec. 8   Big white bands
Dec. 15   Benny Goodman
Dec. 22   Outdated and small Negro bands
Jan. 5   Big Negro bands
Jan. 12   From spiritual to boogie-woogie

The series: $12.50

Each lecture: $1.10

ROBERT GOFFIN. Docteur en Droit, Brussels. Editor, La Voix de France; formerly editor, Alerte, anti-Nazi weekly, Brussels; Music, first jazz magazine. Secretary, P.E.N. Club; former president, association for jazz studies in Europe. Author, Jazz Band; Aux Frontières du jazz; Empress Carlotta; Rimbaud vivant; other books.

LEONARD FEATHER. Conductor of WMCA jazz quizz program, Platterbrains; writer of lyrics, music and arrangements for Count Basie, Duke Ellington and other band leaders. Formerly director, Rhythm Club, London; BBC jazz programs; special recording bands for Decca, Columbia and Victor recording companies in London and New York. Public relations counsel for Louis Armstrong, Lionel Hampton, et al. Contributor to New York Times, Down Beat, Music and Rhythm, and leading music publications; to Melody Maker, and Radio Times, official BBC journal, London.

4.4   Poster announcing Goffin-Feather 1942 jazz lecture series at the New School for Social Research. Joshua Berrett, personal collection.

New York's Metropolitan Opera House—the first such event ever to take place in that venerable arena—with Louis Armstrong and Jack Teagarden among the headliners.[80]

As for Whiteman, he was based in New York from 1943 through the end of the decade, focusing on his work as musical director for the Blue Network—precursor of the American Broadcasting Company. One of his great hopes was to strike gold with another *Rhapsody in Blue;* to that end he commissioned works from a broad range of composers, among them Aaron Copland, Igor Stravinsky, Duke Ellington, Roy Harris, Victor Young, and Leroy Anderson. What Whiteman had in mind was "a dozen or so short pieces, five or six minutes long, each miniature Rhapsodies . . . something between a song and a symphony."[81] And thanks to a Creative Music Fund established at the network, composers received an advance with the proviso that the network retained rights to the first broadcast as well as to performance rights for a period of a year. Only a small number of these commissions have survived in the repertoire, among them Stravinsky's *Scherzo à la Russe,* Leroy Anderson's *Jazz Pizzicato,* and Victor Young's *Stella by Starlight.* The Stravinsky piece, which premiered on a Blue Network broadcast of September 5, 1944, was begun in 1943 as a score for the film *North Star.* At the same time, the commission attests to Whiteman's long-standing admiration for Stravinsky, to whom he had made a similar offer almost twenty years earlier, in 1925, as part of his effort to develop a symphonic jazz repertoire. Perhaps a month before the Blue Network debut, Nadia Boulanger, the renowned teacher of composers from Aaron Copland to Philip Glass, had reportedly conducted a reading of the score with an ensemble in Montreal.[82] Such are the wondrous ways in which media and musical category came to overlap.

Frustrated though he was in his efforts to find his latter-day *Rhapsody,* Whiteman did enjoy some opportunities to bask in the glow of past Gershwin glory. He conducted all-Gershwin concerts, one with the Los Angeles Philharmonic in 1943 and another with his own orchestra at Chicago's Opera House in 1947. But more far-reaching in its impact was the 1945 release by Warner Brothers of the Gershwin "biopic" *Rhapsody in Blue,* with Robert Alda as George Gershwin and Paul Whiteman as himself. Even though the movie offers an easily digested confection of clichés, all but purging the story of African-American influence, the role of Paul Whiteman is well captured in his cameo appearance. Early scenes involving Whiteman span the period from the George White Scandals of 1922, when he and his show band made their debut at New York's Globe Theater and Whiteman first met Gershwin, through the premiere performance of *Rhapsody in Blue* in Aeolian Hall, but suggest absolutely nothing of the nature of Whiteman's Experiment at this historic concert of 1924. Whiteman briefly reappears at the end, helping frame the movie; he directs another performance of *Rhapsody,* cut for dramatic effect but now taking place at New York's Lewisohn Stadium before a vast audience on the occasion of the first anniversary of Gershwin's death. It is a re-creation of the actual event of July 11, 1938, when Whiteman conducted members of the New York Philharmonic before an estimated crowd of nineteen thousand.[83]

While the Gershwin movie represented an important trip down memory lane for Whiteman and his public, it was released at a point when he was living in semiretirement, spending a good part of his time on his estate, Walking Horse Farm, near Rosemont, New Jersey. He was relishing the country life, indulging such passions as Tennessee walking horses, antique firearms, and classic road-racing cars. But he continued to maintain a presence as director of music for the American Broadcasting Company and serve as president of the Paul Whiteman Record Club, which claimed a listening audience of ten million people. He had also helped organize a Paul Whiteman Club for teenagers in Lambertville, near his farm, a model for a wider effort to set up weekly dance parties as a weapon against juvenile delinquency. Then in 1948, with the appearance of his book *Records for the Millions,* Whiteman offered his public a popular history of recording laced with fond reminiscences of his earlier days in the studio and how he had encouraged and supported a wide range of performers and composers. And the discographies he included attest to his broad, inclusive approach. There is a generous sprinkling of suggested recordings of the staples of symphonic, operatic, and chamber music and other repertoires. More important, jazz as a category is subsumed under "Basic Pops for Your Record Library" or "Popular Recordings by Artists." The listing of Bing Crosby recordings is especially comprehensive, but due attention is also given to Louis Armstrong, Nat Cole, Mildred Bailey, Duke Ellington, Benny Goodman, Ella Fitzgerald, and many others. Finally, by 1961 Whiteman had moved to a new home in New Hope, Pennsylvania, where he was to live until his death in 1967.

If 1945 was a banner year for Whiteman with the appearance of the film *Rhapsody in Blue,* 1947 held comparable, if not far greater, significance for Armstrong. The year marked a critical transition in his career, under the influence of a number of forces: the general collapse of the big bands around 1945, a growing attention to bebop, a fascination with singers on the order of Billie Holiday and Ella Fitzgerald, and—most decisive for Armstrong—the New Orleans revival. In truth, the revival had been ongoing since at least

1937, when a documentary had commemorated the twentieth anniversary of the first recordings of the Original Dixieland Jazz Band. Involved in this development around the same time had been the introduction of Dixieland units by such big band leaders as Tommy Dorsey and Bob Crosby, whether in their ballroom, theater, or hotel presentations. One could add the launching of the Commodore record label in 1938 by Milt Gabler of Commodore Music Shop fame, the RCA recordings sessions supervised by Hugues Panassié, the "Spirituals to Swing" concert of John Hammond, and the publication of Smith and Ramsey's *Jazzmen,* which, among other influences, gave a new lease on life to the pioneer jazzman William "Bunk" Johnson.[84] So in many respects Armstrong was riding the crest of an historic wave, a countervailing force to the bebop movement.

Most revealing is what happened within the roughly five-month stretch, from late February to early August 1947. A February date organized by Leonard Feather brought Armstrong onstage at Carnegie Hall, performing Janus-like before a packed house in a dual capacity: in the first half of the concert he was accompanied by the sextet of the clarinetist Edmond Hall, an aggregation anticipating Armstrong's All Stars in most essential details; Armstrong then closed the evening by fronting his own big band. Reviews were generally favorable and prompted other promoters to make arrangements for another concert, this one in New York's Town Hall on May 17. On this occasion, however, only seven musicians, including Armstrong, participated. Among them was the trombonist Jack Teagarden, with whom Armstrong premiered a fascinating number fusing their two names, "Jack Armstrong Blues," a piece clearly affected by the emerging bebop style, with a harmonic and rhythmic language pushing the envelope. Yet almost simultaneously, what epitomized the popular nostalgic surge for Dixieland was the highly publicized release by United Artists on June 9 of the movie *New Orleans,* featuring Louis Armstrong and Billie Holiday, among others.

The story of the making of *New Orleans* is a cautionary tale, testimony to how a director of bold imagination and high principle can be undermined by the studio system. Originally Orson Welles was to direct a film on the story of jazz to be called *It's All True,* with central roles for Louis Armstrong and Duke Ellington. But the film was never completed because the relationship between Welles and RKO turned sour. Ellington was dropped, Holiday added, and as the script was rewritten, Armstrong and Holiday became secondary rather than central characters in what ended up being essentially a love story about a white cabaret owner and an aspiring opera singer. Nick Duquesnes (Arturo de Córdova), the "King of Basin Street" and a connoisseur of jazz, is owner of the city's most elegant casino. He falls in love with Miralee Smith (Dorothy Patrick), the daughter of a New Orleans dowager with strong political connections who disapproves of jazz. But Miralee is captivated by the sound of jazz and persuades her maid, Endie (Holiday), to escort her to the venue where Armstrong performs for Nick, together with such veterans as Barney Bigard, Kid Ory, and Zutty Singleton, on clarinet, trombone, and drums, respectively. Later in the film Miralee is heard performing "Do You Know What It Means to Miss New Orleans?"—a refrain in the movie—while her control-freak mother is in the process of using her muscle to close down Storyville.

Even though the film presents a fictionalized view of the history of jazz and the closing of Storyville in 1917—and contains quite a few egregious anachronisms—it nevertheless dramatizes the validation of a black, primarily Afrocentric music and its acceptance by a predominantly white, educated public. When Nick is asked to explain the origins of jazz, he replies: "Well, it comes from work songs, the Gold Coast of West Africa, little Christian churches, river boats. . . . They made up the music as they went along." Equally telling is the scene in which a tuxedo-clad Armstrong, now in Paris, performs to the warm approval of royalty in the audience. We also see Miralee congratulating Armstrong backstage after one of his concerts and holding up a copy of his first autobiography, *Swing That Music.* Literature has, in effect, elevated jazz to the status of art.[85]

One further event during 1947 added to Armstrong's visibility and the championing of the New Orleans Dixieland tradition. On August 13 Louis Armstrong and the All Stars made their debut at Billy Berg's club in Los Angeles—the ensemble consisting of a front line of trumpet, clarinet, and trombone, backed by a rhythm section of piano, bass, and drums. On hand that night were such celebrities as Hoagy Carmichael, Woody Herman, Benny Goodman, and Johnny Mercer. There was also major press coverage. In its September 1 issue *Time* put it succinctly: "Louis Armstrong has forsaken the ways of Mammon and come back to jazz." Others raved: "Satchmo's superb stage presence binds together a showcase of jazz stars into a jazz production that warmed the hearts of nostalgic music lovers (Louis is playing and singing with more heart and inspiration than he has for years)."[86]

These qualities of "more heart and inspiration" were to carry Armstrong and the All Stars to the zenith of international fame during the years of the Cold War. Certainly by the mid-1950s "Ambassador Satch" was a force to be reckoned with, even by the U.S. State Department. What helps make his vital role more comprehensible is the profound influence at the time of the Marshall Plan in shaping both American foreign policy and the general perceptions of the United States abroad. In fact, the basic concept of the Marshall Plan was initially publicized on June 5, 1947, some two months before the All Stars first opened at Billy Berg's.

In 1948 the causes of justice for African-Americans and of jazz as a product of their labor, as well as the future of American democracy itself, were brought together in a united front. Concluding his Marxist book, *Jazz: A People's Music,* Sidney Finkelstein had this to say:

> Jazz is the living embodiment of the creative powers of the people. It is especially the product, and gift to America, of the most poverty-stricken, hounded and exploited of the country, the Negro people. . . . Jazz is the product of labor, in that the musician today is largely a kind of laborer. The free, creative and humanly expressive music that is hot jazz is the sign of the constant desire of the laborer to break out of the chains of mechanical production, to create a product that is worthy of him, one that bears the stamp of his mind and personality. Through the work of the musician it becomes the expression of the people from whom he comes and for whom he creates. . . . Its content is of the life of those who are in the front line of the struggle to conquer nature. . . . It is one of America's most precious cultural possessions, and its continued life is bound up with our life as a free people.[87]

Finkelstein was part of a generation of jazz writers once derided as "a bunch of Ivy League Marxists" by Bernard Wolfe, one-time personal secretary in Mexico to Leon Trotsky and coauthor with Mezz Mezzrow of *Really the Blues* (1946). Included in this group were Rudi Blesh (Dartmouth), Wilder Hobson (Princeton), John Hammond (Yale), Frederic Ramsey (Princeton), and Marshall Stearns (Harvard and Yale). Arguably the most outspoken was Rudi Blesh, who in his *Shining Trumpets* (1946) includes a fairly elaborate comparative table organized under two headings and purporting to show the corrupting influence of capitalism and European culture: "African Survivals in Negro Jazz" (essentially hot jazz) and "Deformations of Negro Jazz."[88]

The coup de grâce to Whiteman's regal stature was the *Time* cover of February 21, 1949, featuring Louis Armstrong, resplendent in bow tie, smiling as he looked heavenward, his head adorned with a crown of gold trumpets. Inside was a feature article celebrating Armstrong's preeminence as a jazz icon, tracing his journey from rags to riches, delineating his vital role in the history of jazz, and remarking on his participation in New Orleans as King of the Zulus Parade. The article concluded with a thought by Armstrong about what he would do at the Pearly Gates. "I'm gonna blow a kiss to Gabriel."[89]

A new "King of Jazz" was now on the throne.

5 SHARED MEMORY

Sovereign though they were in their respective kingdoms, our two kings of jazz were rulers of domains with open borders. There one could find a free flow of cross-influences, of various sidemen, and sundry movers and shakers who were all part of a collective experience—an experience transcending religion, race, class, and category, with a shared memory of intersecting personal relationships and a common musical repertoire. Much of this memory was shared by a generation that saw a precarious balance between the contingencies of race—one thinks of the pervasiveness of Jim Crow and the terror tactics of the Ku Klux Klan—and the need to maintain order and civility. The nursing of interracial grudges and the "dissing" of whites for appropriating and exploiting a black musical treasure were urges largely repressed. It was within this world that Whiteman showed himself to be a man with a racial conscience far greater than is commonly recognized. Connie and George Immerman (owners of Connie's Inn), Tommy Rockwell, and the president of the American Federation of Musicians alleged that Armstrong was guilty of breach of contract and caused him to file a deposition in the U.S. District Court, Southern District of New York, claiming "irreparable injury" to his reputation. Whiteman's staunch defense—a sworn affidavit in 1931 that "Louis Armstrong is outstanding"—helped tip the scales of justice in his favor.

Whiteman's treatment of Earl Hines is another case in point. The great pianist with whom Armstrong made such historic recordings as "West End Blues," "A Monday Date," and "Weather Bird" had much to thank Paul Whiteman for. Hines, the resident pianist and bandleader at Chicago's Grand Terrace, was on the verge of being fired by the mercurial night club entrepreneur Ed Fox. Fox could hit the ceiling one minute, agree the next to pay $3,000 so that Hines could have the Bechstein piano of his choice, then later threaten to dump him and his band. He was all too suggestible, often swayed by what waiters or self-promoting bandleaders had to say about the competition. After one of Fox's threats to fire Hines, Whiteman showed up at the club in the company of two of his most accomplished musicians, the vocalist Mildred Bailey and the pianist-arranger Roy Bargy. Whiteman reportedly snapped back at Fox: "Are you out of your goddamned mind? You've got the world's greatest piano player." Bargy struck fear into Fox by warning: "You make a change and you'll lose all the business you get from other entertainers."[1] Others, like Red Norvo, master of the xylophone and vibraphone, another member of the Paul Whiteman Orchestra from the late 1920s to the early 1930s and one-time husband of Mildred Bailey, have corroborated the basic story. "The guy was definitely thinking about firing him! It was Whiteman who convinced him to keep Hines. Then Whiteman went further. He had a Steinway sent out to the Grand Terrace [on loan] from the NBC studios, and arranged for nightly NBC network broadcasts by Hines. Then he even had the leading Chicago announcer assigned to handle the remotes from the Grand Terrace. That was Whiteman. If he thought you were good, he'd go all out. And he knew all the jazz guys."[2]

While Whiteman deserves considerable credit for helping make possible Hines's ten-year residency at the Grand Terrace from 1928 to 1938, he was inclined to maintain the status quo on the bandstand. Earl Hines has borne out this assessment in a statement both pointed and poignant: "Paul Whiteman loved my playing, and he would have liked me to join him, but he always had to qualify his admiration by saying, 'If you were only white . . .'"[3] This state of affairs continued into the 1940s, when the highly accomplished reed player Garvin Bushell applied for the position of bassoonist in Whiteman's radio orchestra. Upon arriving he was told by the contractor that his secretary had made a mistake and that a flute player was actually being sought. Bushell reported this act of race discrimination to the union representative and was assured that he had a strong basis for a lawsuit. But he decided to "just let it slide" for fear of forfeiting future chances for a staff position on radio.[4]

But otherwise no one could fault Whiteman for his generosity of spirit. In

1924, after finishing his evening at New York's Palais Royal, he would stop by around the corner at the Kentucky Club to soak up the sounds of Duke Ellington and his Club Serenaders. Ellington himself later recalled: "Whiteman came often as a genuine enthusiast, listened respectfully, said his words of encouragement, very discreetly slipped the piano player a fifty-dollar bill, and very loudly proclaimed our musical merit."[5] Some two years later, in a piece of advance publicity for Ellington's summer tour of New England, he was hailed as "The Paul Whiteman of Colored Orchestras."[6] Then in his August 27, 1927, column for the leading black newspaper, the *Chicago Defender*, Dave Peyton reported on a previous article describing Whiteman's reaction to Ellington's band of the day: "One evening in particular this writer sat in the night club and saw Paul Whiteman offer the Washingtonians $100 to play 'I Love You' in their inimitable way. When Paul Whiteman recognizes another orchestra's superiority they must be very good. It is very unusual for Paul to seek musical information. He usually gives it."[7] Some years later, in 1939, in the course of offering thumbnail tributes to various bandleaders—his tone has been compared to that of "a toastmaster's speech at an awards banquet"—Ellington gave the following assessment of Whiteman: "Mr. Whiteman deserves credit for discovering and recognizing ability or genius in composers whose works would not normally be acceptable to dance bands. Whiteman makes it possible to commercialize these works. We confess he has maintained a 'higher level' for many years, and we think there is no doubt but that he has carried jazz to the highest position it ever has enjoyed. He put it in the ears of the serious audience and they liked it. He is still Mr. Whiteman."[8]

In 1943, five years after Whiteman had featured his commissioned piece "Belles of Harlem" (also known as "Blue Belles of Harlem") at his Eighth Experiment in Modern Music, Ellington lavished praise on Whiteman for his promotion of symphonic jazz. "Our band came along just when Paul Whiteman and his orchestra had popularized the symphonic style. And don't let them kid you about Whiteman. He has been a big man in our music. He's done a lot for it, especially with his concerts where he gave composers a chance to write new, extended works."[9] At the same time, like Armstrong, Whiteman always had an abiding commitment to his public, to please them regardless of any labels, "symphonic" or otherwise. Nothing shows this more clearly than the musicians' embrace of the music of Guy Lombardo. In Whiteman's case, we will recall, it meant a relationship extending over forty years, beginning in 1927, when he recommended Lombardo to take over his failing Club Whiteman in New York; Lombardo and his Royal Canadians had, however, already been lured away by a more tempting offer from the Granada Café on Chicago's South Side. Whiteman and Lombardo were to work together in various capacities over some four decades, on the Committee of Five for the Betterment of Radio during the 1930s, in joint publishing ventures, and on the Blue Network, on which Whiteman, the musical director, had Lombardo's orchestra perform. As for Armstrong, he was enamored of the Lombardo sound, "the sweetest sound this side of heaven." He was first smitten when he and the drummer Zutty Singleton were "wined and dined until the wee hours of the morning" by Lombardo at the Granada Café in 1928.[10] Lombardo's was a relaxed, soothing sound that Armstrong sought to emulate in his pop-song recordings starting in 1929, as in such numbers as "Ain't Misbehavin'," "When You're Smiling," and "Some of These Days."

Those titles are part of a common repertoire shared by Armstrong and Whiteman—some three dozen titles that both performed in the course of their careers. Others, in alphabetical order, include "All of Me," "Basin Street Blues," "Body and Soul," "Dinah," "I Can't Give You Anything But Love," "I've Got a Gal in Kalamazoo," "Jeepers Creepers," "Rockin' Chair," "St. Louis Blues," "Sugar," "Sweet Georgia Brown," "Sweet Sue," "Tiger Rag," and "When It's Sleepy Time Down South." Helping keep the music alive were various important sidemen who at different times worked with both men. One thinks of such Whiteman alumni as Mildred Bailey, Eddie Lang, Joe Venuti, the Dorsey brothers, and particularly Bing Crosby and Jack Teagarden, two musicians with whom Armstrong had an especially long-standing and intimate working relationship.

These standards belong to a core repertory—a larger group of favorite pieces upon which musicians have improvised time and time again, and for which a rich variety of arrangements will often exist. Indeed, so widely are these pieces collectively shared that even musicians who have never worked together can be expected to perform them on the spur of the moment. Some have gone so far as to tabulate the number of recordings issued of a given standard and have concluded that these are pieces of music "that may be shown empirically to have been favorites in a given period of time."[11] Studying the performance history of such pieces, primarily on the basis of recordings, can often yield rich insights about the interface of musical category and commerce, the blurring of jazz and the popular, personnel and personality, the breaching of racial barriers, and more. James T. Maher has recalled in a poetic turn of phrase the impact of big band standards on his youthful days. Though his comments refer specifically to the interracial partnership of Fletcher Henderson and Benny Goodman, they have much broader application: "Song is the wind-chime of memory, and these were our songs. They were part of the daily ordinary, and this is what took Benny over the gap . . . into the American parlor."[12]

This core repertory encompasses a stylistic spectrum covering everything from blues to various examples of the Tin Pan Alley popular song. And more than anything else, these standards exemplify an abiding commitment on the part of both Armstrong and Whiteman to keep their public happy. As the distinguished jazz historian and trumpet player Richard Sudhalter has observed:

> My inclination is to link Armstrong and Whiteman through their shared belief that the public deserved what it paid for. For each (and Louis enunciated this countless times throughout his career), making the people happy (and that includes keeping 'em dancing) was the prime imperative. It certainly trumped any self-conscious idea of purism in art. . . .
>
> I've become so weary of hearing Whiteman belittled because his orchestra didn't serve up "genuine" hot jazz. He understood, as did Louis, that a lay audience would only accept something new if it were packaged in familiar (i.e., reassuring) form. Whiteman excelled here: let Bix, . . . Teagarden, and the rest have their moments, but within a framework that wouldn't leave listeners shaking their heads. Armstrong too: I've heard too many people who should know better assert decisively that Louis's decline began in 1929, when he started recording pop songs.[13]

A key figure in this history, a major mover and shaker straddling the worlds of jazz and popular music of the day, was Hoagy Carmichael (1899–1981). His was the voice of the American heartland, one endowed with a unique gift for evoking the down-home, rural landscape of fond memory. He was a native of Bloomington, Indiana, active as songwriter, singer, pianist, and bandleader, working alongside and helping shape the repertoires of not only Whiteman and Armstrong but also Jack Teagarden, Bix Beiderbecke, Tommy and Jimmy Dorsey, Mildred Bailey, Bing Crosby, and many others in their orbit, whether in performing, recording, publishing, or film. His was a pervasive cross-racial influence flowing naturally from a style filled with appropriated black elements going back to his earliest years, and operating on the cusp of jazz and popular music.

There was a hardscrabble quality to Carmichael's early life. As he once bluntly put it, "We were poor white trash." Hoagland Carmichael—he was named after a circus troupe stranded in Bloomington—was the first child and only son of Howard Clyde ("Cyclone") Carmichael, who made an uncertain living running horse-drawn taxis and subsequently worked as an electrician, and Lida Robison Carmichael, a highly capable pianist who accompanied silent movies and was often in demand at weekend dances on the Indiana University campus. One of her specialties was what proved to be Scott Joplin's most famous ragtime piece, "Maple Leaf Rag," published some two months before Carmichael was born. According to John Edward Hasse, "Ragtime pieces were Hoagland's lullabies, for his mother would often take him to fraternity dances, where he would fall asleep on a board placed between chairs as she beat out the jagged syncopations." He later wrote of his mother: "Her life was lived in ragged time, on the ragged edge, but she was always there. Eighty pounds of solid rock which nothing could dismay."[14]

The rhythms of ragtime were to course through Carmichael's musical veins for much of his life—something absorbed not only from his mother but from other sources as well, particularly the black ragtime pianist Reg DuValle, "the elder statesman of Indiana jazz." Carmichael bonded with DuValle during a crisis in his teens. A downturn in his father's fortunes had required Carmichael to quit high school in Bloomington and move with his family to Indianapolis in early 1916. Those were bleak times, with the family living at "the thin dark side of a double-fronted place," as he later remembered it. He enrolled at Manual Training High School only to quit after "little more than one miserable year." What followed was work on a construction crew and various other jobs, including a stint at a meat-packing plant cleaning the entrails of freshly slaughtered pigs in "a forgotten dungeon, a hell-hole full of death."[15] What saved the young Carmichael was the black nightlife on Indiana Avenue. It was there that he met DuValle, soon becoming a frequent visitor to the DuValle home on the predominantly black south side of Indianapolis. The impact was deep and long-lasting. "Reggie had the new black music tricks and he made ragtime sound old hat. With his head hanging to one side, as if overcome with ecstasy, he'd play and play—and grin. 'You listening, boy?' I would sit, absorbed, watching the movements of his crazy hands."[16]

By the spring of 1919 Hoagy Carmichael was back at Bloomington High School, receiving his diploma the following year and enrolling as a freshman at Indiana University in September 1920 with the avowed intention—under pressure from his mother—to study law rather than music. But the siren call of the extracurricular life won out, and his pledging the Beta Theta chapter of Kappa Sigma fraternity had far more to do with the future direction of his career than any classes he ever attended. In the course of the social whirl his focus shifted ever more to jazz and hot music, a process that would within a few short years bring about lifelong relationships with Whiteman and Armstrong.

It was in early 1922 that the Kappa Sigma fraternity house was abuzz with news of a style of playing called "sock time"—that is, "a way of playing four steady, equally weighted beats to a bar that seemed lighter and smoother than what most other bands were doing." And the source of all the excitement was a motley crew playing in a Chicago basement cabaret called the Friars' Inn, billed as the "Land of Bohemia Where Good Fellows Get Together." Hailing from New Orleans and from the farm belt stretching from Iowa to Ohio, these youngsters were the ticket to lively entertainment at a time when Prohibition was the law of the land. They were known as the Friars' Society Dance Orchestra, an early incarnation of what by 1923 would become the New Orleans Rhythm Kings. Sounding like a smitten young beau, Carmichael confessed: "The thought of what I might hear when an entire band was playing this stuff made me weak." He was struck to the core upon actually hearing the sounds of the group's clarinet and cornet players, in particular, when he visited Friars' Inn in April or May of 1922: "The notes smacked me in the face and at unexpected moments; they went right on through my gizzard and dropped on the floor, making my feet jump."[17] Such was the force of the budding New Orleans Rhythm Kings, a group whose sound blended the white with the black—that of the Original Dixieland Jazz Band and King Oliver's Creole Jazz Band, including "Little Louis" on second cornet. There was, in addition, an encounter that night at Friars' Inn which Carmichael later elevated to the level of a personal epiphany, his meeting an "extremely young kid in a belted pile coat and cracked patent leather shoes."[18] This was Bix Beiderbecke, fresh from a cornet gig, with a reddened upper lip and the odor of gin on his breath.

Here were two flaming youths who would soon become kindred spirits, each besotted by the music, muggles, and booze of club, cabaret, and fraternity life of the American Midwest of the day. And in keeping with their bohemian ways, each soon ran afoul of the academic establishment where he was enrolled. In May 1922 Beiderbecke was dismissed from Lake Forest Academy, just north of Chicago, where his parents had sent him in vain hopes that academic rigor would be the right medicine for their wayward son. But the young Beiderbecke's curfew violations, among them climbing down the dormitory fire escape after lights-out, proved to be the last straw for the powers-that-be. As for Carmichael, by early January 1923, simply unable to meet tuition and loan payments, he had withdrawn from Indiana University without completing even a single semester. He did, however, maintain an ongoing presence in campus life, especially at popular haunts like the Book Nook, where one could see "the skimpy kid in a yellow slicker who jerked and bobbed at the piano like a man with St. Vitus's dance."[19] Aside from the Kappa Sigma fraternity house, this college hangout—saturated with the sounds of jazz and the voices of debate about poetry, the arts, dating, the relative merits of gin and home-brewed beer, and more—was the center of Carmichael's Bloomington world; "that little gink over there flogging the piano—that's me. The one with the long nose and exerted red face."[20]

Their passion for hot music brought Beiderbecke and Carmichael to Chicago's Lincoln Gardens on the city's South Side some time in the fall of 1923 to hear Armstrong blow. Carmichael's recollections take on the quality of another epiphany. "As I sat down to light my first muggle, Bix gave the sign to a big black fellow, playing a second trumpet for Oliver, and he slashed into 'Bugle Call Rag.' I dropped my cigarette and gulped my drink. Bix was on his feet, his eyes popping. For taking the first chorus was that second trumpet, Louis Armstrong. Louis was taking it fast. . . . 'Why,' I moaned, 'why isn't everybody in the world here to hear that?' I meant it. Something as unutterably stirring as that deserved to be heard by the world. Then the muggles took effect and my body got light. Every note Louis hit was perfection." There was apparently more. Like a demon possessed, Carmichael had to take the place of Lil Hardin at the piano as the band swung into "Royal Garden Blues." He goes on to say: "I had never heard the tune before, but somehow I knew every note. I couldn't miss. I was floating in a strange, deep-blue whirlpool of jazz."[21]

In the early 1920s history was being made in Richmond, Indiana, in a single-story gray outbuilding belonging to the Starr Piano Company and located alongside a spur of the Chesapeake and Ohio Railroad. It was in this unlikely place that the Gennett label had its studio, where floor-length draperies and an old rug were used in a feeble attempt to dampen the sound, and where they would make recordings of William Jennings Bryan or the Ku Klux Klan one day, and black jazzmen the next. This was where, as we have seen, Louis Armstrong and King Oliver's Creole Jazz Band had put their sound on wax for the very first time on April 5, 1923. The following February found Bix Beiderbecke and a plucky group calling themselves the Wolverine Orchestra of Chicago on hand for their first session. On May 6 they brought along Hoagy Carmichael to record his maiden effort as a composer. As Beiderbecke explained to the recording engineer, Carmichael "hadn't written it down: he could neither read nor write music, really. But they'd been playing fraternity house dates he'd booked for them, and he'd worked this thing out on the piano at . . . the Book Nook."[22] The fledgling piece was called "Free Wheeling," but because it reminded Beiderbecke of the Mississippi riverboats near his hometown of Davenport, Iowa, and the banjo player found it had a "shuffle" feel, it was promptly renamed "Riverboat Shuffle"; and the name stuck.

Pretty soon, because of its catchy rhythm and its four engaging solo breaks, it became a standard of area white jazz bands, not to mention later Chicago and Dixieland revival groups. And almost three years later to the day, Hoagy Carmichael, together with Bix Beiderbecke and Frankie Trumbauer, were to make an even stronger recording. In the meantime Carmichael and his group, the Collegians, were going full steam ahead with dance gigs. There were "at least fifty advertised dates around Bloomington during academic year 1924–25 and even more in 1925–26. At times they appear to have averaged between three and five a week (often two a day), including fraternity and sorority dances, theater engagements, Charleston contests, jazz band 'battles,' football games, and other campus events."[23]

The paths of Carmichael and Whiteman were to cross rather soon. Although Paul Whiteman and his Orchestra had appeared in Bloomington on April 17, 1925, for a reprise of his historic Aeolian Hall concert of the previous year—he was now in the midst of a major transcontinental tour—it was only on October 27, 1927, that the two men finally met, when Whiteman was appearing at the Indiana Theater in Indianapolis. The occasion was a defining one for each of them; for it was at this concert that both Bix Beiderbecke and Frankie Trumbauer joined Paul Whiteman's Orchestra. The addition of "Bix" and "Tram," not to mention Bill Challis, Eddie Lang, Joe Venuti, and the Dorsey brothers from the top dance band of Jean Goldkette's collapsing empire, translated into a hotter style of music making. And it was also at this 1927 concert, Carmichael has claimed, that Beiderbecke and Trumbauer took him to meet the King of Jazz himself. "I'll always admire him for the warm reception he gave. . . . I liked him right off the bat. Then he told me what he thought of my scratchy Gennett record of 'Washboard Blues' . . . went to a piano to have a rendition. . . . I did 'Washboard Blues' the best my squeaky voice could do it. Paul looked at me and said: 'You're coming to Chicago next week to make a concert record of that thing with me, and you're going to sing it, you screwy guy."[24]

Accounts of the initial meeting of Carmichael and Whiteman actually differ somewhat. In one rather far-fetched version Carmichael is said to have played an earlier Gennett recording long-distance over a telephone at a fraternity house. In another, a biographer of the Dorsey brothers has Carmichael invading Whiteman's hotel room with a small portable organ. As Carmichael played and sang "Washboard Blues," Whiteman is reported to have said to

Bill Challis: "Get this down; we'll do it in Chicago."[25] Challis subsequently repeated much the same story, though remembering the hotel room as his own. But what is crucial is that the newly hired Bill Challis was brought into the act, arranging now for an orchestra with a hotter sound and one sporting the talents of Beiderbecke, Trumbauer, and the Dorsey brothers. In fact, Whiteman's recording of Carmichael's "Washboard Blues" of November 18, 1927, with the composer doing both piano and vocals, not only launched Carmichael's career on records with the top bandleader of the day but also marked Beiderbecke's first session with Whiteman. And the arrangement of Challis, showcasing the special gifts of Beiderbecke in a hot chorus, raised the hackles of the veteran trumpet player and master of muted effects Henry Busse. Even though Busse was one of Whiteman's stars harking back to his Palais Royale days and had played a vital part in such recorded hits as "Hot Lips" and "When Day Is Done," Whiteman ultimately decided in favor of Challis. Challis himself later put it this way: "I'd pared down the instrumentation quite a bit to get the effect I wanted, and Henry Busse was not included. Busse found out about it and hit the ceiling. He went to Paul and said he had a contract that called for him to make every Whiteman record. I told Paul that my contract allowed me freedom in arranging."[26]

The resulting arrangement, with piano solos and vocals by Hoagy Carmichael, is a masterpiece in miniature, a tone poem achieving a remarkable sense of both tension and balance within just over four minutes. The "blues" in the title, rather than signifying a piece built on the conventional form of twelve-bar choruses, has far more to do with a sense of melancholy, relieved in this case by flashes of hope. A brief slow introduction featuring Jimmy Dorsey's clarinet in the throaty chalumeau clarinet register embedded in a gently warm string sound evokes that once-upon-a-time feeling. It is followed by a solo piano interlude that harks back to the worlds of Zez Confrey's novelty piano and the stride style of Fats Waller, but is disrupted by a manic passage in double time. Shortly after the orchestra enters with the first chorus there is, in the bridge, a disruption of the regular four-beat measure—suggesting what is sometimes called "secondary rag"—as a recurring three-note motif is heard five times. Carmichael's ensuing rendition of the verse and chorus, a vocal with solo piano, is a poignant, utterly sincere statement of world-weariness—"a grievance coupled with dignity in a way that is absolutely heartbreaking," in the words of James T. Maher.[27] The lyrics, written in black dialect by Fred B. Callahan, an Indiana gravestone cutter, open as follows:

Mornin' comes with cloudy skies and rain;
Mah po' back is broke with pain.
My man's sleepin', I'se a-scrubbin';
Chillun weepin', I'se a-rubbin';
Pain a-creepin', clothes a-tubbin'
All day long.

A transition—it consists of the rhymed couplet "never get me gone from here, / Scrubbin' dirty clothes all year"—leads to a recitative-like passage presented in halting phrases and accompanied by strings and bass clarinet, as our protagonist for a fleeting moment, maybe in a delirium, dreams of better times:

New clothes, in my city clothes, in raggedy clothes,
And buy me clothes,
That's all I know, up and down, back and forth, all day long,
Oh lordy, won't you hear my song?

Good times and the bright lights of the city are briefly evoked in the ensuing doubletime chorus, very much in the spirit of the Charleston, as Bix Beiderbecke is given his chance to shine. But we are then abruptly brought back to a bleak landscape as Carmichael in a concluding verse and chorus expresses a faint hope for a brighter future: "goin' down to that river some day, hurry day, hurry."

In the context of the times, this traversal of "Washboard Blues" speaks volumes for the artistic judgment and inclusiveness of Paul Whiteman, his capacity to straddle the worlds of white and black. Not only is it in a dramatically different universe from such hits of the day as "Dinah," "Sweet Georgia Brown," "Tea for Two," or "Yes, Sir, That's My Baby," the 1927 recording itself dates from a time of extreme racial violence in Indiana. The Ku Klux Klan had approached its peak of influence barely three years before when Grand Dragon David Curtis Stephenson ("I am the law in Indiana") was lording it over many areas of state government. At the Republican state convention in 1924 many who were to win elective office—from school board candidates, to the mayor of Indianapolis, to the state governor—clearly owed allegiance to the Klan. But by 1928 Stephenson had been convicted of murder, many of his cronies had been indicted, and the ranks of the Klan were in disarray. That same year the *Indianapolis Times* won the Pulitzer Prize for its exposé of political corruption tainted by Klan connections.[28]

As for the relationship between Armstrong and Carmichael, it was a

5.1 Hoagy Carmichael and Louis Armstrong in Los Angeles, July 3, 1970, together for the last time at Armstrong's birthday party. Photo by L. Levine.

warm and enduring one spanning close to fifty years. As we have seen, it began sometime in the fall of 1923 when a youthful, muggle-inhaling Carmichael came to hear his hero at Chicago's Lincoln Gardens and reportedly ended up on the bandstand playing piano in "Royal Garden Blues." They last saw each other in Los Angeles on July 3, 1970, at a party held the day before what was assumed at the time to be Armstrong's seventieth birthday. Even more telling are the Carmichael compositions that helped define Armstrong's work as the preeminent soloist of the day, performing on the very cusp of the worlds of jazz and popular music—titles such as "Georgia on My Mind," "Star Dust," "Rockin' Chair," "Jubilee," "Lazy River," and "Lazybones."

No piece in the Carmichael canon illustrates these features more vividly than one popularized by both Whiteman and Armstrong, "Rockin' Chair," which for the composer represented a sequel to "Washboard Blues." We are again transported to a rural setting as the protagonist—indeterminately male or female, black or white—infirm and in fullness of days, is reminiscing, facing the coming deliverance of death with a stoic resignation. The bridge of the song says it all:

> My dear ol' Aunt Harriet
> How long in heaven she be
> Send me sweet chariot
> For the end of these troubles I'll see.

More than anything else, it is a song permeated with "the idea of home, a place where wandering ceases and the heart comes to rest."[29] "Rockin' Chair" dates from 1929, from Carmichael's time in California, after he had come to realize that there was little point in hanging around Indiana, especially with the advent of sound in the movies. Hollywood was beckoning, and he had nothing to lose. "I put part of my little bank account into National City Bank stock . . . drew the rest, and was away to set Hollywood on fire. . . . I didn't see that any disillusionment could harm me. If so, I felt it might be a man's coming of age. I bought a ticket west."[30] His timing could not have been more opportune. In mid-June, Paul Whiteman and his whole entourage arrived in Hollywood to start the filming of Universal's *King of Jazz*. Frankie Trumbauer, Bix Beiderbecke, Bing Crosby, and his fellow Rhythm Boys, not to mention some friends from Indiana, were on hand, and the partying could begin. One such party, thrown by Mildred Bailey for Paul Whiteman and his Orchestra, proved to be a turning point when one of the Rhythm Boys, Al Rinker, introduced Hoagy Carmichael to his big sister, the hostess herself. This party, as we have seen, was all part of a stratagem for an audition, with calls for Bailey to "give us a song" once Paul Whiteman had knocked back some of her homemade beer.[31] The ruse worked: Whiteman was captivated and hired her on the spot as the first full-time female band singer. She was to work with him from 1929 to 1934, and like Louis Armstrong became identified with such Hoagy Carmichael numbers as "Georgia on My Mind" and "Rockin' Chair."

A sense of timing and the conjunction of personalities helped create "Rockin' Chair," a standard memorable for breaking the barriers of race and category. Bailey's thyroid condition and chronic weight problems had fired

Carmichael's imagination: she "struck Hoagy as well suited to an unfettered loll in a rocking chair." And in the course of the next few weeks in California, Carmichael was to play and sing his new song for Mildred Bailey, who took a strong liking to it. Some measure of the impact that her rendition was to later have can be gauged by what happened in May 1931 following a broadcast with Whiteman's band from the Edgewater Beach Hotel on Lake Michigan, a plush country-club setting just outside Chicago, with one thousand rooms and such amenities as a nine-hole putting green, tennis courts, beach, and promenade. "The response from listeners was phenomenal. Western Union received so many enthusiastic messages that the company was unable to deliver all the telegrams."[32] But no air checks have apparently survived from those days, so it is impossible to pinpoint what it was about Bailey's vocals, the qualities of timbre, nuance, and inflection that so excited the listening audience. We can at best only extrapolate from two Bailey recordings of "Rockin' Chair" made almost five years apart during this general period. The first, with Whiteman, from August 18, 1932, brought Bailey to the Victor studios in her debut recording of the standard, with her third-husband-to-be, Red Norvo, playing the vibes behind her. A brief introduction on vibraphone, wistful and modal, ushers in the vocals as Bailey communicates a sense of world-weariness and a resignation to the inevitable, treating "Rockin' Chair" with great expressivity, but in the manner of a period pop song. The 1937 Bailey remake, however, in an Eddie Sauter arrangement, shows to perfection her ability to capture the nuances of blues coloration—"'fore I tan your hide" is one of several illustrative phrases—and improvisatory freedom on the reprise of the chorus. One is reminded here that Mildred Bailey, part Coeur d'Alene Indian and born near Tacoma, Washington, had shown early on a passion for hot music, at the same time thinking instrumentally, "as if a lead instrument had somehow acquired the capacity of articulating words . . . [adopting] not only the black musician's way with a phrase, but also his way with a word and his vocal sound, including the pronounced nasal resonance." The veteran critic of the voice Henry Pleasants, who enjoyed playing recordings of Bailey to unsuspecting guests, both black and white, and asking them to describe the singer, has claimed that without exception each would respond: "Well, to begin with, she's Black."[33]

Even though Mildred Bailey came to be called the Rockin' Chair Lady, she was not the first to record the song, not by a long shot. In fact, close to two dozen versions were committed to wax before hers, starting in 1929, including a notable session on December 13 featuring Hoagy Carmichael and Louis Armstrong. This performance, at Okeh's Union Square studios, took place

5.2 Front cover of "Paul Whiteman's Favorite Modern Rhythmic Spirituals as featured by Mildred Bailey." Joshua Berrett, personal collection.

fairly soon after Carmichael's arrival in New York from California, where he had come near to running out of money without making any inroads into the movie industry. With the approach of Labor Day, he had decided to throw in his lot with the Whiteman crowd by hiding as a stowaway aboard the Old Gold Special, sharing berths with Bing Crosby and Andy Secrest, or else sequestering himself in the men's toilet, as they all headed back east to New York. Carmichael's performance with Louis Armstrong and his Orchestra established a precedent-setting dialoguing routine, redolent of minstrel show comedy, essentially trading one- or two-measure phrases of the vocals, as Carmichael played the role of the aging father, Armstrong that of the son.

Pointed comparison of these performances reveals some striking differences. The Mildred Bailey recordings show far greater sophistication in terms of form—evocative introductions, among other things—harmony, orchestration, and rhythmic interest, including the distinctive vibraphone counterpoint provided by Red Norvo in the 1932 version with Paul Whiteman; and her 1937 traversal, in the arrangement by Eddie Sauter, provides the distinct benefit of a poignant, bluesy rendition and subtle touches of melodic improvisation. In the 1929 Armstrong-Carmichael rendition the spotlight is clearly on the soloists. Armstrong, fresh from his triumphs in such numbers as "Ain't Misbehavin'" from Connie's *Hot Chocolates,* dominates with his trumpet from the very outset, hewing fairly close to the original melody and backed by a rather limp, pedestrian-sounding group from the Luis Russell band, with more than a few touches of whinnying saxophones. But compensating for these deficiencies are the contrasting vocals of Carmichael and Armstrong, providing a sense of dramatic verisimilitude and humor as father and son seek to upstage each other. At the same time, however, the shortcomings of the Luis Russell orchestra exposes what was to be a sore spot for Armstrong as he fronted big bands from 1929 to 1947. The clarinetist Barney Bigard, who played in both the Duke Ellington Orchestra and Armstrong's All Stars, has recalled just how raw emotions could sometimes become, especially backstage:

Louis was a wonderful man to work with. I mean, he'd say a lot of things. He can raise hell with you. Now in too few seconds he's forgotten all about it and even what it was all about. I kidded him. One time, for no reason whatsoever, we were at the Blue Note in Chicago and he came off the stand. He said, "Cats think because they played in a big band that they are the best musicians in town. . . . They think they're hell and everyone thinks he was with Paul Whiteman, he's hell too." So I'm listening. I said, "What's all this about?" And

I hadn't even said one word to him. Neither has Jack [Teagarden]. Nobody. And he's mumbling all this in his dressing room. So I said, "Well, I know you must be hinting at me. . . . I'm sure glad I was with the greatest band in the world, because your band wasn't nothing." I said, "You had the world's worst band." And he kept quiet. . . . Oh, boy. That's the truth. He had good men in his band, but they didn't have no good arrangements, nothing.[34]

Beginning in 1929 and over the course of the next forty-odd years, Armstrong was to record "Rockin' Chair" a total of twenty-nine times; his last version dates from January 1971, barely six months before his death, when he performed this signature piece with trombonist Tyree Glenn. But for most of Armstrong's performance history of this song, his gin-swilling partner in musical crime and favorite male vocal foil was the trombonist Jack Teagarden. Like Armstrong, Teagarden had a warmth of personality and comedic flair that was contagious, and he would communicate a distinctive bluesy languor, whether on trombone or with his vocals. And as one can readily hear in their historic New York Town Hall performance of May 17, 1947, which featured a nascent form of the first All Stars, they could also riff with wicked glee on such phrases as "fetch me that gin son / 'Fore I tan your hide," and "just sittin' here grabbin' / At the flies round this rockin' chair"—all enlivened by rapid-fire exchanges, as when Armstrong says "I ain't got no gin, father." Things positively heat up as they say the word *grabbin'* five times in five seconds. It is all part of a delicious moment with "the two of them singing back and forth in liquor-sodden brotherly love."[35] They were able to bring that same kind of energy to a performance for a much wider audience during the 1957 Christmas season as part of NBC's *Timex Show* from New York's Copacabana.

Teagarden's was a vibrant presence, a ready mix of music and high spirits, significant to the career of Paul Whiteman between 1933 and 1938 and a key player in his fiftieth anniversary concert of 1956. As for Armstrong, his professional association with Teagarden began as early as 1929 as part of a series of interracial recording dates for the Okeh label when Armstrong also worked alongside Eddie Lang, Eddie Condon, and Tommy and Jimmy Dorsey. Their association continued sporadically during the 1930s and early 1940s, resumed with Armstrong's All Stars from 1947 to 1951, and was followed by special appearances until 1958. A native of Vernon, Texas, where he was born in 1905, Teagarden's first contact with Armstrong was as an inebriated teenager who had just been making the rounds of the French Quarter of New Orleans; this was sometime between 1919 and 1921, when Armstrong was playing with Fate Marable's band aboard the Streckfus Steamboat Line. Teagarden recalled: "I couldn't see anything but an excursion boat gliding through the mist back to port. Then the tune was more distinct. The boat was still far off. But in the bow I could see a Negro standing in the wind, holding a trumpet high and sending out the most brilliant notes I had ever heard. It was jazz; it was what I had been hoping to hear all through the night. . . . It was Louis Armstrong descending from the sky like a god."[36] Armstrong was to return this compliment from the "fine young white boy," later writing: "The first time I heard Jack Teagarden on the trombone I had goose pimples all over; in all my experience I had never heard anything so fine. Jack met all the boys in my band. . . . I did not see Jack Teagarden for a number of years after that first meeting, but I never ceased hearing about him and his horn and about the way he was improving all the time. We have been musically jammed buddies ever since we met."[37]

Teagarden's five years with Paul Whiteman have often been dismissed as a sell-out, or at least a time when he was forced to make strategic compromises that undermined his chances to attain true stardom. And what he sometimes put to his lips during those years was not the mouthpiece of his instrument. According to Whiteman's biographer Thomas A. DeLong, during 1938 the bandleader overindulged more than ever: "He eagerly joined the heavier drinkers in his band. He often grabbed Jack Teagarden as a companion in a marathon round of elbow bending. In fact, Paul so often sought his presence that Jack protested: 'It doesn't look good. The boys will think you're playing favorites.' 'I'm paying you, ain't I?' Whiteman snapped. 'Ain't I paying you?' Teagarden admitted he was. 'Then come along and don't give me any backtalk.'"[38]

Yet some fine Teagarden performances from those Whiteman years deserve more attention. One of these is a Victor recording from 1935 in which he takes a full vocal chorus in the popular song of Fats Waller and Andy Razaf "Ain't Misbehavin'," a number on which Armstrong had scored so handsomely in the 1929 production of the show *Hot Chocolates*. The obvious sophistication of the 1935 Whiteman arrangement—it was the only time he recorded "Ain't Misbehavin'"—with its contrast among sections, its countermelodies and key changes, all conspicuously absent in Armstrong's 1929 version, helps add luster to Teagarden's vocal, not to mention the full-toned, wonderfully agile playing of the lead trombone player Bill Rank, formerly a regular companion to Bix Beiderbecke in Jean Goldkette's top orchestra. But in the larger context of the discographic history of "Ain't Misbehavin'" and its place in the core repertory, it is Armstrong's body of recordings of this song that assumes greater significance. Not only was his rendition the most memorable to be preserved during 1929 in a rash of no fewer than thirteen recordings by various performers that year, he left to posterity twenty-one subsequent versions, starting in 1938 and continuing through December 1965, when he shared vocal honors with Mike Douglas on his TV show.

Returning to the Carmichael canon itself, no song has shone more brightly than "Star Dust," one of the most recorded of popular songs, translated into some forty languages. The title itself, as well as its lyrics, have inspired the naming of innumerable nightclubs, bars, cafés, movies, and books, not to mention the two memoirs by Carmichael himself—*The Stardust Road* (1946) and *Sometimes I Wonder* (1965). Although most widely known as an introspective ballad of lost love, "Star Dust" was initially a jazz instrumental, uptempo to the point of often being confused with a rag or stomp.[39] Carmichael originally wrote his own lyrics—there were additional drafts by an Indiana classmate—but they were soon to be superseded by the 1929 text of Mitchell Parish, who incorporated a number of phrases from the earlier drafts. Parish was a staff member of Mills Music, Carmichael's publisher at the time and an arm of the empire of Irving Mills, who had recently acquired Duke Ellington as a client. This entity, in turn, was an offshoot of the Rockwell-O'Keefe Theatrical Agency, run by Tommy Rockwell and Cork O'Keefe. Rockwell and O'Keefe were soon to mentor an up-and-coming protégé, Joe Glaser, Louis Armstrong's manager from 1935 until the time of his death.

Now within the larger context, "Star Dust" represents a richly layered statement about memory. It is not simply a conventional ballad of love lost but rather a song about a song, and the evocative power of that song, as a lover, solitary and forlorn, gazes at the stars, humming it in his head all the while. Partly self-referential, with its phrase "beside a garden wall, when stars are bright"—presumably an allusion to a "spooning wall" alongside a campus lovers' lane in Bloomington, Indiana, on a starlit night—the chorus of "Star Dust" is the stuff of consolation as our protagonist spends "the lonely night," his reverie haunted by the melody, made all the more memorable by its seamless phrases and atypical form.

By the end of 1931, fairly early in the song's history, both Louis Armstrong and Bing Crosby had made their definitive recordings within a few months of each other, Armstrong immortalizing it as a somewhat brisk quasi-stomp—very close in tempo to Carmichael's original 1927 recording—and Crosby as a slow, sentimental ballad. Armstrong's version, which consists of only the chorus, depends, like virtually all of his work with big bands from

1929 to 1947, on a publisher's "stock" arrangement, and presents a rather stodgy rhythm section—there is perceptibly heavy accenting on the first and third beats, coupled with rather stereotypical mooing saxophones. Yet by the same token, precisely this kind of backing helps to dramatize the wonderful immediacy of Armstrong's trumpet solo and vocal. Especially telling are Armstrong's evocation of breathlessness with his touch of double time in the opening trumpet chorus, not to mention his subtle rhythmic manipulation and vocal paraphrase as he sings behind the beat. He inserts phrase repetitions and halting isolated words as they float like wisps of memory: "Sometimes I wonder why I spend such lonely nights, oh baby, lonely nights, / Dreaming of a song—melody—memory—and I'm once again with you." And his final lines take on special poignancy as he sings

> Though I dream in vain
> In my heart it will remain, remain
> My star dust melody, . . .

fading away on the words "oh memory," heard three times.

Bing Crosby's "Star Dust" session (August 19, 1931) took place at a point when he was no longer with Paul Whiteman—he had quit sixteen months earlier, presumably in late April 1930, following mounting tensions between the two of them.[40] Here now was Crosby the crooner, the master of the mellow, offering a haunting ballad treatment of the standard, singing both verse and chorus, exchanging phrases with Jimmy Dorsey on alto saxophone—like him, a recent Whiteman alumnus—and inserting touches of scat as well as whistling. We should recall, by the way, that earlier in his career Crosby had been smitten with Armstrong's sound, and that he and Al Barris would "dress up their rhythm songs" by imitating the duetting cornets of Armstrong and Oliver, interpolating unison scat breaks.[41] Around the time he joined Paul Whiteman in Chicago in December 1926, Crosby was, like so many "hip" musicians, swept away by Armstrong's hit record "Heebie Jeebies." But the sheer lyricism of Crosby's vocal heard here, not to mention the slowed tempo, are integral to the full-bodied "Star Dust" arrangement of Victor Young—complete with suggestive washes of celesta, both in the opening verse ("meadows of my heart" and "a song that will not die") and at the close ("the memory of love's refrain"), as if stars above were still there twinkling.

There is yet another layer of memory that helps define the essence of "Star Dust." It involves a haunting melodic plunge first heard in the key phrase "dreaming of a song," which perhaps serves as a metaphor for star dust touching the heart of the forlorn lover down on earth.[42] Circumstantial evidence points to the likely source as the stop-time chorus from Armstrong's "Potato Head Blues" of May 10, 1927—it predates Carmichael's initial recording by almost six months—where an identical trumpet figure is unmistakably heard. We should recall that Carmichael not only tried to get his hands on every available Armstrong record, he also made frequent trips up to Chicago to hear him in the flesh. More than that, this kind of harmonic usage suggests a prior source for this kind of melodic usage, drawing attention again to the classically trained Lillian Hardin's pivotal role at this time in helping raise Armstrong's general level of musical literacy and knowledge of music theory. Hoagy Carmichael himself has hinted at some of this honing of Armstrong's skills at the hand of Hardin, though without spelling out much in the way of detail: "Lil worked the fat off Louis. She got a book of the standard cornet solos and drilled him. He really worked, even taking lessons from a German down at Kimball Hall."[43]

In the same period of the late 1920s we find another important instance of shared memory that brings together two other intersecting career paths—those of Louis Armstrong and Tommy Dorsey. Dorsey had recently joined forces with the guitarist Eddie Lang, who, like him, had recently left the Whiteman band, shortly after the shooting of *King of Jazz*. A case in point is a 1929 session with Eddie Lang and his Orchestra in which we hear the young Dorsey on trumpet—he was, of course, later identified with the trombone—performing the Billy Rose–Lee David number "Hot Heels," and in the process doing an imitation of Armstrong's solo on the Hot Five "The King of the Zulus" ("At a Chit'lin' Rag").

Not to be ignored are Whiteman-Armstrong cross-influences, which date back to Whiteman's earliest recordings as leader of a fox-trot-focused dance band. His 1920 hit record "Whispering," with its engaging slide whistle solo, was imitated in the 1923 recording of "Sobbin' Blues," in which Armstrong, as sideman in King Oliver's Jazz Band, can be heard performing on both slide whistle and cornet. There are, in addition, Armstrong's 1926 Hot Five recording of "Who'Sit," with its slide whistle chorus played against a gurgling clarinet countermelody, and the 1921 Fanny Brice Ziegfeld Follies showstopper, "My Man," recorded by Whiteman that year with Henry Busse and Hale Byers on trumpet and saxophone. It finds its counterpart in the dialogue, replete with the signature Busse wah-wah imitation, of Don Redman and Coleman Hawkins in Fletcher Henderson's October 1924 recording of "Go 'Long Mule" that was made shortly after Armstrong had joined the trumpet section.[44] In fact, Henderson himself, even before departing his native Georgia for New York, came to relish the sounds of Paul Whiteman and his Orchestra.[45]

It was largely thanks to the initiative of two key people—Jack Kapp and Victor Young—that Crosby's 1931 Brunswick session of "Star Dust" came about at all; and they were individuals whose careers intersected with those of Armstrong, Crosby, and Whiteman in important ways. The producer Jack Kapp (1901–49) had gotten his first taste of the record business in his early teens, working in his family's Chicago store, the Imperial Talking Machine Shop. Here was a man with his finger on the popular pulse—his instincts were reputedly infallible—who was apt to frame things in terms of the accusatory question: "Where's the melody?" He is said to have understood records "the way Irving Thalberg understood movies."[46] During his tenure as general manager at Brunswick, Kapp developed an impressive roster, including, among others, Cab Calloway, Duke Ellington, the Mills Brothers, Guy Lombardo—an avowed favorite—and Victor Young. Familiar with Crosby from his Whiteman days, Kapp had no hesitation in signing him in the spring of 1931 to a six-month contract with a renewal option.

But by the end of 1933 Kapp had moved on to Decca, soon making it the second-biggest label in the United States. He brought a Midas touch to his marketing by pricing his records at only thirty-five cents, while such competitors as Victor and Columbia were charging seventy-five cents. And it all coincided with the repeal of Prohibition in December 1933 just as Kapp began producing precisely the kind of product that operators were looking for to stock their new, proliferating electric multiselection jukeboxes. It was in this context that Kapp was able to promote releases, mainstreaming the work of such musicians as Victor Young, Count Basie, the Andrews Sisters, Jimmy Dorsey, Guy Lombardo, and especially Bing Crosby and Louis Armstrong. The extent of his mainstreaming was such that certain commentators have complained: "Realizing that in Armstrong and Crosby he had the two founding fathers of modern pop music, Kapp devised a way for them to expand both their musical horizons and their popularity, turning them into all things for all people, covering all musical genres."[47] In 1938 Paul Whiteman himself became part of this Decca mix. He had been with Victor from the start of his recording career in 1920, then signing with Columbia eight years later. Now he turned to such repertoire as "I'm Comin' Virginia" and "Aunt Hagar's Blues" (with Jack Teagarden and the Four Modernaires), as well as such middlebrow fare as Gershwin's *Cuban Overture, An American in Paris,* Second Rhapsody—all quite new to him, at least in the recording studio—and his signature piece, *Rhapsody in Blue.*

As for Victor Young, he was immensely successful as a conductor and composer of the middlebrow. By the same token, he shows up only sporadically in standard jazz sources—sometimes out and sometimes in—raising anew the issue of where the lines of category are to be drawn.[48] He came to work on some three hundred films and had to his credit such hits as "Sweet Sue," "Stella by Starlight," and "My Foolish Heart," all of which became jazz standards; he was also a man with whom Bing Crosby enjoyed an especially close, long-lasting professional rapport. And like Paul Whiteman, he was a classically trained violinist—he had studied in Poland at the Warsaw Conservatory—and earlier on had entertained serious hopes of a solo career, only to be lured away after World War I by the worlds of dance and movie theater orchestras. While direct contact between Young and Whiteman appears to have been sporadic at best, Victor Young did contribute his arrangement of "Valencia" to Whiteman's Fifth Experiment in Modern Music (Carnegie Hall, January 25, 1933)—sharing program billing with William Grant Still and Ferde Grofé among others—and also later premiered his hit-to-be "Stella by Starlight" on one of Whiteman's Blue Network broadcasts of 1944.

Outside of the pieces in the Hoagy Carmichael canon already discussed at some length, Victor Young's "Sweet Sue" stands as one of several core repertory numbers common to both Whiteman and Armstrong. Published in April 1928, it was recorded by Whiteman barely five months later, then again in late 1932, while Armstrong first put it on wax in 1933—one of only three versions in his entire discography. The differences between Whiteman's and Armstrong's treatments could not be more telling as we compare Whiteman's performance of September 18, 1928, with Armstrong's dating from April 26, 1933.

Running to some four and a half minutes and originally issued in a twelve-inch recording, Whiteman's 1928 recording is essentially an exercise in "symphonic jazz" rather than a version made for dancing. The arrangement by Bill Challis is among the more elaborate that he created to showcase the special gifts of Bix Beiderbecke while also allowing for solo and sectional turns by members of Whiteman's large ensemble. The introduction, including the opening verse, adroitly contrasts brass colors, the reed section (not to mention solos for oboe—a relative rarity), and strings, to evoke an old-time, somewhat saccharine quality. Once the first chorus begins, an imaginatively voiced muted trombone quartet—the melody is in the middle voice—wafts one along to a comfortable fox-trot beat. The transition which follows recalls much of the opening material, but with the added star dust of celesta sound. A brief bridge passage for solo piano moves the music a half-step higher—from C to D-flat, the key of choice for Jack Fulton as he sings the lyrics of Will Harris in his sweet, effeminate style to the celesta countermelody and with

rhythmic underpinning on piano. Another transition follows, this one bringing some modern-sounding brass which "foreshadow[s] swing band writing
in a rather remarkable way."[49] We then arrive at the third and final chorus (in
A-flat), as Beiderbecke does his hot uptempo star-turn playing—"away from
the score," as Armstrong would say—with the support of only the rhythm
section. Things are then neatly wrapped up in a coda by the full ensemble.

There is a quirky anecdote about a Whiteman radio performance of
"Sweet Sue" some years later, on the Philco Radio Hall of Fame in 1944. It
harks back to the kind of question Jack Kapp would repeatedly ask. Whiteman
had decided to introduce a "Now and Then" segment as an audience-building
feature, juxtaposing original and updated arrangements of such numbers as
"Whispering," "Avalon," and "Sweet Sue." On one such occasion, a somewhat
querulous Eddie Condon, who was in the studio audience, was heard to com-
plain to his companion: "They're always asking me: 'Where's the melody?'
Now, I'm asking, 'Where the hell's the melody up there with those guys?'"[50]
Incidentally, back in March 1929, when Armstrong was beginning to record
more mainstream pop material such as "I Can't Give You Anything But Love,"
the banjo player Condon was one of his sidemen, together with Jack Teagarden and Eddie Lang, in one of the first interracial jazz ensembles.

Armstrong's 1933 recording of "Sweet Sue" tells a very different story. It
is faster-paced, clocking in at just under two-thirds the length of Whiteman's
version, and in his hands the song becomes hilarious—a mischievous statement reeking of marijuana! Its central feature is a "viper's chorus" in which
Armstrong trades phrases of pig Latin scat—"get a load of this viper's language"—with Budd Johnson, "my tenor man." Johnson was a highly accomplished clarinet and tenor sax player as well as an arranger. And *viper*, of
course, was jargon for marijuana smoker. Buttressing all this "viper's" business are an opening vocal and an out chorus on trumpet, both delivered with
panache by Armstrong.

Needless to say, what is deliciously affirmed here is Armstrong's professional self-image as "actor and musician," as one who was forever "laying it
on the public." And the recording dates from a time when memory was surely
still fresh of Armstrong's nine days in jail after having been busted for smoking marijuana in the parking lot of Frank Sebastian's Cotton Club in Culver
City, California.[51] In fact, during the period that this recording was made, on
April 26, 1933, two days after their making "Laughin' Louie," Armstrong was
working with a group of fellow "vipers": in addition to Budd Johnson, the
trumpet player Zilner Randolph, the pianist Teddy Wilson, and the reed
player Scoville Brown. As Budd Johnson has recalled: "We wouldn't allow

anybody in the recording sessions because Louis would like to get high, and he'd like for the band to get high. So he says, 'We're going to record "Laughin' Louie" today, gentlemen. I want everybody to smoke a joint.' . . . We were floating when we made that 'Laughin' Louie' and Louis played that trumpet like a bird."[52]

At first blush, Victor Young's "Sweet Sue" is what might be called a "treacle title." If simply taken together with the original lyrics, which can sometimes border on musical molasses, it becomes sticky business trying to separate the saccharine from the sentimental; its opening phrase is characteristic—"Ev'ry star above knows the one I love, Sweet Sue, just you. / And the moon up high knows the reason why, Sweet Sue, just you." But at the same time it actually belongs to a huge body of tunes with the "sweet" epithet, such as "Sweet Lorraine," "Sweet Adeline," "Sweet Baby Doll," "Sweet Savannah Sue," as well as two numbers by the songwriter Maceo Pinkard, a key figure in African-American musical theater of the first quarter of the twentieth century—"Sweet Georgia Brown," from the show *Bubbling Brown Sugar*, and the more mainstream "Sugar"—where issues of race and skin color are never too far behind.

The recorded performance history of "Sugar," as successively interpreted by Whiteman (1928), by Armstrong (1946), and finally by the duo of Armstrong and Crosby (1960), tells a fascinating story of changing times. For all the skill the Challis arrangement for Whiteman shows in handling a large ensemble and spotlighting key soloists, it is very much a period piece. It is essentially a dance number, with plenty of pep provided by the rhythm section and the bouncing bass of the tuba, and conforms to the prescribed length of around three minutes for a ten-inch "78" of the day. The brief introduction evokes an impressionistic atmosphere with its close voicing of parallel chords in the upper brass and reeds, while also hinting at harmonic wisps of Beiderbecke's piano solo, "In a Mist," of the previous year. The four choruses are notable for the way they provide for variety "inside the strain," the second and third in particular. It is there that we are treated to three cornet solos by Beiderbecke alternating with ones by Bill Rank on trombone and Frank Trumbauer on clarinet. It is a general pattern that is carried through the out chorus as well, where the string sound is contrasted with solo turns on saxophone and cornet.

Somewhat surprising is that Armstrong's 1946 version of this 1927 song was the first he ever recorded. But how exactly this came about remains a mystery. Leonard Feather, the producer of this session, might have brought it to his attention. Feather, we will recall, was a highly visible champion of jazz at the time. In 1942 he had initiated with Robert Goffin the highly publicized adult education jazz lecture series at New York's New School for Social Research, and, with the enthusiastic support of Arnold Gingrich, editor of *Esquire*, had launched the annual critics' poll in the magazine, not to mention the "Esquire All Stars" concerts starting in 1944. And Armstrong himself was in 1946 on the cusp of change, looking to the past as well as to the future. In fact, the date of this Los Angeles session, September 6, 1946, coincided with the start of shooting in Hollywood for the movie *New Orleans,* that fanciful, romanticized account of jazz in its Storyville days. The recording ensemble assembled for the occasion, dubbed Louis Armstrong and his Hot Seven, was unmistakably a throwback to his heady days in 1920s Chicago, while at the same time, Janus-like, looking ahead in its instrumentation to his All Stars, the combo to be launched in 1947. Indeed, there was an intricate web of crisscrossing career trajectories, something that was key in illuminating intersecting personal relationships, some of many years' standing. Musicians for the "Sugar" session, such as the reed player Barney Bigard, the drummer Zutty Singleton, and the bassist Red Callender were known quantities to Armstrong. They were tried and true sidemen who had worked extensively with him, whether in the early Chicago days or when he had fronted a big band through the 1930s. Along with Billie Holiday, they were all busy in Hollywood that fall of 1946, filming *New Orleans.* Holiday herself, as we have seen, had recently collaborated with Paul Whiteman in the studios of Capitol Records in Los Angeles, turning out such numbers as "Trav'lin' Light" to great acclaim. And Barney Bigard, whose credits included some fifteen years with Duke Ellington and who was soon to enjoy a tenure of about the same duration with Armstrong's All Stars, had recently appeared with Louis Armstrong, Jack Teagarden, and Whiteman's one-time star vocalist Mildred Bailey at the 1944 First Esquire All American Jazz Concert at New York's Metropolitan Opera House.

Armstrong's recording here amply demonstrates his unique dual gifts as the Gabriel of trumpet players and as vocalist. The basic sentiment of the song is captured in the opening chorus, as the sound of Armstrong's richly resonant trumpet fills one's ears, with the clarinet and trombone providing harmony in sustained notes, while the rhythm section maintains a perky but steady four beats to the bar. The second chorus, Armstrong's vocal, sweet and without guile, opens with the phrase:

Oh sugar, I call my baby my sugar.
I never maybe my sugar, because my sugar is so confectionary.

Funny, she never asked for my money,
All I can give her is honey . . .

There are solo turns by trombone and clarinet in the third chorus, followed by an out chorus—actually a half-chorus, in which Armstrong returns in his solo glory, with the final eight bars given over to a joyous burst of Dixieland polyphony.

The Armstrong-Crosby "Sugar" session of 1960 for MGM brings together several shards of shared memory—career paths, traditions of the minstrel show, and hints of Rhythm Boys routines of earlier Whiteman days, all neatly wrapped in an arrangement by Johnny Mercer, a man who had been given a boost back in 1934 when he was one of Whiteman's vocalists. Mercer was to return the favor by having Whiteman record for his newly established label of Capitol Records, which he had cofounded with Buddy de Silva in 1942. Mercer's plush big band arrangement, heard to full advantage in the brief introduction, in interludes, and in the out chorus, gives Armstrong and Crosby ample room to breathe in the course of four choruses. Crosby takes the first of these, his vocal tinged with blues color and hints of the sound he had cultivated so well in such earlier Whiteman recordings as "Mississippi Mud" or "Tain't So, Honey, Tain't So." With the second chorus comes a compelling statement of how the minstrel show tradition of exchanges between the straight man (interlocutor) and the end man can become transmogrified. It has here become a routine filtered through the experience of Crosby's work with Bob Hope on all those *Road* movies from the 1940s and 1950s. More than that, it seems to gently poke fun at popular TV shows of the 1950s, especially those with intellectual pretensions—quiz shows like "Twenty Questions" and perhaps even the scandalous "Twenty-One" that saw the meteoric rise and fall of the Columbia University professor Charles Van Doren during the 1956–57 season. Even more to the point, the aggressively promoted sugarless, saccharin-based sweetener Sweet 'n Low appeared in 1958. So what one hears in this second chorus is a series of exchanges as a single word or phrase sung by Armstrong elicits a professorial-sounding comment spoken by Crosby. It all goes something like this:

Sugar
THAT'S A SIMPLE CARBOHYDRATE
I call my baby my Sugar
GLUCOSE, DEXTROSE, LACTOSE
I never maybe my Sugar
THEN, OF COURSE, THERE'S SUCARYL FOR WEIGHT WATCHERS.

In the third chorus Armstrong expands on matters with his melodic para-phrase on trumpet as Crosby chimes in with his countermelody—"Sugar's what she puts in my coffee, a lump and a half will do, then stir it up—dining like a real gourmet." And by the time we arrive at the out chorus Armstrong's vocals have become humorously self-referential, opening with some charac-teristic punning—"Sugar raises Cain with my diet"—and continuing with "the calories break my heart" and "Sugar's got to be my downfall"; we should recall that he and Lucille had recently gone public with their *Lose Weight the Satchmo Way.*[53] Armstrong and Crosby then go out in a blaze of glory as they sing in unison "unadulterated and crystalline, every bit sweet and superfine, that ever-loving Sugar of mine."

All is sweet in the world of "Sugar." But more often than not, what lingers in the human breast are those "torch songs," those statements of love gone sour, love unrequited, and a sense of abandonment. No song in the Whiteman-Armstrong canon epitomizes these qualities better than "Body and Soul," which features one of the most beloved and most-played melodies in jazz. It has been characterized as feeling "more like a pop tune that already has its jazz ornamentations built into it," with richly fertile harmonies to match.[54] The music is by Johnny W. Green, who first came to public attention around 1922, when he was a fourteen-year-old pianist leading a juvenile dance band on local New York radio. By the summer of 1927, already a junior in economics at Harvard, he was working in Chicago as an arranger for Guy Lombardo, the bandleader so beloved of both Whiteman and Armstrong. The following year, thanks to a nudge or two from Guy Lombardo and his brother Carmen, Green copyrighted what proved to be his first hit, "Coquette." It be-came a core repertory standard following the first-ever recording made of it by Whiteman in 1928. Whiteman was soon to promote other Green works as well, most notably *Night Club,* a series of six Gershwinesque impressions of a cabaret—from 7 P.M. to 2 A.M.—composed for three pianos and orchestra, which premiered at Whiteman's Fifth Experiment in Modern Music, Carne-gie Hall, January 25, 1933.

This was a concert vividly illustrating Whiteman's commitment to sym-phonic jazz and the cultivation of the middlebrow. The program, as we have seen, also included William Grant Still's "Land of Superstition" from *Africa,* and was replete with such programmatic pieces as Ferde Grofé's *Tabloid—Four Pictures of a Modern Newspaper,* his increasingly popular "On the Trail" from his *Grand Canyon Suite,* and numbers like Robert Braine's *Concerto in Jazz,* "The Peanut Vendor," "Valencia," and a pop arrangement of Franz Liszt's "Liebestraum."

In the early 1920s the visiting musical comedy star Gertrude Lawrence had been sufficiently impressed by Johnny Green, this "musical boy wonder," to hire him as her accompanist. Lawrence was soon to make a dramatic splash in Gershwin's 1927 *Oh, Kay!*—especially with the showstopper "Someone to Watch Over Me"—and shortly thereafter in Noël Coward's *Private Lives,* which set both London's West End and New York's Broadway on fire. Shortly before her premature death Gertrude Lawrence took the female lead of Anna opposite Yul Brynner's King of Siam in Rodgers and Hammerstein's *The King and I* (1951). By the late 1920s Green had started working with two lyricists, Edward Heyman and Robert Sour. Learning of this budding songwriting team, Gertrude Lawrence put in a request for new material, and one of the songs that came about was "Body and Soul." So taken was she with the piece that she not only sang it but, as Green later put it, decided to buy "an interest in this song at a low but welcome figure."[55] She promptly took it back to London, where it was soon broadcast, and she recorded it twice by the end of March 1930.

The song's title and lyrics have long been associated with the theme of love unrequited. As we learn from the opening quatrain of the chorus:

> My days have grown so lonely
> For I've lost my one and only
> My pride has been humbled
> But I'm yours body and soul.

The words "body and soul" have a much deeper resonance, having long been inseparable from the very idea of survival itself, the struggle to keep body and soul together. In terms of the black experience, there is no better example in American literature than *Uncle Tom's Cabin*, in which Uncle Tom tells Simon Legree: "My body may belong to you, but my soul belongs to God." And closer to the time of the song's creation, we have the 1925 Oscar Micheaux movie *Body and Soul*, which featured Paul Robeson in the dual role of a fast-talking, glib pastor—a wolf in sheep's clothing—and his brother, the pure innocent.

The early history of "Body and Soul" is a story of a certain transatlantic rivalry just as the big band era was being born in the United States, and of the involvement of Whiteman and Armstrong in promoting it. On September 10 and October 9, 1930, barely a month apart, but at opposite ends of the continental United States, Whiteman and Armstrong recorded their respective versions in New York and Los Angeles. Given its strong fox-trot beat and its conventional duration of around three minutes, it is tempting to hear Whiteman's rendition of "Body and Soul" as primarily a dance number. But the way the arrangement knits together the introduction, the initial chorus, a fairly lengthy transition, and the subsequent out chorus represents a small triumph of musical skill while also showing acute sensitivity to the lyrics. The tonally unstable introduction itself is built on fragments of the bridge—"What lies before me / The future is stormy"—and the opening phrase of the chorus as it enters off the beat. Running just under half a minute, this introduction serves as a metaphor for the nervous anxiety of our abandoned lover, just as the orchestration shifts every two bars. When Jack Fulton takes the opening chorus, whatever his effeminate sound might lack in expressiveness is compensated for at least in part by the cushion of strings, the rock-steady rhythm, and punctuating strokes on vibraphone. The out chorus, in a contrasting key, epitomizes Whiteman's passion for variety "inside the strain" as the saxophone section is brought into play, followed by a hot cornet solo in the bridge by Bix Beiderbecke's successor and near-clone, Andy Secrest.[56]

Armstrong's version has the distinction of being the first on record showcasing a major jazz soloist.[57] It also came at a time when, more than ever, he was pushing the envelope of category, recording such numbers as "Blue Yodel No. 9" with the country music singer and guitarist Jimmie Rodgers and the Cuban rumba hit "El Manisero" ("The Peanut Vendor"). Following a brief introduction poignantly mixing minor with major, we hear Armstrong taking the opening chorus and doing something that was a real rarity for him, playing the trumpet with straight mute. It is an inspired touch that perfectly captures the sense of vulnerability of the song's lyrics. The expressive power is further enhanced as Armstrong, playing behind the beat, is supported by the warm sound of the saxophone choir—a sonority associated with Guy Lombardo. When Armstrong takes the vocals in the second chorus, we are treated to another masterstroke as he lags behind a muted trumpet on the bandstand, singing about how he has grown so lonely and lost his one and only, inserting an "oh babe." There is a certain lack of resolution appropriate to the sentiments of the song, as they then all go out with a half-chorus and tag.

Comparing these Whiteman and Armstrong performances of "Body and Soul," not to mention their renditions of any number of other standards, inevitably throws into bold relief certain basic differences in their style. As the quintessential trumpet soloist and vocalist, Armstrong, the self-identified actor and musician, was committed to "laying it on the public" and was content to depend on the backing of a band playing stock arrangements much of the time. While he certainly wanted to be paid his fair share, Armstrong forever gave relatively low priority to money matters. His priorities were set early on, dating back to his early days in the New Orleans Colored Waif's Home; his instrument became his talisman. We recall that it was then that his life was transformed when he was made leader of the band—"I jumped straight into the air"; he felt real pride in his position as bugler, shining the instrument and making it "the gleaming bright instrument instead of the old filthy green one." And as he later said: "I have always been wrapped up in my music and no woman in the world can change that. Right until this day my horn comes first."[58] Whiteman, however, as the nonpareil entrepreneur-promoter-bandleader, one who uniquely fused a shrewd business sense with bonhomie, was never really a soloist at all but rather placed his stock in the work of a raft of arrangers and star instrumentalists on his payroll. In his focus on the ensemble, on "symphonic jazz," and the showcasing of soloists, he attached a much lower priority to his vocalists. Aside from the brief tenures of Bing Crosby and the Rhythm Boys, or Mildred Bailey, or his occasional work with a singer of the stature of Billie Holiday, we find Whiteman offering his public the nondescript and distinctly unmemorable efforts of a Jack Fulton, Austin "Skin" Young, Peggy Healy, Jane Vance, or others. Yet he was not one to stand still; he was forever alert to new possibilities and ways of reaching his public.

Within the core repertory as a whole there is no standard that can quite match W. C. Handy's "St. Louis Blues." Published in 1914, it became the biggest hit in the annals of jazz discography, with 165 recordings tabulated for the period ending in 1942.[59] There are three different recordings of it issued for Whiteman between 1926 and 1938, while Armstrong can claim a staggering total of forty versions in the course of his career. At the same time, its composer, William Christopher Handy (1873–1958), also a cornetist, bandleader, and one who spent much of his life in the music-publishing business, represents something of a paradox—a paradox touching on crucial issues of class, race, musical category, and shared memory. Similarly, "St. Louis Blues" itself is an anomaly in its combination of blues and tango elements, and its history, no less than the cultural memory into which Handy himself tapped, provides the context in which to properly compare the respective performances by Whiteman and Armstrong. Even though he has long held the iconic status of "Father of the Blues"—and in 1969 the U.S. Postal Service issued a stamp perpetuating that very image—Handy has also been judged, perhaps too harshly, as a "black Rockefeller [who] like the oil baron . . . made his pile by tapping into natural resources, in this case not in the ground but in the air . . . the melodies that emanated from his own people."[60]

Coming from the black upper class in Florence, Alabama—his grandfather and father were Methodist ministers—Handy received precious little encouragement from parents or teachers to pursue a career in music. "Son, I'd rather see you in a hearse," his father told him. "I'd rather follow you to the graveyard than to hear that you had become a musician."[61] Unbowed, the young Handy began operating in secret; he acquired a cornet and began taking lessons at a local barber shop. By his mid-teens he had taught himself to play well enough to join a touring minstrel troupe. This training, combined with what he had learned from singing in the choir of Florence District School for Negroes, not to mention a burning ambition, was enough to get him started. In 1896 he became cornetist with Mahara's Minstrels. Subsequently he became bandleader, and with the troupe toured widely in the United States, Canada, Mexico, and Cuba, while also acquiring valuable experience in arranging, composing, and conducting. In addition, these years included a stint as bandmaster at Alabama A & M College in Montgomery. Throughout this period, into the first decade of the twentieth century, his focus was squarely on music for the minstrel troupe or on organizing, booking, or leading military and dance bands.

Most important, Handy came into his own at a time when the word *jazz* did not even exist. As he recalled in an interview with Leonard Feather: "I've played with many novelty musicians. Even in the minstrel days we played music similar to jazz, but we didn't call it jazz."[62] In a sense he stumbled upon it, an experience that suggests a rough parallel to what transformed Whiteman's life on California's Barbary Coast. In his autobiography, *Father of the Blues*, Handy tells the story of what happened when he and his band—"all musicians who bowed strictly to the authority of printed notes"—showed up for a dance gig in Cleveland, Mississippi. Sometime during the evening "an odd request" reached the bandstand: more of "our native music." The band tried to oblige with "an old-time Southern melody, a melody more sophisticated than native," but was greeted by another request for a local colored band to come up and play some dances. Handy and his men agreed to take a break, allowing an instrumental trio to take over the stage with "a battered guitar, a mandolin and a worn-out bass." What Handy heard was "one of those over-and-over strains. . . . Thump-thump-thump went their feet on the floor. Their eyes rolled. Their shoulders swayed." Something then happened that stayed with him for life. Musically literate and upwardly mobile, he came to realize the extent to which a folk music tradition was ripe for commercial exploitation. Speaking of this tradition, Handy has confessed that each one of his blues "is based on some old Negro song of the South—some old song that is a part of the memories of my childhood and of my race."

A rain of silver dollars began to fall around the outlandish, stomping feet. The dancers went wild. Dollars, quarters, halves—the shower grew heavier and continued so long I strained my neck to get a better look. There before the boys lay more money than my nine musicians were being paid for the entire engagement. Then I saw the beauty of primitive music. They had the stuff the people wanted. It touched the spot. Their music wanted polishing, but it contained the essence. Folks would pay money for it. The old conventional music was well and good—but there was no virtue in being blind when you had good eyes. That night a composer was born, an *American* composer.[63]

A good part of "St. Louis Blues" was adapted from the "primitive music" Handy had heard, music from his memory bank that was given some "polishing," with the sheet music then being published by his company in 1914—a piece that some forty years later was earning Handy annual royalties in the range of $25,000. This blues, in which his avowed aim was to "combine ragtime syncopation with a real melody in the spiritual tradition," consists of three discrete elements, each of them vitally important in helping one appreciate the differing interpretations by Whiteman and Armstrong.[64]

The first part is made up of two twelve-bar choruses, each sung to a single rhymed couplet with the first line repeated—fairly standard—starting with "I hate to see de evenin' sun go down." It is a phrase resonant with the personal memory of hard times, harking back to a point when Handy and his group were down on their luck and had to sleep "on the cobbles down by the river in St. Louis." What follows is an echo of something Handy heard in Havana at the turn of the century in the course of his Cuban tour with his minstrel troupe, a sixteen-measure tango (or the eponymous habanera). It is sung to a quatrain consisting of two rhymed couplets introduced by the phrase "St. Louis woman wid her diamon' rings . . . " New material then comes with yet another twelve-bar blues and with three rhyming lines of text containing the "hook" of the song. "Got de St. Louis blues, jes as blue as I can be / Dat man got a heart lak a rock cast in de sea . . . " Handy has claimed that the second line, in particular, was inspired by a black St. Louis woman he ran into on the city's streets who was distraught over the cold indifference of her absentee husband.

Somewhat ironically, Handy, the entrepreneurial, literate black—he was sometimes called "Fess" ("professor") for that reason—used dialect in the lyrics precisely because that was what was marketable. A parallel can be drawn with Eubie Blake's insistence, in preparing for performances of *Shuffle Along,* that his orchestra perform the score from memory so as to foster the myth of blacks as illiterate creatures of instinct. Handy was also mindful of expressive values. "Negro intellectuals were turning from dialect in poetry as employed by Paul Lawrence Dunbar. I couldn't follow them, for I felt then, as I feel now, that certain words of Negro dialect are more musical and more expressive than pure English."[65] Perhaps even more fascinating is that the music for this final strain was apparently borrowed from a Handy instrumental number, "Jogo Blues"—"jogo" is black jive for "colored"—which in turn, according to one source, was based on a melody he heard as a boy, one his preacher sang when he passed around the collection plate.[66] But because this specific blues strain is riff-based and often sounds so rhythmically energized, there are those who speculate that it might have helped spark such dance crazes as the shimmy and such "Shim-Me-Sha-Wabble." In short, these elements play out in strikingly different ways in the Whiteman and Armstrong recordings under discussion, which span almost thirty years—to riff on the blues or tango qualities.

Speaking of the tango, Handy himself has written about what he saw happening on the dance floor "at a sort of sun-tanned Coney Island" in Memphis. Talking about the dancers' response to a number by William H. Tyers— a colleague of James Reese Europe—and the effect on the tango rhythm, he observed "that there was a sudden, proud and graceful reaction to the rhythm. Was it an accident, or could the response be traced to a real but hidden cause? I wondered. White dancers . . . took the number in stride. I began to suspect that perhaps there was something Negroid in that beat, something that quickened the blood."[67] Acting on his conviction, he soon introduced the rhythm into such compositions as "St. Louis Blues." Once again, there is an analogy to be made, this time with a point raised earlier about Paul Whiteman. At locales like New York's Palais Royale, Whiteman would seek to be on the same level, close to the dancers, rather than being isolated on the stage. By that means "he personalized the band by channeling the enthusiasm of the dancers to the players."[68]

The earliest of the recordings of "St. Louis Blues" under discussion is Armstrong's classic version of January 14, 1925, made in New York with Bessie Smith in one of her most memorable sessions. It came at a point when Armstrong was with Fletcher Henderson and attests to the intense pace and work ethic that defined Armstrong's life. It also reminds us of how various career trajectories could intersect. We should recall that this session came about shortly after he had arrived in New York and been offered work by Clarence Williams, the pianist-composer-entrepreneur from New Orleans. Now installed as head of the Clarence Williams Publishing Company in the Gaiety

Theater Building at 1547 Broadway, a few blocks down from the Roseland Ballroom, where Armstrong was appearing with Henderson's band, Williams was working out of a building that was a hub of the African-American entertainment business. Bert Williams, Will Vodery, and the Pace and Handy Music Company maintained their offices there.

Louis Armstrong and Bessie Smith complement each other perfectly, with harmonic backing provided by Fred Longshaw on reed organ. They open with a double statement of the first blues—that is, two choruses of twelve bars each, using the same music, but sung to different lyrics, starting, respectively, with "I hate to see that evenin' sun go down," and "Feelin' tomorrow lak I feel today." What follow are the sixteen-measure tango ("St. Louis woman wears her diamon' rings") and the second blues ("Got the St. Louis blues, jes as blue as I can be"). The result is a rendition of poignant power, slow and pensive, as Smith and Armstrong linger over each phrase, underscoring the melodic and spiritual qualities of the piece. With Whiteman's purely instrumental version, however (March 29, 1926), the piece has become a richly orchestrated but snappy tango dance number, obsessed with the "Latin tinge"; it is replete with opening castanets, touches of accordion—with hints of "Lady of Spain"—and cloying, mock-sentimental breaks on piano. Placed in context, this particular version is animated by much the same rhythmic vitality as the 1925 hit "Jalousie," the "tango tzigane" of Danish composer Jacob Gade.

With his 1929 version, Armstrong has moved to a very different universe from the one he inhabited some four years earlier, with perhaps a hint of Whiteman influence. Certainly "St. Louis Blues" has now become an ebullient dance number fusing a Latin quality with a gutsy, funky blues sound, to the point of anticipating what was to come more than twenty years later with early rock 'n' roll, and even the closing choruses of such Miles Davis classics as "Walkin'." Plunging in with half of the tango chorus, Armstrong and his Orchestra launch into two statements of the first blues—an exercise in rollicking Dixieland polyphony. What follows is the tango chorus on the earthy gutbucket trombone of J. C. Higginbotham, backed by the incisive castanets of Paul Barbarin. The balance of the performance is a wonderful riff—good for seven choruses—on the second of the blues. Armstrong does a star turn on vocals, throwing in some scat for good measure, with some animated responses from Henry "Red" Allen on trumpet. After more of Higginbotham and some bluesy business, we arrive at the two climactic choruses where Armstrong can be heard punching out no fewer than twenty-one high Gs and five high Ds.

Friday night, December 2, 1932, found Paul Whiteman and his Orchestra catering to the genteel crowd at New York's Biltmore Hotel. What has been preserved for posterity is a fast-paced recorded medley of twelve selections which runs just under ten minutes and was designed by Victor to neatly fit on both sides of a twelve-inch 78 rpm disc. Rich in memory and variety, Whiteman's medley includes such early signature pieces as "Whispering," "Japanese Sandman," and "When Day Is Done." Also to be heard is "Mississippi Mud," a onetime specialty of Bing Crosby, Harry Barris, and Al Rinker, but performed here by a reconstituted Rhythm Boys, the original group having long since departed. Sandwiched between "When Day Is Done" and "Sweet Sue" is a truncated "St. Louis Blues" running to slightly over one minute and including the tango introduction and two statements of the second blues chorus. Despite its relative brevity, this rendition captures very well the vocal of Irene Taylor, who does a creditable job of imitating the nuances of a black-inflected bluesy sound.[69]

There are two Armstrong performances of "St. Louis Blues" from the 1950s that are especially resonant with memory. The first of these, from July 13, 1954, is the opening track on a major retrospective album of Handy standards, and one of the greatest in the annals of jazz discography, issued by Columbia Records in its Great Jazz Composers Series. A project of the veteran producer George Avakian, it brings together Louis Armstrong, Velma Middleton, and the All Stars for a marathon version of "St. Louis Blues" running to about nine minutes and taking advantage of what was then the relatively new medium of the long-playing record. All the vital ingredients are kept in wonderful balance: the glorious sound of Armstrong's solo trumpet, Middleton's down-home blues feeling, Armstrong's own vocal, his vaudeville-inspired duet with Middleton, the wailing glissando of Barney Bigard's clarinet, the gutbucket sound of Trummy Young's trombone, the climactic Dixieland polyphony of the final choruses, and the drum break of Barrett Deems.

George Avakian has vividly captured the emotions flooding the studio during playback as the aging W. C. Handy was overwhelmed by what he heard, Louis Armstrong at his side:

Up on the top floor of the Columbia Records building on upper Times Square, in a studio converted to an editing room, a handsome old gentleman sat listening to the tapes of this record, tears streaming from his sightless eyes. "I never thought I'd hear my blues like this," W. C. Handy said again and again. "Truly wonderful! Truly wonderful! Nobody could have done it but my boy Louis!" Louis Armstrong sat at his side, doing quite a job of looking proud and

5.3 Armstrong (wearing Star of David necklace), W. C. Handy, and George Avakian in studios of Columbia Records, July 1954. Institute of Jazz Studies, Rutgers University.

modest at the same time. He kept saying what fun the sessions had been. "Ain't no work, making records like this! Them old time good ones, they play themselves, Mr. Handy. You get to blowing those beautiful changes right, and you have to play good. We was just having a ball, that's all."[70]

Emotions ran high again on July 16, 1956, when Handy made what was one of his last public appearances, two years before his death. Performing "St. Louis Blues" at New York's Lewisohn Stadium were Louis Armstrong and the All Stars with members of the New York Philharmonic under Leonard Bernstein. The event was filmed by CBS-TV as part of *Satchmo the Great,* a tribute to Armstrong covering his world tour of 1955–56, with interviews and commentary by Edward R. Murrow. While it is tempting for certain purists to dismiss "St. Louis Blues (Concerto Grosso)" as an overblown affair and a rather pretentious effort at symphonic jazz, the performance does give ample latitude to Armstrong and the All Stars, providing for some glorious solo moments as Armstrong's trumpet soars above the orchestra. Besides, Handy himself has spoken most positively about this kind of jazz. His memories of Paul White-man and his approach to symphonic jazz, let alone his treatment of "St. Louis Blues," all attest to this. Though initially skeptical about James Weldon Johnson's prediction that the blues would form the basis for symphonic structure, Handy later admitted to having been proven wrong.[71] "His [Johnson's] prophecy was fulfilled when Paul Whiteman played a program at Carnegie Hall a few years later, where for the first time I heard and enjoyed Gershwin's *Rhapsody in Blue* with Gershwin at the piano. Whiteman has played and recorded many symphonic arrangements of "St. Louis Blues," but to my mind his most outstanding arrangement was played at the Hippodrome, December 1, 1936, by his orchestra in combination with the Philadelphia Orchestra."[72]

Handy has also expressed warm memories of "when I dined at the home of a friend in the company of Gershwin . . . and Whiteman, and of how we had discussed the great potentialities and possibilities of American music." Finally, Handy fondly remembered an episode at the Memphis Cotton Carnival of 1936, where he was the toast of the town: at the Floral Ball in the Municipal Auditorium, "amidst five thousand enthusiastic cheering people," Paul Whiteman and his orchestra struck up "St. Louis Blues." He added: "Due, however, to faulty vision which I feared would prevent proper reading of the score, I declined Whiteman's proffered baton as the press photographers snapped us there in front of his band."[73]

Ranking a fairly close second to "St. Louis Blues" within the core repertory is "Tiger Rag," with a total of 136 recordings for the period ending in 1942. Discographic tabulations alone, however, barely begin to tell the story of this piece and all that it represents in the way of shared memory. In truth, the origins of "Tiger Rag" are understood to date in part from a pre-twentieth-century French quadrille, with subsequent adaptations and additions—"Praline" (or "No. 2 Rag") among them—being made by a range of New Orleans musicians, presumably within the first two decades of the twentieth century. In the process this standard took shape as essentially a multistrain piece in the general spirit of a rag, with the third strain becoming especially memorable for the tiger "growl" on trombone and the band's response, "Hold that tiger!" We should recall too that this development coincided with a mercurial period of change for what was primarily an aural tradition—the very word *jazz* had barely gained currency and at best signified something peppy and uptempo. And it was within this general context that rival claims to authorship could erupt, whether by the Crescent City's African-American, Creole, or Italian-American musicians in the person of Bunk Johnson, Jelly Roll Morton, or Nick LaRocca, cornetist of Original Dixieland Jazz Band fame, to name a few.

The initial ODJB recording of March 25, 1918, in all its visceral and wild abandon, became identified with early Dixieland, exciting both the young Louis Armstrong—we know he owned their recordings at the time of their initial release, when he first acquired a wind-up Victrola—and Bix Beiderbecke, who began by learning "Tiger Rag" on the piano before teaching himself the notes on the cornet. We come across the first recorded versions by Armstrong and Whiteman some twelve years later, both of them released and produced in New York within a little more than two months of each other, on May 4 and July 25, 1930, respectively.[74] Armstrong was to record it thirty-five more times, the last time in 1968, three years before his death.

Armstrong's 1930 rendition, in the same driving duple ragtime rhythm as the ODJB original, but even faster by a hair or two, provides for not only some impressive clarinet acrobatics and solos on trombone and saxophone but also riveting work by Armstrong. His closing choruses serve as a fascinating demonstration of how he was able to draw upon his rich store of memory by superimposing on the original chord changes a series of quotations from three discernible sources: "Irish Washerwoman," "Singin' in the Rain," and "Vesti la giubba" from Leoncavallo's *Pagliacci*.[75] There were often times when Armstrong's performances could pander to the primitive, as we learn from this spoken introduction to a 1932 version: "Now ladies and gentlemen, we have a little novelty here for you this evening. We're goin' to take a little trip through the jungles you know, and we want you all to travel with us. Because that tiger's running so fast . . . takes about seven choruses to catch that baby. So I want you all to count with me. I'm goin', I'm goin'."[76] Then there were reportedly those occasions when Armstrong's wild ride could push some of his sidemen over the edge: "He'd make me so mad on 'Tiger Rag' that I wouldn't know what to do. He'd want me to ride the cymbals on the last three choruses. I'd grab the cymbal around the eighth chorus and start riding it, and by the end of the tenth it would sound good to him and he'd hit with one finger, which would mean one more chorus . . . and he'd play ten more choruses. . . . That guy worked me to death."[77]

By contrast, Whiteman's "Tiger Rag" emphasizes the skill of his large ensemble. An arrangement by Roy Bargy for eighteen pieces, it is a tour de force of timbral and textural variety, all of it driven by the brisk rhythm of the initial ODJB recording. The music is replete with clarinet breaks in the old-time New Orleans tradition, the "trading of twos"—two-measure exchanges by brass and reeds—a stunning chorus of feathery lightness showcasing the reeds, "novelty" circuslike effects as brass phrases are punctuated by gong, crash cymbal, or slide whistle, and the galloping rhythm of the "hold-that-tiger" chorus. Is the beast, one wonders, perhaps going to get away? What we do know is that this Whiteman recording from 1930 represents but one layer in his performance history of "Tiger Rag." In a Don Redman arrangement of "Sensation Stomp" performed by the Whiteman forces in a recording of August 11, 1927, the group can be heard playing with stunning virtuosity at full throttle. About a minute and a half into the piece Jimmy Dorsey treats us to an entire chorus built on the chords of "Tiger Rag"—"a model of fleet, assured playing, full of swooping, hill-and-dale phrases, nimble 'false' fingering, and other tricks of the saxophonist's trade." It soon became an exemplar, a paradigm to be memorized note for note to the point where it could be flawlessly recalled years later. Richard Sudhalter mentions a 1976 rehearsal for the Whiteman commemorative concert when three saxophonists "astonished fellow-bandsmen by reeling off the chorus from memory, in faultless unison."[78]

What Jimmy Dorsey achieves here is a more highly developed form of Armstrong's superimposition of quotations from opera and sundry sources on the original chord changes of "Tiger Rag." It is in fact very much part of a larger time-honored practice among jazzmen of using the harmonies of pre-existing pieces, or parts of them, as the basis for creating new ones, known in the trade as "contrafacts." In his book *Jazz*, Whiteman tackles with relish the related issue of "pilfered music," effectively deflating the puffery surrounding the merits of lowbrow vs. highbrow:

> When you are listening to your favorite jazz tune, you are most likely absorbing strains that are most classic of all the classics. Do you not know that more than half of the modern art of composing a popular song comes in knowing what to steal and how to adapt it—also, that at least nine-tenths of modern jazz music turned out by Tin Pan Alley is frankly stolen from the masters? That's why a good many of the jazzists chuckle over lowbrows who say they can't abide classical music and highbrows who squirm when they hear jazz. Pretty nearly everybody knows now that Handel's *Messiah* furnished the main theme of the well-known "Yes, We Have No Bananas." Perhaps it is not such general knowledge that most of the "banana" song which wasn't taken from . . . *Messiah* came from Balfe's famous "I Dreamt That I Dwelt in Marble Halls." Chopin supplied "Alice Blue Gown." "Avalon" was *Tosca* straight. . . .
>
> There is no legal limit to this kind of lifting, so long as the model chosen has not been copyrighted.[79]

Whiteman is touching here on a pervasive practice that has defined the history of music for many centuries—from the so-called "sacred" polyphony of medieval and Renaissance Europe to Igor Stravinsky, Elvis Presley, and beyond—that of trawling the ocean depths for shards and detritus of every shape and stripe. Recycling of the past and sampling were facts of musical life long before the advent of hip-hop culture and rap. Some of the most familiar tunes—"God Save the King/Queen" and its American counterpart, "America" ("My Country! 'Tis of Thee"), "The Star-Spangled Banner," or "Happy Birthday"—are in fact stolen goods. In a song thesaurus of major scope, two intrepid scholars have compiled, among other things, intriguing lists of political campaign songs and their pilfered sources, as well as an inventory of more than two hundred "elegant plagiarisms," by no means complete, extending back to the mid-1700s.[80] Their evidence skewers any of the puffery inflating "great" music and suggesting that it somehow breathes a purer, more rarefied air. And it was this very broadly based tradition and its deep reservoir of memory which so effectively helped anchor so much of what both Whiteman and Armstrong presented as they were able to "lay it on the public"—as Armstrong would put it—where mainstreaming and blurring the distinction between "high" and "low," between the classical and the popular, were the norm. For this reason it is well to recall one of those revealing statements of the opera-quoting Armstrong: "Anything you can express to the public is jazz."[81] Similarly, Whiteman had no qualms about recycling Rimsky-Korsakov, Massenet, or MacDowell, in such numbers as "Song of India," "Meditation," or "I Love You," to mention a few. Such appropriation was inseparable in his mind from the practice of "jazzing" the classics, promoting the cause of symphonic jazz, and catering to the middlebrow taste of his public.[82]

Whiteman and Armstrong each had their own signature tunes, those "theme songs" rich in memory with which both they and their public identified. In the case of Whiteman it was the E-major "Love theme" from Gershwin's *Rhapsody in Blue*—that work whose very commissioning and world premiere has long been inseparable from his name. For Whiteman the work as a whole was perhaps as close as he had to a talisman, being programmed by him time and time again as the paradigm for his idea of symphonic jazz and the music of a busy modern urban America, whether in concert, on the radio, or in such of his major movies as *King of Jazz* and *Rhapsody in Blue*.

Armstrong's signature piece was the song "When It's Sleepy Time Down South"—a 1930 jazz ballad opening an important window into his stage persona and self-image. It is a song true to its title, offering an idealized romantic portrait of "a sleepy time down South," with images of the pale moon, crooning folks, soft winds, a life of ease, steamboats on the Mississippi, ringing banjos, and an expressed yearning to be in "mother's (or mammy's) arms." Armstrong first recorded it in Chicago on April 20, 1931, soon after its publication, initiating what would prove to be a staggering number of ninety-eight recordings of the song in the course of his career, whether in toto or in abridged form as part of a medley or concert opener or closer. In his initial recording the proceedings are prefaced by an opening phrase of the chorus followed by spoken dialogue between Armstrong and his pianist, Charlie Alexander: "There's a guy coming up the street . . . looks like he's from my hometown"; after a brief exchange of pleasantries we learn that Armstrong is "going back home." Although this introduction was dispensed with in later versions, the basic presentation remained essentially the same, except for adopting slower, more lingering tempos, and changing such lines as "darkies are crooning songs soft and low," to the more politically correct "folks are crooning . . . " Incidentally, usages like *darkies* were perfectly acceptable during the 1920s and early 1930s. The word can be heard in the early versions of "Ol' Man River" from *Showboat* (1927), and in Paul Whiteman's own version of "When It's Sleepy Time," recorded some six months after Armstrong, in October 1931, with Mildred Bailey providing the vocal southern comfort.

In reality, of course, it was very rarely "sleepy time," whether down south or any number of other places—such as when Armstrong was crossing the Atlantic in July 1933 in the company of his drunkard manager, Johnny Collins. With his great gift for using earthy humor and cool judgment, Armstrong was able to contain his justifiable rage in the face of racism to defuse a crisis.

When it comes to the marketing of musical memory on a mass scale, there is no medium that can quite match that of film. And the sheer number of jazz movies is striking—or movies about entertainers with a tangential connection to jazz—"story movies," if you will, that were released in the United States during the 1940s and 1950s, with some spillover into later decades. Such jazz biopics have been likened to black-and-tan fantasies, harking back in turn to what Duke Ellington once said about his own "Black and Tan Fantasy," explaining that what he had in mind was a place "where people of all races and colors mixed together for the purpose of fulfilling their social aspirations."[83] For starters one thinks of such titles as *Rhapsody in Blue* (1945), *The Fabulous Dorseys* (1947), *The Glenn Miller Story* (1954), *The Benny Goodman Story* (1955), *The Eddy Duchin Story* (1956), and *The Gene Krupa Story* (1959). One can readily add films from the early 1940s to the late 1960s that feature Armstrong and Whiteman, including two rare instances, *Birth of the Blues* (1941) and *Atlantic City* (1944), of their appearance in the same movie. Then again, as in the case of *New Orleans* (1947), there is a distinct nostalgic strain running through a number of these films as they evoke the world of the early-twentieth-century America. Indeed, the powerful countervailing force of memory drives not only these films but also the sensibility of American musical theater and ballet during the troubled times of World War II and the years immediately after. Familiar examples include Rodgers and Hammerstein's *Oklahoma* (1943) and *Carousel* (1945), Irving Berlin's *Annie Get Your Gun* (1946), and Aaron Copland's *Appalachian Spring* (1945).

Birth of the Blues, a melodrama set in New Orleans and loosely based on the rise to stardom of the Original Dixieland Jazz Band, can be paired with the roughly contemporaneous *New Orleans*. But instead of an essentially black music accepted enthusiastically by a predominantly white educated public, what we see in *Birth of the Blues* is jazz presented as the undeveloped language of black primitives that requires the polishing of the white musician. The agenda is clearly spelled out in the rather unsubtle coded message that appears directly after the opening credits have rolled: "Dedicated to the musical pioneers of Memphis and New Orleans who favored the 'hot' over the 'sweet'—those early jazz men who took American music out of the rut and put it 'in the groove.'" Within moments we hear the lad Jeff Lambert (Bing Crosby plays this protagonist as an adult) improvising on clarinet with great flair behind the cotton bales on the Basin Street levee, effortlessly providing a countermelody to a band of folk ("ear") musicians playing "Georgia Camp Meeting." The black clarinet player is dumbfounded. How is it possible that "his own hot licks" seem to be coming out of his horn when he is not even blowing? When the precocious young Lambert is presently discovered behind those bales, he explains how he learned to play. "Oh, I just picked it up hanging around Basin Street." The black clarinetist is duly impressed. "White boy, come sit beside me. There's a few things I want to pick up." In due course Lambert puts together his combo, the Basin Street Hot Shots, and is joined by the singer Betty Lou (Mary Martin), who becomes the love interest of both Lambert and his cornet player. Jack Teagarden, the band's trombonist and occasional vocalist, is added to the mix as we hear such standards as "St. Louis Blues," "St. James Infirmary," "Melancholy Baby," and "Tiger Rag." Not all is plain sailing; there are the fisticuffs and threats as the musicians encounter the mob and have to face rejection. But they ultimately prevail. The closing sequence effectively helps frame the underlying thesis of the movie as we hear Crosby singing the title song accompanied by a montage of jazz notables presented in quasi-evolutionary order, moving from black to white: Ted Lewis, Duke Ellington, Louis Armstrong, the Dorseys, and Benny Goodman, culminating in George Gershwin and Paul Whiteman. The message is unmistakably reactionary for 1941, espousing a position redolent of the 1920s: the music is understood to have come of age only when the civilizing sweetener of Paul Whiteman is added.

Set during the years from 1915 to 1920, *Atlantic City* (1944) tells the fictional story of the young Bradford Taylor (Stanley Brown), the visionary entrepreneur who is intent upon transforming the oceanside community into "the playground of the world." But all his ambitious real estate development, not to mention the initiation of an annual beauty pageant, serve as merely a backdrop to a succession of musical and vaudeville acts in which both Paul Whiteman—he is, after all, revisiting the scene of his early triumphs—and Louis Armstrong have conspicuous roles. Whiteman is in his element, briefly heard playing violin, leading with the bow, and even singing a duet with Marilyn Whitaker (Constance Moore), the love interest of Taylor as they reprise the number "On a Sunday Afternoon" of Harry von Tilzer. Whiteman is also the suave emcee as he introduces Gus Van and Charles Marsh, who do their comic routine "That's How You Can Tell They're Irish," and he serves as the smooth accompanist in Moore's rendition of "I Ain't Got Nobody." Armstrong re-creates his 1929 role in *Hot Chocolates,* performing "Ain't Misbehavin'" in Taylor's Apollo Theater opposite the lithe and leggy Dorothy Dandridge, who has introduced him: "From the land where the blues were born comes the man with the horn." This scene, framed by "Harlem on Parade" and "Rhythm for Sale," is charged with the eroticism of Dandridge's body language, with Armstrong "fully cognizant of Dandridge's sexual presence" and directly addressing her with lines like "your kisses are worth waiting for." There is also a telling moment when he stoops down, blowing his horn directly into the camera as the bell of his instrument fills much of the screen.[84]

An elegant romp set in the moneyed milieu of Newport, Rhode Island, MGM's *High Society* (1956) is an updated version of Philip Barry's *The Philadelphia Story* (1940), with music and lyrics by Cole Porter. As a sequel of sorts to *Time*'s 1949 mainstream magazine coronation of Armstrong, it represents a celluloid celebration of his arrival in society, a parallel to what *King of Jazz* accomplished for Whiteman in 1930. In fact, the film was released when "Ambassador Satch" was at the zenith of his international fame and undertaking a world tour. We first see Armstrong seated at the back of the bus, resplendent in suit, tie, and Panama hat. Taking puffs of a cigarette and flanked by his All Stars, he sings "High Society Calypso," intoning, "Can you dig ol' Satchmo swinging in the beautiful high society!" With Armstrong's segue, "End of song, beginning of story," we are alerted to his role as narrator in prose and song as he comments in the manner of the Greek chorus on the life and loves of the movie's male lead, the popular jazz musician and sponsor of the Newport Jazz Festival, C. K. Dexter Haven (Bing Crosby).

Toward the movie's end the strategically inserted segment "Now You Has Jazz" provides a gloss on the party held on the wedding eve of Tracy Samantha Lord (Grace Kelly), ex-wife of Haven. Parenthetically, in a delightful plot twist, Tracy and Dexter will retie the knot the very next day, for she has come to learn that to err is human, and that she would rather spend her days with the warm but fallible Dexter—she has come to see him as a man of character, not simply a "jukebox hero"—than with her rigid, dull fiancé, George Kittredge (John Lund), who is apt to place her on a pedestal. In any event, the vocals of Crosby are backed by the wonderfully energetic playing of Armstrong and his All Stars. Addressing the "dear gentlefolk of Newport, or maybe I should say hats and cats," he assures them that they will "hear some really shimmering sharps and flats . . . for these cozy virtuosi, just about the greatest in the trade, are fixing to show you now precisely how, or approximately, jazz music is made." And we soon learn that "from the north to the south, from the east to the west, jazz is king, jazz is the thing the folks dig most."

The assembled guests respond enthusiastically—testimony that jazz is being taken seriously by an affluent and elite audience—an allusion to the Newport Jazz Festival itself. Incidentally, *High Society* was the last film in which Armstrong and Crosby appeared together. As such it taps into the memory of Crosby and Armstrong's working relationship, both on and off the screen, and the process of breaching of racial barriers harking back to the Whiteman days. Perhaps emboldened by his portrayal in *High Society,* Armstrong, soon after the movie's release, was to shake up the establishment.

Two highly publicized events of 1957 point to this. While on the road in North Dakota in September, Armstrong caught some late-breaking TV stories about events in Little Rock, Arkansas. He summarily canceled a State Department–sponsored tour of the Soviet Union, telling reporters, "The people over there ask me what's wrong with my country. What am I supposed to say? The way they are treating my people in the South, the Government can go to hell." Armstrong was outraged, accusing President Eisenhower of having "no guts" and dismissing Governor Orval Faubus as an "uneducated plow boy." Then in a despairing tone he added: "It's getting almost so bad a colored man hasn't got any country."[85] He refused to take back a word, despite less than unanimous support from fellow blacks, among them entertainers like Sammy Davis, Jr. The impact of Armstrong's strong stand against racial discrimination and his putting President Eisenhower on notice speaks volumes

5.4 Publicity still from *High Society* (MGM, 1956) showing C. K. Dexter Haven (Bing Crosby) being entertained by Armstrong and the All Stars. Joshua Berrett, personal collection.

for his stature as a civil rights pioneer. Earlier that year, on July 4, the Newport Jazz Festival was the scene of an Armstrong birthday party that was on the verge of self-destructing.[86] It was then that Armstrong stood his ground and cursed, balking at the efforts of producers and his own manager to have him appear with almost every act on the bill, without his regular vocalist, and without prior rehearsal. As Dan Morgenstern put it: "Like an ancient African king, he smites them with his righteous wrath."[87]

During his final years Armstrong was able to smite the opposition with two hit singles—"Hello, Dolly!" and "What a Wonderful World." "Hello, Dolly!," the title song from a hit Broadway musical, bumped the Beatles from the number 1 spot on the *Billboard* chart in May 1964 and received a further boost when Armstrong performed it with Barbra Streisand in the 1969 movie version. He made nearly two dozen recordings, in the studio or live, between December 1963 and January 1971, some six months before his death. The richness of allusion that can be heard in some of these recordings from his twilight years speaks volumes for the power of shared memory; by some

5.5 Whiteman helps Armstrong celebrate his birthday onstage, July 1966 at Lambertville Music Circus. From left, Tyree Glenn (trombone), Armstrong, Whiteman, St. John Terrell (producer), his assistant. Photo by Ed Berger.

strange alchemy, the events of daily life and those of Armstrong's creative process are melded. On July 4, 1966, on the occasion of his birthday as it was then celebrated, Armstrong appeared with members of his All Stars at a relatively obscure venue, the Lambertville Music Circus in western New Jersey, just across the Delaware River from New Hope, Pennsylvania. The proximity of New Hope is significant in that Paul Whiteman was then living there in retirement. That day he showed up onstage at Lambertville, fiddle in hand, making what was one of his last public appearances—he died on December 29, 1967—playing "Happy Birthday," a very special toast from one king of jazz to another. This rare moment was captured for posterity in the only photograph known to have been taken of the two of them together.

Wondrous too are the workings of Armstrong's mind. Several shards of musical memory have been found embedded in five contemporaneous recordings of "Hello, Dolly!" made by him in Berlin, Paris, and New York between 1965 and 1967. Not only can we hear excerpts from "Mahogany Hall Stomp," "Way Down Yonder in New Orleans," and "Struttin' with Some Barbecue," but there are three instances when he quotes from a standard—in the case of one recording it can be heard twice—that has no known precedent in his entire discography. The standard alluded to turns out to be one of Whiteman's own very earliest hits from 1920, "Japanese Sandman."[88]

One king was returning a compliment to another.

6 OUT CHORUS

Our kings of jazz, each affectionately known as "Pops," were the twin fathers of American popular music, and their enduring commitment to making their public happy trumped any idea of self-conscious purism in their art. As children of the "Jazz Age," each of them came into his own during the 1920s, swept up in the headlong rush of modernism as the United States freed itself from the cultural domination of Europe to embody "The American Century" and become an international force in its own right. Even though this characterization of the twentieth century harks back to a 1941 editorial of American triumphalism by Henry Luce, the founder of *Time, Life,* and *Fortune*—it was written as part of an appeal to Americans to commit themselves to the service of mankind—it has since been applied most persuasively to the twentieth century as a whole.[1] And no music was more vital to that century's soundtrack than jazz. "Any gangplank interview with European luminaries visiting the United States during the 1920s, whether with Stravinsky, Bartók, or Ravel, revealed . . . that American jazz, not concert music, was what interested them."[2]

U.S. News and World Report, in its issue of December 27, 1999, featuring twenty-five Americans who shaped the modern era, had this to say: "If jazz was the American Century's soundtrack, then Armstrong was its ambassador, the living embodiment of the nation's living art form." As one of nature's supreme gifts to twentieth-century American culture, Armstrong helped shape modern lingo—words like *cat, gig, jive, dig, hustle, chick,* and many more. He has become so identified with words and expressions that have since become part of the argot of the jazz world that his vividly illustrative usages have been cited in major reference works on slang.[3] He was also an inspiration to visual artists and photographers, among them Romare Bearden, Arthur Dove, Edward Steichen, Al Hirschfeld, Gordon Parks, Lisette Model, Irving Penn, Miguel Covarrubias, and Leroy Neiman.[4] Then there were those Paris dadaists like Tristan Tzara who claimed to hear in Armstrong's scat vocals the sound poetry of the avant-garde. But above all, it was with his personal charisma and the sound of his solo horn that he became renowned, a veritable Gabriel standing in sharp contrast to bandleader-entrepreneur Paul Whiteman and his focus on the ensemble. The trumpet—actually it was initially the bugle and cornet—was Armstrong's talisman. His close identification with his horn, we should remember, harks back to a miraculous turn of events during his early New Orleans years at the Colored Waif's Home. It was there, under the tutelage of Peter Davis, that he became bugler—"I was in seventh heaven"—quickly graduating to cornet player and leader of the band—"I jumped straight into the air."

In the words of Wynton Marsalis, the sound of Satchmo's horn was "a pure spiritual essence, the sound of America and of freedom."[5] Armstrong took a vital cue from his early New Orleans mentor, King Oliver, who said: "If a cat can swing a lead and play a melody, that's what counts." And swing he did, helping transform the very nature of jazz, from a music of ensemble improvisation to one defined by a theme (head)–solo choruses–theme format. He was indisputably the first great soloist, establishing the paradigm for expanding upon "breaks" and improvising on chord changes. In the process he created solos lasting a whole chorus or more, drawing upon a "bag" of "licks" coming from a wide range of sources—all animated by a sense of operatic bravura, and a distinctive passion and intensity.

Armstrong had little use for the minutiae of money and managing a band. He was perfectly happy to blow his horn peacefully and not have to deal with "too much quarreling over petty money matters." By contrast, Whiteman's was a corporate mentality. In his focus on the ensemble and arrangements he epitomized the savvy dance band or orchestra leader as well as the entrepreneur and promoter par excellence. It was as if he were taking his cue from Calvin Coolidge, who in a 1925 speech before the Society of American Newspaper Editors originated the dictum "The business of America is business."

Unlike Armstrong, Whiteman was ahead of the Coolidge curve. It was as though the hard lessons about contracts and money he had learned as a child from his domineering father paid off handsomely as he became a musical entrepreneur. As early as 1921, boosted by his successes at Atlantic City and the sales of his first Victor recordings, he formed the company of Paul Whiteman, Inc., essentially a booking organization located at 160 West 45th Street, with the express goal of developing and supplying outstanding satellite dance bands for cabarets, clubs, and luxury liners. By the early years of the decade he commanded a satellite empire consisting of some twenty bands performing in venues ranging from the New York metropolitan area to Massachusetts to Ohio to ocean liners bound for Cuba and Jamaica.[6] The rise of that empire contributed to a bullish growth in his annual income, from around $156,000 in 1924 to some $800,000 the following year. "Although the big money poured in for many more years, Paul never topped 1925 in dollars earned."[7] One further measure of his resources is provided by his weekly payroll. The week ending January 20, 1928, is a case in point, when a total of $7,440 was disbursed to thirty-six employees. Nor was Whiteman immune to some unabashed boosterism—the payroll reads like the inflated annual report of a CEO—caught up as he understandably was in the giddy excitement of the decade. "Jazz . . . is bulking increasingly large in economics. There are today more than 200,000 men playing it. The number of jazz arrangers is around 30,000. . . . They are lucrative industries, too. . . . Jazz has made fortunes and bought automobiles, country houses and fur coats for many a player, composer, and publisher. . . . The accessories of jazz figure conspicuously in the buying and selling of the nation. In 1924, the United States spent $600,000.00 for music and musical instruments."[8]

Although widely separated by geography, not to mention factors of race, class, and financial backing, Armstrong, in August 1922, was to cut a path comparable in significance to that traced by Whiteman, if not more so. The telegram from his surrogate father and mentor, Papa Joe Oliver, summoning him from New Orleans to Chicago was the defining moment of his early career. And barely eight months later, in April 1923, Armstrong made his first recordings with King Oliver and his Creole Jazz Band in the studios of Gennett in Richmond, Indiana. So it is that we have two transcontinental journeys of Paul Whiteman and Louis Armstrong—Whiteman's from the West Coast to Atlantic City (and very soon, New York), Armstrong's from New Orleans to Chicago—representing intersecting axes joining the major jazz centers of the day.

Armstrong and Whiteman shared a common core repertoire—titles such as "Body and Soul," "St. Louis Blues," "Rockin' Chair," "Tiger Rag," "Sweet Sue," and a number of others. We have also seen various Whiteman influences exerted on Armstrong in such selections as "Sobbin' Blues," "Who'Sit," and "Go 'Long Mule"—all of them among the shards of shared memory. They were joined in myriad ways by the intersecting career trajectories of such musicians as Guy Lombardo, Hoagy Carmichael, W. C. Handy, Bing Crosby, Mildred Bailey, Eddie Lang, Joe Venuti, Jimmy and Tommy Dorsey, and Jack Teagarden, to name a few. It was something that all happened within a larger context of how they understood their public roles and the music they purveyed. Indeed, one of my important goals here has been the development of a fuller appreciation of how for both Whiteman and Armstrong the idea of *jazz* was broadly inclusive and far-ranging, encompassing much of what was loosely defined as popular, light classics, and the middlebrow. Whiteman speaks of having dodged for years the question of what jazz is, unable to arrive at an adequate answer. He does, however, briefly and broadly refer to such defining characteristics as question and answer, syncopation, and "the manner of saying it," and he speaks of jazz as "a new musical language, expressing new meanings—fresh combinations of old meanings . . . a method of saying the old things with a twist . . . strictly speaking, . . . instrumental effects."[9] And what Whiteman had in mind was not simply the "jazzing" of such classics as "Meditation" from Massenet's opera *Thaïs* or Rimsky-Korsakov's "Song of India." He was also deeply committed to a much more ambitious agenda of fostering the growth of "symphonic jazz," bequeathing a legacy which, as we shall soon see, has yet to receive its due.

For Armstrong the idea of *jazz* was not anything he ever wanted to "mess with." When he was asked to define what exactly jazz was, his answers often assumed the tone of an oracular warning—such statements were ascribed to him as "If you have to ask what it is, you will never know," or "If you don't know what it is, well, just don't mess with it." In 1932, we should recall, upon filing an application for a passport on the eve of his first trip to Europe, Armstrong identified his occupation as "actor and musician"—the word *actor* to be taken in the spirit of the minstrel show and vaudeville. As a human being with a rare generosity of spirit, Armstrong transcended the barriers of religion, category, and race. "As far as religion, I'm a Baptist and a good friend of the Pope, and I always wear a Jewish star for luck. Those people who make the restrictions, they don't know nothing about music; it's no crime for cats of any color to get together and blow." Discussing the niceties of "art" as opposed to "entertainment" held no interest for him; they were synonymous. Commitment to his audience—"The music ain't worth nothing if you can't lay it on the public"—was with him throughout his performing life. There was deeply ingrained in him a work ethic, an ethic so strong that it could sometimes put his health in serious jeopardy. Nothing illustrates this more vividly than the exchange described earlier between him and his personal physician, Gary Zucker, at the time of his last gig at New York's Waldorf Astoria in March 1971. Even though he was suffering from congestive heart failure and shortness of breath and risked dying onstage, Armstrong was not to be deterred from going ahead with the performance. Zucker has spoken of the chill he felt going up and down his spine as Armstrong, assuming the position of holding his horn, looked up at the ceiling and uttered words coming from the core of his being: "Doctor, you don't understand. My whole life, my whole soul, my whole spirit, is to b-l-o-w this h-o-r-n. My people are waiting for me. I cannot let them down."[10]

What he offered his public was music of vast stylistic breadth, richly diverse in content. In the course of a 1962 interview Armstrong, after spontaneously launching into singing the opening of "Serenade" from Sigmund Romberg's 1924 operetta *The Student Prince,* bluntly says: "That's jazz. That's the way I look at it. Anything you can express to the public is jazz."[11] Embedded in his improvisations, and deeply internalized from his listening to the recordings of opera singers in his personal collection—singers such as Caruso, Galli-Curci, and Tetrazzini—are quotations from such operas as Verdi's *Rigoletto,* Bizet's *Carmen,* and Leoncavallo's *Pagliacci.* Here was a unique, mercurial figure, driven by an intensely strong work ethic. On a given day he might be accompanying singers at a morning recording session, then playing scores for silent pictures in the afternoon under the direction of Erskine Tate at Chicago's Vendome Theater, performing arrangements of Suppé's overture, "Poet and Peasant," or the "Intermezzo" from Mascagni's *Cavalleria Rusticana.* And in the evening he might be found doing his bit at a venue like the Dreamland Café. Then again he was also party to the creation of pieces attributed to Lil Hardin, such as "Struttin' with Some Barbecue" and "Skid-Dat-De-Dat," with their elements of European classical music. He also made many appearances on television and in short films, not to mention twenty-three feature films from 1931 to 1969. His output ranged from his collaboration with Jimmie Rodgers on "Blue Yodel No. 9," to "I Wish I Could Shimmy Like My Sister Kate," to the quintessential rumba number "The Peanut Vendor" ("El Manisero"), to "West End Blues," to the two hits at the end of his career, "Hello Dolly" and "What a Wonderful World."

Turning again to Whiteman, posterity has not judged him kindly. He now earns little more than honorable mention in most surveys for having commissioned and premiered *Rhapsody in Blue* and having hired players like Bix Beiderbecke. As part of an effort to keep his memory alive, a few years after Whiteman's death in 1967, the indefatigable Richard Sudhalter and some committed kindred spirits gave a series of concerts in 1974 and 1975 and issued two recordings with the billing of the New Paul Whiteman Orchestra. This was followed in 1983 by the publication of Thomas A. DeLong's richly anecdotal biography *Pops: Paul Whiteman, King of Jazz* and the appearance twenty years later of the first of two volumes of Don Rayno's magisterial study. But for the most part the name of Paul Whiteman and all that he achieved have slipped from popular memory. Wider recognition is long overdue for his tireless efforts to nurture and generously reward talent, and to come to the defense of those suffering at the hands of abusive or indifferent managers, notably Louis Armstrong and Earl Hines. One also thinks of such nurtured talents as Hoagy Carmichael, Johnny Mercer, William Grant Still, Bix Beiderbecke, Frank Trumbauer, Bing Crosby, Tommy and Jimmy Dorsey, Eddie Lang, Joe Venuti, Jack Teagarden, Florence Mills, and many others. All too rare is the kind of bold statement made by the vibraphonist Red Norvo, a former Whiteman band member and onetime husband of Mildred Bailey: "Don't you dare ever bad-mouth Whiteman. We all owe him plenty."

This sorry state of affairs was brought home by the glaring oversight of 1990, the centennial of Whiteman's birth—the very opposite of what happened in 2001, when well over one hundred celebrations worldwide honored the memory of Louis Armstrong. The snub prompted the following incisive remarks from Richard Sudhalter:

> The opprobrium attached to Whiteman's name, especially among jazz critics, has persisted. This became painfully obvious in 1990, when the centenary of the leader's birth occasioned not a single event—concert, television program, even newspaper or magazine feature. It was as if a world which had come to understand "jazz" as synonymous with "African-American" music were holding Whiteman hostage to his long-ago "King of Jazz" billing. It hardly needs explaining that, to the public of the 1920s, "jazz" had a much more generalized meaning, one within which the "King" title had some relevance. Whiteman's domination of the light music world of his day was beyond dispute: and if, for most Americans, this was indeed the "jazz" age, he had more than passing claim to its rulership.[12]

Yet the neglect of Whiteman by the larger world in the centennial year of his birth should not have come as a complete surprise. By 1990 some sixty years of history had eroded his position, and the head wearing the crown had

6.1 The New Paul Whiteman Orchestra performing in London, October 1974, with Richard Sudhalter, center, on trumpet. Photo by Dennis Austin, courtesy of Richard M. Sudhalter.

long since become uneasy. As early as 1928, the year when Brecht and Weill's *Threepenny Opera* premiered and the Comintern made its first pronouncements on racial inequality in the United States, developments were set in motion that would have a lasting effect on the writing of jazz history. We have seen how *The Daily Worker,* the writings of Charles Edward Smith, the furor surrounding the case of the Scottsboro Nine, and the activism of John Hammond were key factors in that process as three overlapping themes came to be articulated again and again: negro oppression, jazz as folk art, and the idea that hot jazz is the only genuine article.

The entry of the United States into World War II in 1941 brought in its wake some radical changes for African-Americans—among them the banning of discrimination in defense industries, the founding of the Congress of Racial Equality (CORE), the founding of *Ebony* magazine, and the arrival of Jackie Robinson on the Brooklyn Dodgers. We are reminded, too, of the Afrocentric course in the history of jazz offered by Robert Goffin and Hugues Panassié at what was then known as the New School for Social Research, and the enthusiastic support to the cause lent by Arnold Gingrich of *Esquire.* Yet Whiteman was hardly invisible in the 1940s: the Gershwin biopic *Rhapsody in*

Blue, orchestral concerts in Los Angeles and Chicago, recordings with Billie Holiday for Capitol, and his work as music director for the Blue Network all helped maintain Whiteman's public profile. But to a large extent he was basking in the glory of things past, hoping perhaps, especially with his radio work of the time, to discover a latter-day Gershwin who would create another *Rhapsody in Blue.*

By the time of the 1950s and 1960s Whiteman was living in semiretirement. There were the sporadic appearances—he conducted a three-concert series of Gershwin at Hollywood Bowl in 1954, took part in the revue *Newcomers of 1928* in Las Vegas in 1958, appeared—together with Jack Teagarden, Peggy Lee, Bing Crosby, and Buster Keaton—on a 1960 CBS-TV show, on the occasion of his seventieth birthday, and showed up onstage at the Lambertville Music Circus in New Jersey, fiddle in hand, to toast Armstrong on his birthday in 1966. When he was not reliving past glories, Whiteman's focus was on such hobbies as Tennessee walking horses, antique firearms, and classic cars, rather than engaging in any of the musical developments of the day. Certainly his decision in 1958 to sell his New Jersey farm and move to the newly built "Coda Cottage" in New Hope, Pennsylvania, where he was to live out the rest of his days, made his priorities all too clear.

Armstrong meanwhile was, of course, moving into overdrive. We recall that, following the debut in 1947 of the All Stars, he reached the zenith of international fame during the Cold War, while also being praised for playing and singing with more heart and inspiration than he had in years. As "Ambassador Satch," Armstrong was a highly prized commodity at a time when the Marshall Plan was critical to shaping both American foreign policy and general perceptions of the country abroad. The impact of Armstrong's 1955–56 world tour and his highly publicized cancellation in September 1957 of his State Department tour of the Soviet Union to protest integration in Little Rock, Arkansas, are among the more vivid demonstrations of his stature. He also made many appearances on TV shows, with Ed Sullivan, Bing Crosby, Danny Kaye, Steve Allen, and Johnny Carson, among others. Nor can one overlook his roles in a dozen feature films following *New Orleans* (1947)—such movies as *A Song Is Born, The Glenn Miller Story, High Society, Paris Blues,* and *Hello, Dolly!* In fact, more than half of Armstrong's total output of feature films dates from the period of 1947 to 1969.

Even more remarkable is the extent to which Armstrong was able to achieve a balance between hewing to a certain traditionalism with his All Stars and embracing elements of modernism—bebop and such substyles as cool jazz and Third Stream music—as he collaborated with such musicians as

Dizzy Gillespie and Dave Brubeck. But despite such evidence, Armstrong was sometimes accused of being a "moldy fig," a traditionalist, not to mention an Uncle Tom.[13] For all the acrimony, simplistic generalities, and media hype, his music making from 1945 through much of the 1960s provides ample proof of a mind alert to the modernist possibilities of bebop and its substyles, as well as a genial relationship with many of its practitioners. Important examples include "Jodie Man," "I Wonder," "Jack Armstrong Blues"—a joint creation of Louis Armstrong and Jack Teagarden from the historic 1947 Town Hall concert—and "Umbrella Man," as heard in a joyous performance with Dizzy Gillespie on the CBS-TV *Timex All Star Show* in 1959; that duet came at a time when Armstrong and Gillespie lived in the same neighborhood of Queens, New York, their wives socializing as well. This particular appearance attests as does nothing else to the genuine affection between these two jazz greats, affection borne out by a letter Armstrong wrote to Gillespie a few months later, and by Gillespie's subsequent confession in his 1979 autobiography of having previously misjudged Armstrong.[14] While riffing on Armstrong and modernism, one has to also include a major project of 1961 with Dave and Iola Brubeck, "The Real Ambassadors," signaling "something of a musical accord between modernists and traditionalists," while also communicating a poignant power in its commentary on American racism and social injustice. And Armstrong was certainly operating in Whiteman's bailiwick, on the turf of symphonic jazz, when in July 1956 he played "St. Louis Blues Concerto Grosso" with members of the New York Philharmonic under Leonard Bernstein in Lewisohn Stadium and in the presence of W. C. Handy. The following December found him in Royal Festival Hall, London, with the Royal Philharmonic Orchestra in a benefit for the Hungarian and Central European Relief Fund.

The civil rights movement of the 1950s and 1960s, and much of the attendant racial strife, inevitably affected the world of jazz—certainly to the extent of valorizing the "African" half of the African-American epithet and effectively excluding someone like Paul Whiteman. Many were frustrated by this climate. The jazz pianist and lecturer Billy Taylor begins a 1957 essay on a highly provocative note: "Strange as it sounds, American Negroes who created jazz music, today hardly know anything about it." At the same time, he is quick to acknowledge that jazz has become "the medium of expression of all types of Americans and, to a surprising degree, musicians from other lands and other cultures," and proceeds to single out for praise such "serious-minded, creative artists" as John Lewis, a founding father of the Modern Jazz Quartet and one who helped set Third Stream music on its course, and the cool jazzman Dave Brubeck. Taylor addresses the need for instilling racial pride and speaks approvingly of a number of jazz writers—among them Hugues Panassié, Robert Goffin, Leonard Feather, and such "Ivy League Marxists" as Rudi Blesh and Sidney Finkelstein, all of whom championed an African-American jazz agenda in general, and musicians like Louis Armstrong in particular.[15]

Arguably the angriest and most acerbic voice of the time was that of the saxophonist, composer, and playwright Archie Shepp. In a 1965 *Down Beat* article, "An Artist Speaks Bluntly," he claims to speak "with some authority about the crude stables (clubs) where black men are groomed and paced like thoroughbreds to run till they bleed" and refers to the United States as "one of the most vicious, racist social systems in the world." Shepp finally throws down the gauntlet with the following outburst:

> Give me leave to state this unequivocal fact: jazz is the product of the whites—the ofays—too often my enemy. It is the progeny of the blacks—my kinsmen. By this I mean: you own the music, and we make it. By definition, then you own the people who make the music. You own us in whole chunks of flesh. When you dig deep inside our already disemboweled corpses and come up with a solitary diamond—because you don't want to flood the market—how different are you from the DeBeers of South Africa or the profligates who fleeced the Gold Coast? All right, there are niggers with a million dollars but ain't no nigger got a *billion* dollars.[16]

Some thirty years later Shepp was still spewing venom. On January 10, 1996, in the course of a program on jazz and race on National Public Radio's *All Things Considered*, he was heard deploring the very word *jazz* and its connotations of sex and racism, insisting that jazz was "founded on Afro-American blues idioms," while finding such European elements as tonality, harmony, form, or instrumentation "incidental." No matter—one may note in the spirit of Armstrong's "cats-of-any-color" credo—that Shepp had performed at defining moments of his career with such white musicians as the trombonist Roswell Rudd, the clarinetist Perry Robinson, and the bassist Cameron Brown. One could add to the list the name of John Tchicai, a Danish saxophone player born to a Congolese father and Danish mother.

Very different in tone on the program was the voice of the white guitarist Jim Hall, coming to the defense of his colleague the saxophonist Joe Lovano, who had been attacked for playing "white jazz." Hall deplored the very notion of "white jazz" as a divisive ploy to sell newspapers and magazines, and one at odds with his forty-year experience of playing with the likes of such black musicians as Ron Carter and Sonny Rollins. The veteran black trumpeter and Armstrong contemporary Doc Cheatham sounded like the lone voice of reason when he said: "I don't know what they mean by black music. . . . I've seen black notes on white paper." And Dan Morgenstern, the eminent writer, critic, and director of the Institute of Jazz Studies at Rutgers University, spoke of jazz as a hybrid of many disparate musical and cultural elements—European, African, Latin, and more. He concluded: "To say that jazz is a black music that was ripped off by the mainstream culture is entirely wrong."

The National Public Radio program coincided with the week that BET on Jazz, the first twenty-four-hour cable channel for jazz, owned and operated by Black Entertainment Television, was launched in Washington, D.C. At the same time, the NPR program was presented as part of an effort to untangle the strands of myth—powerful perceptions, truths real or imagined—that have defined the very nature of some one hundred years of jazz history. Is it true that white guys can neither jump nor swing and have no business playing jazz? Questions such as these were framed in the context of a recent personnel dispute. Wynton Marsalis had been accused of reverse discrimination in his role as artistic director of the jazz program at New York's Lincoln Center, hiring virtually no whites and programming works featuring only black composers. Even though inequities in the problem had since been corrected, what seemed to linger was the stinging comment of Marsalis to the effect that the great innovators in jazz were all African-American, and that it was imperative to concentrate on that group before moving on to the lesser contributions of whites.

Marsalis's position was not without foundation. One can point to at least four developments in Washington, D.C., between 1973 and 1990 that helped foster the idea of a federally sanctioned image of jazz as an African-American art form defined by a canon of predominantly black-composed masterpieces. The process began with the release in 1973 of the Smithsonian Collection of Classic Jazz—a recorded anthology of eighty-six selections, of which only three showcase white performers. In 1987 a resolution of the 100th Congress of the United States began: "Whereas jazz has achieved preeminence throughout the world as an indigenous American music and art form, bringing to this country and the world a uniquely American musical synthesis and culture through the African-American experience . . ." The following year afforded scholars the first opportunity to explore the treasure trove of Ellington manuscripts and scores acquired by the Smithsonian National Museum of American History. In 1990 came the founding of the Smithsonian Jazz Masterworks Orchestra. Meanwhile, in New York the start of the decade brought the birth of Jazz at Lincoln Center, with Marsalis as director. By December

1995 the Lincoln Center Board had "awarded the institution's jazz department, Jazz at Lincoln Center, equal status with the New York Philharmonic, the Metropolitan Opera, the New York City Ballet and the other so-called constituents of the Center."[17]

Within this larger context, the racially charged and highly publicized exchange between Marsalis and James Lincoln Collier in the early 1990s—a major victory for Marsalis—was inevitable. Besides, animosity toward Collier had been building in the jazz community since the release of his 1983 biography of Armstrong, *Louis Armstrong: An American Genius.* Collier had depicted Armstrong as a pathetically dependent soul who "failed his talent" in forever seeking applause.[18] A similar dysfunctional subtext came to define Collier's 1987 study of Duke Ellington, who is characterized as too "lazy" to take composition seriously. Matters finally came to a boil with a scalding letter by Wynton Marsalis in the *New York Times Book Review* of December 19, 1993, written in response to a largely favorable review of yet another Collier book, *Jazz: The American Theme Song* (1993). In his letter Marsalis accused Collier of being "a poseur who attempts to elevate himself above his subject," one who "continues to posture as an authority while disseminating misinformation . . . a viper in the bosom of blues and swing." He challenged Collier to go public and defend himself. Sure enough, there was a donnybrook arranged by Marsalis at Lincoln Center on August 7, 1994; Collier was clobbered, even though Marsalis failed to refute certain charges—that there had never been a tribute concert for such figures as Bix Beiderbecke or Benny Goodman, and that the agenda of Jazz at Lincoln Center had become a strategy to present jazz as a tradition built on the accomplishments of "black greats" in an effort to attract major corporate funding.

With the release of the vigorously promoted nineteen-hour PBS documentary series of Ken Burns, *Jazz: A History of America's Music,* in 2000—heavily funded by General Motors—Marsalis seemed once again to be using the prestige of his position to advance the cause of dead jazzmen, primarily black, limiting most coverage to the period ending around 1960 and making Louis Armstrong perhaps the central figure in an epic narrative of struggle, triumph, and decline. In all fairness, the companion book, cowritten by Geoffrey C. Ward and Ken Burns, is more nuanced and strives for better racial balance—enhanced by perceptive essays by Dan Morgenstern, Gerald Early, Gary Giddins, and Stanley Crouch, as well as interviews with Marsalis and Albert Murray.

What is most telling for our purposes is how Armstrong and Whiteman are portrayed, their respective legacies assessed, in this highly publicized history of America's music released on the cusp of the millennium. The rags-to-riches story of Armstrong is told in loving detail—from his humble beginnings in New Orleans, to his stardom in Chicago and New York, to his challenges of the status quo, to his bonding with Joe Glaser, to his European and world tours, to the hits of final years such as "Hello, Dolly!" Quite special are the anecdotes and asides of Doc Cheatham, Dan Morgenstern, and Wynton Marsalis. Cheatham, for example, tells of an occasion when he was asked by Armstrong to sit in for him at the Vendome Theater and perform the number "Poor Little Rich Girl" with the forces of Erskine Tate. "The people started screaming. You couldn't hear, I mean, I never saw anything like it in my life—for one second. Then it stopped, it died. The whole applause died, died right down . . . because they noticed that I wasn't Louis. I felt like dropping dead." Responding to a question about what puts Armstrong in a category all his own, Wynton Marsalis says: "When you talk about Louis Armstrong, well you're talking about the deepest human feeling, and the highest level of musical sophistication in the same man. . . . [He] invented a new style of playing. He created the coherent solo, fused the sound of the blues with the American popular song." Dan Morgenstern recalls the time he received the greatest compliment from Armstrong after sending him an advance copy of a special issue of *Down Beat* honoring him on his seventieth birthday with tributes from around the world. "Within days, a letter arrived in that familiar hand (Pops always addressed his envelopes himself). 'I received the magazine,' it said, 'and it knocked me on my ass!' No raves from 'critics' could ever top that."[19]

Within the world of the Ward-Burns book, Paul Whiteman is assigned a predictably marginal place, the discussion of his achievements confined largely to the 1920s. At the same time, he is given a nuanced, sympathetic treatment as the authors recount the details of his early years in Denver, San Francisco, and Atlantic City, his influences from such bandleaders as Art Hickman and Paul Specht, and the role of Ferde Grofé in doing his arrangements. Especially revealing are the comments made about Fletcher Henderson, "the Colored King of Jazz," who found a role model in Paul Whiteman. Like Whiteman, Henderson is dismissed as being a leader of "a popular dance orchestra specializing in cheerful light music with only a judicious jazz seasoning." Yet Don Redman's Whiteman-inspired arrangements for Henderson are just the ticket, according to the quoted comments of Dave Peyton in the *Chicago Defender:* "soft, sweet and perfect, not the sloppy New Orleans hokum, but peppy blue syncopation in dance rhythm . . . not at all like the average Negro orchestra, but in a class with the good white orchestras such as Paul Whiteman."[20]

Better yet, Whiteman is presented—accurately—as having aroused few if any grudges among black musicians. If anything, he elicited words of praise from the likes of Duke Ellington, who admired Whiteman for attracting first-rate musicians and running his band with managerial flair. Alluding to the title of King of Jazz, Ellington remarked: "No one as yet has come near carrying that title with more certainty and dignity. . . . I used to hear Whiteman records taking the snobbishness out of . . . music and opening doors."[21]

We have already seen how the centennials of Whiteman and Armstrong's years of birth and their respective legacies were celebrated in utterly different fashion. And the relative neglect of Whiteman has not simply been a symptom of a predominantly African-American jazz perspective shaped by the ideologies of the 1930s or the changes wrought by the civil rights movement of the 1950s and beyond. It has also been the casualty of a failure to acknowledge Whiteman as the father of an often-overlooked tradition—that of symphonic jazz. In its fusion of jazz and classical European music it is a tradition with an honorable lineage extending from Whiteman to Igor Stravinsky's "Scherzo à la Russe" for Whiteman, to his "Ebony Concerto" for Woody Herman, to an impressive array of works by such composers and arrangers as John Lewis, Gil Evans, Leonard Bernstein, Duke Ellington, J. J. Johnson, Stan Kenton, and Artie Shaw. As someone who has studied the work of Whiteman's arrangers more closely than most, Richard Sudhalter has drawn attention to the links connecting the Third Stream achievements of Artie Shaw's orchestras with Whiteman:

> Shaw organized two successive large orchestras and turned for arrangements to [Lennie] Hayton and William Grant Still, both alumni of [the] Whiteman ensemble. What Gunther Schuller has labeled the "Third Stream" efforts of various Shaw orchestras, blending jazz and other, more disparate, ingredients, can be traced directly to the Whiteman orchestra, *Jahrgang* 1927–30. Exhaustive research in the Whiteman Collection of arrangements, housed at Williams College in Massachusetts, has shown that the scores recorded by the orchestra in that four-year period represented only a fraction—and not necessarily the most creative fraction—of work being done by its arranging staff. A major assessment of this orchestra's achievements and its influence on the popular music world of its own and subsequent times (an assessment uncontaminated by latter-day racial politics) is long overdue.[22]

By accident or design—perhaps it was Manifest Destiny—something happened in the world of American music during the final two decades of the twentieth century to provide it with an exquisite symmetry. This development, embodied in the career of Wynton Marsalis, now the artistic director of Jazz at Lincoln Center, achieved a synthesis of Armstrong's transcendent solo trumpet playing and Whiteman's commitment to symphonic jazz composition, both supported by an elaborate program of educational outreach, command of the media, and vast financial resources.

As a musician born in New Orleans in 1961, at the beginning of the decade when Paul Whiteman died and Louis Armstrong's performing career wound down, Wynton Marsalis brings a special symmetry and synthesis to this whole study of the two kings of jazz. Born in the cradle of jazz, Marsalis the trumpet virtuoso and latter-day archangel Gabriel rose to prominence in the mid-1980s, around the time that jazz was approaching its centennial. Jeff Levenson, a veteran jazz writer and former executive at Columbia and Warner Records, has put it very succinctly: "This kid emerges who's a hotshot . . . and the whole thing has a kind of symmetry to it. Louis Armstrong starts things off—trumpet player, New Orleans, turn of century. Wynton closes it out—trumpet player from New Orleans."[23] Like Armstrong, he is reportedly extraordinarily disciplined, driven by a strong work ethic and an urge to excel. Taking up the trumpet at age six, he received a broad-based musical education under the tutelage of his father, Ellis Marsalis, a trained pianist and jazz musician. By age fourteen he had performed Haydn's Trumpet Concerto in public; he attended the Berkshire Music Center at Tanglewood three years later and entered the Juilliard School in 1979. Around that time he was recruited to join the band of Art Blakey and the Jazz Messengers, making his recording debut as a bandleader three years later. In both 1983 and 1984 he won Grammy Awards in both the jazz and classical music categories. As a composer he has carried the tradition of symphonic jazz initiated by Whiteman to unprecedented heights by creating ballet scores for the New York City Ballet and the Alvin Ailey Dance Company, written such Third Stream compositions as *At the Octoroon Balls* (1995) for the Orion String Quartet and the Chamber Music Society of Lincoln Center, earned the Pulitzer Prize in music for his oratorio *Blood on the Fields* (1997), and composed an elaborate twelve-part work fusing richly diverse styles, *All Rise* (1999), that was commissioned and premiered by the New York Philharmonic and first performed by them together with the Lincoln Center Jazz Orchestra and Morgan State University Choir in December 1999.

Changes in programming policies of Jazz at Lincoln Center show a heightened awareness of the need for inclusiveness at every level, whether the music of Pixinguinha, Brazil's founding father of the samba, the work of such whites as Lee Konitz, Gil Evans, or Woody Herman, or of African-

Americans like Thelonious Monk, Ornette Coleman, Count Basie, or Mary Lou Williams. And included in the mix as well are formerly excluded players such as the saxophonist Joe Lovano. Marsalis's comments on *All Rise* reflect a similar vision as he speaks of the hope for a new musical world order as we begin the twenty-first century:

> The twentieth has been the century of communication. The twenty first will be the century of integration. Now there's more talk than ever about the global community. The search is on, and when we finally find each other, the head of recognition will cause souls to rise. We will truly be at home in the world. *All Rise* celebrates togetherness and ascendance. It has dance movements, introspective sections, and other portions that aim to demonstrate basic units of music like the blues that speak of a common human heritage.[24]

NOTES

INTRODUCTION

Epigraph: Lewis Carroll, *Through the Looking-Glass.*

1. Stanley Dance, "Duke Ellington," *Stereo Review,* December 1969, 69.
2. Gerald Early, "Pulp and Circumstance: The Story of Jazz in High Places," in *The Culture of Bruising* (Hopewell, N.J.: Ecco, 1995), 166.
3. Arthur M. Schlesinger, Jr., *The Disuniting of America* (New York: Norton, 1992), 47.
4. Quoted in Bill Kirchner, ed., *The Oxford Companion to Jazz* (New York: Oxford University Press, 2000), 102.
5. Hendrik Hertzberg and Henry Louis Gates, Jr., "The African-American Century," *New Yorker,* April 29–May 6, 1996, 10.
6. "Paul Whiteman," *Jazz: The Rough Guide* (London: Rough Guides, 2000), 826.
7. "Russian jazz," ibid., 886–87.

1 BEGINNINGS

Epigraph: Paul Whiteman and Mary Margaret McBride, *Jazz* (New York: J. H. Sears, 1926), 32–33.

1. Wilberforce Whiteman was born on September 1, 1857, on the family farm near Fairhaven in Preble County, just west of Dayton, on the southwestern Ohio frontier. Significantly, the previous year Wilberforce University, the first institution of higher education in the United States to be owned and operated by African-Americans, was founded a short distance just east of Dayton. Given the proximity of these two events in space and time, it seems highly plausible that Wilberforce Whiteman's parents were inspired in naming their infant son by a certain idealism and spirit of tolerance associated with the founding of the university and its eponymous English abolitionist. Yet the racist attitudes toward jazz and African-Americans that Wilberforce Whiteman came to express later in life certainly belied the hopes of his parents.
2. Gene Fowler, *A Solo in Tom-toms* (New York: Viking, 1946), 239–40.
3. B. E. Lloyd, *Lights and Shades in San Francisco* (San Francisco: A. L. Bancroft, 1876), 78–79.
4. *New York Journal and American,* November 20, 1938, 2-E.

5. Fowler, *Solo in Tom-toms,* 231.

6. Quoted ibid., 233.

7. Ibid., 234.

8. Michael Kimmel, *Manhood in America: A Cultural History* (New York: Free Press, 1996), 177.

9. Whiteman and McBride, *Jazz,* 21.

10. "Pops Whiteman Returns Home," *Rocky Mountain News,* April 29, 1956.

11. *St. Louis Star and Times,* November 9, 1933.

12. Unattributed manuscript (ca. 1936), Paul Whiteman Collection, Williams College, Williamstown, Mass.

13. Thomas A. DeLong, *Pops: Paul Whiteman, the King of Jazz* (Piscataway, N.J.: New Century, 1983), 21.

14. Unattributed manuscript (ca. 1936).

15. Marshall Stearns and Jean Stearns, *Jazz Dance: The Story of American Vernacular Music* (New York: Oxford University Press, 1968), 96.

16. *San Francisco Examiner,* November 29, 1910.

17. Stearns and Stearns, *Jazz Dance,* 96.

18. Sylvia G. L. Dannett and Frank R. Rachel, *Down Memory Lane* (New York: Greenberg, 1954), 75.

19. Remark by Max Morath in television series *Ragtime Years* (KRMA-TV, Denver, April 1961).

20. Eric Lott, *Love and Theft: Blackface Minstrelsy and the American Working Class* (New York: Oxford University Press, 1993), 6. The emotional extremes to which Lott refers have been tragically real. Song-and-dance routines imitating or satirizing blacks are one thing. But the ugly manifestations of "panic, anxiety [and] terror" are quite another.

21. Thornton Hagert, liner notes to *An Experiment in Modern Music* (Smithsonian Collection, RO 28, 1981), 1, 3.

22. The first two verses reproduced here were reprinted in the *New York Journal-American,* May 16, 1960, 19. My thanks to James T. Maher for bringing this citation to my attention.

23. Mervyn Cooke, *The Chronicle of Jazz* (New York: Abbeville, 1998), 38. Original catalog in Hogan Jazz Archive, Tulane University, New Orleans.

24. Lawrence Gushee, "How the Creole Band Came to Be," *Black Music Research Journal* 8, no. 1 (1988): 85.

25. *San Francisco Examiner,* April 11, 1928, 6.

26. These citations are included in Dick Holbrook, "Our Word JAZZ," *Storyville* 50 (December 1973–January 1974), 46–58.

27. Richard M. Sudhalter, *Lost Chords: White Musicians and Their Contribution to Jazz, 1915–1945* (New York: Oxford University Press, 1999), 423.

28. James T. Maher and Jeffrey Sultanof, "Pre-Swing Era Big Bands, Jazz Composing, and Arranging," in *The Oxford Companion to Jazz,* ed. Bill Kirchner (New York: Oxford University Press, 2000), 269.

29. My thanks to James T. Maher for generously sharing the results of his unpublished research on the life of Art Landry.

30. Carl Johnson, *Paul Whiteman: A Chronology* (Williamstown, Mass.: Williams College, 1988), 13. See also unattributed sheet, "Financial Structure for Early Bands" (1919–21), box T, folder 18, Whiteman Collection, Williams College, Williamstown, Mass.

31. Whiteman later signed with such labels as Columbia, Decca, and Capitol.

32. Oral history of Tom Whaley (no. 3, 59), Institute of Jazz Studies, Rutgers University, Newark, N.J.

33. Eugene de Bueris's letter of September 8, 1915, to the *Globe* was subsequently reprinted in James Weldon Johnson's "Views and Reviews" column in *New York Age,* September 23, 1915, 4.

34. *Billboard,* March 14, 1925, 53.

35. Louis Armstrong, "Louis Armstrong and the Jewish Family in New Orleans La. The year of 1907." Louis Armstrong Archives, series ms. no. 1/5, 7.

36. Findings of Tad Jones as summarized by Ralph Blumenthal in "Digging for Satchmo's Roots in the City That Spawned Him," *New York Times,* August 15, 2000, E2.

37. Quoted in Joshua Berrett, *The Louis Armstrong Companion: Eight Decades of Commentary* (New York: Schirmer, 1999), xiv.

38. Louis Armstrong, *Satchmo: My Life in New Orleans* (New York: Da Capo, 1986), 159.

39. Quoted in Berrett, *Companion,* xv.

40. *Louis Armstrong: A Self-Portrait,* interview by Richard Meryman (New York: Eakins, 1971), 24. Henry Burr, alias Harry McClaskey, was a "soft-voiced popular singer of sentimental songs." His career, which began around 1910, spanned nearly thirty years. For more on Burr/McClaskey, see Roger D. Kinkle, *The Complete Encyclopedia of Popular Music and Jazz,* vol. 2 (New Rochelle, N.Y.: Arlington, 1974), 649. The broad range of music that Armstrong heard when only in his teens is further indicated by a remark from an interview included in a documentary on his New Orleans years (prod. WYES-TV, New Orleans, 1990; WNYC-TV, New York, February 17, 1992). Talking about his days in Peter Davis's band at the Colored Waif's Home, Armstrong says that they played arrangements of Liszt, Bach, Rachmaninoff, Mahler, and Haydn.

41. Louis Armstrong Archives, series ms. no. 1/5, 7 (March 31, 1969).

42. Quoted in Berrett, *Companion,* xiv–xv.

43. Armstrong, "Louis Armstrong and the Jewish Family," 16.

44. Armstrong, *Satchmo,* 35.

45. Ibid., 46.

46. Armstrong on the occasion of a visit to the home of the Anger family, Vancouver, B.C., July 1951, cassette no. 5, Louis Armstrong Archives, Queens College, City University of New York.

47. Quoted in Nat Shapiro and Nat Hentoff, *Hear Me Talkin' To Ya* (New York: Dover, 1966), 48–49.

48. Sidney Bechet, *Treat It Gentle* (New York: Da Capo, 1976), 92.

49. Thomas Brothers, ed., *Louis Armstrong in His Own Words* (New York: Oxford University Press, 1999), 174, 175.

50. Quoted in Berrett, *Companion,* 120.
51. Danny Barker, *A Life in Jazz* (New York: Oxford University Press, 1986), 27.
52. Armstrong, *Satchmo,* 142.
53. Piron's groups had far-reaching influence. His New Orleans Orchestra, for example, included the distinguished Creole sideman, clarinetist Lorenzo Tio, Jr., who taught many of the city's notables of the next generation, among them Jimmy Noone, Albert Nicholas, Omer Simeon, and Barney Bigard. After a stint with King Oliver at Chicago's Plantation Club, Bigard became a fixture in Duke Ellington's band from about 1928 to 1942. This fourteen-year association was followed by three stints with Louis Armstrong's All-Stars (1947–52, 1953–55, 1960–61).
54. Ernie Anderson, "Louis Armstrong: A Personal Memoir," *Storyville,* December 1, 1991.
55. Lawrence Gushee, "New Orleans–Area Musicians on the West Coast, 1908–1925," *Black Music Research Journal* 9, no. 1 (1989): 1–18.
56. *Indianapolis Freeman,* July 22, 1918. See also Gene Anderson, "The Genesis of King Oliver's Creole Jazz Band," *American Music* 12, no. 3 (Fall 1994): 289.
57. Anderson, "Genesis," 290–91.
58. *Chicago Whip,* February 12, March 5, April 9, 1920.
59. *Chicago Defender,* April 2, 1921.
60. Al Rose, *Storyville* (University: University of Alabama, 1974), 67–69. See also Gene Anderson, "Johnny Dodds in New Orleans," *American Music* 8, no. 4 (Winter 1990): 405–40.
61. *Chicago Defender,* April 29, 1922.
62. Ed Garland interview with Burt Turetzky, January 1977, Jazz Oral History Interviews, Institute of Jazz Studies, Rutgers University, Newark, N.J.
63. Quoted in Brothers, *Louis Armstrong,* 37–38.
64. The Goffin Notebooks, a series of reminiscences, were sketched out by Armstrong between 1943 and 1944 for the Belgian jazz writer-lawyer-polymath Robert Goffin. The idiosyncrasies of Armstrong's capitalization and other quirks appearing in the manuscript have been preserved in this transcription by Brothers in *Louis Armstrong,* 87. The originals are now among the holdings of the Institute of Jazz Studies at Rutgers University, Newark, N.J.
65. Quoted in Geoffrey C. Ward and Ken Burns, *Jazz: A History of America's Music* (New York: Knopf, 2000), 90.

2 CIVILIZATION ON TRIAL

1. Kyle Crichton, "Thar's Gold in Them Hillbillies," *Collier's,* April 30, 1938, 24.
2. Ronald C. Foreman, *Jazz and Race Records, 1920–1932,* Ph.D. diss., University of Illinois, Urbana-Champaign, 1968, 92.
3. F. Scott Fitzgerald, *The Great Gatsby* (New York: Scribner's, 1925), 13.
4. Jeff Todd Titon, *Early Downhome Blues* (Urbana: University of Illinois Press, 1979), 228–31.
5. Alain Locke, "The New Negro," *The Norton Anthology of African American Literature,* ed. Henry Louis Gates, Jr., and Nellie Y. McKay (New York: Norton, 1997), 962.

6. J. A. Rogers, "Jazz at Home," in *The New Negro: An Interpretation* (New York: Johnson Reprint, 1968), 217, 218.

7. David Levering Lewis, "Harlem's Visible Man," *New York Times,* August 2, 2001, A21.

8. James Lincoln Collier, *The Reception of Jazz in America* (Brooklyn: Institute for Studies in American Music Monograph no. 27, 1988), 20.

9. "Mr. Gershwin Replies to Mr. Kramer," *Singing* 1, no. 10 (October 1926): 17.

10. The phrase "make [or made] a lady out of jazz" has been attributed to the great conductor and music educator of the day Walter Damrosch. In Merle Armitage's 1938 book *George Gershwin* Damrosch is quoted on page 189 as having said: "Gershwin has made a lady out of jazz."

11. Transcribed from recording *Satchmo and Me* (Riverside RLP 12-120).

12. Ibid. Beiderbecke was attending Lake Forest Academy at the time, just outside Chicago. He was not to join the Paul Whiteman Orchestra until 1927.

13. Bill Crow, *Jazz Anecdotes* (New York: Oxford University Press, 1990), 207.

14. William Howland Kenney, *Chicago Jazz: A Cultural History, 1904–1930* (New York: Oxford University Press, 1993), 78.

15. New York *Clipper,* August 10, 1923, 21.

16. Abel Green's comments in *Variety,* September 24, 1924, 26, and November 26, 1924, 50.

17. Kenney, *Chicago Jazz,* 70, 71.

18. *Satchmo and Me.*

19. Ibid.

20. Max Jones and John Chilton, *Louis: The Louis Armstrong Story, 1900–1971* (London: November Books, 1971), 80.

21. Hugues Panassié, *The Real Jazz* (New York: Barnes, 1960), 198.

22. Winthrop Sargeant, *Jazz: Hot and Hybrid* (New York: Da Capo, 1975), 201.

23. Walter C. Allen, *Hendersonia: The Music of Fletcher Henderson and His Musicians* (Highland Park, N.J.: Jazz Monographs no. 4, published by Walter C. Allen, 1973), 113.

24. *New York Clipper,* February 22, 1924, 37.

25. Robert Kimball, liner notes to *Shuffle Along,* New World Records (NW 260), 3.

26. Thomas J. Hennessey, *From Jazz to Swing: Black Jazz Musicians and Their Music, 1917–1935,* Ph.D. diss., Northwestern University, Evanston, 1973, 19–20.

27. Nathan Irvin Huggins, *Harlem Renaissance* (New York: Oxford University Press, 1971), 3.

28. Howard Scott, interviewed by Chris Albertson, Washington, D.C., March 18, 1979. Transcript in Jazz Oral History Project (JOHP), Institute of Jazz Studies, Rutgers University, Newark, 13, 15.

29. *Chicago Defender,* October 31, 1925, 6.

30. Scott interview, March 18, 1979, 12.

31. J. R. Taylor, liner notes to *Fletcher Henderson: Developing an American Orchestra 1923–1937* (Smithsonian Collection, R006, 1977), 5. See also Lewis Porter, *Jazz: From Its Origins to the Present* (Englewood Cliffs, N.J.: Prentice-Hall, 1993), 122.

32. Paul Whiteman and Mary Margaret McBride, *Jazz* (New York: J. H. Sears, 1926), 219.

33. The Goffin Notebooks, [book 3], 1925, as included in *Louis Armstrong in His Own Words*, ed. Thomas Brothers (New York: Oxford University Press, 1999), 93. Armstrong's quirky capitalization and phrase structure have been deliberately preserved.

34. Quoted in Nat Shapiro and Nat Hentoff, *Hear Me Talkin' To Ya* (New York: Dover, 1966), 204.

35. Quoted ibid., 203.

36. Jeffrey Magee, "Before Louis: When Fletcher Henderson Was the 'Paul Whiteman of the Race,'" *American Music* 18, no. 4 (Winter 2000): 391–425.

37. Quoted in Jones and Chilton, *Louis*, 211.

38. *Record Changer*, July–August 1950, 15.

39. The two sessions, both for major race labels of the day, were as follows: December 22, 1924, with the Red Onion Jazz Babies (Gennett) and January 8, 1925, with Clarence Williams's Blue Five (Okeh). Singers were Alberta Hunter and Eva Taylor, respectively.

40. Quoted in Robert Gottlieb, *Reading Jazz* (New York: Pantheon, 1996), 742, 746.

41. Goffin Notebooks, in Brothers, *Louis Armstrong*, 94.

42. Dan Morgenstern, personal communication, August 7, 2001.

43. Quoted in Jones and Chilton, *Louis*, 211.

44. Whiteman and McBride, *Jazz*, 10.

45. Quoted ibid., 66.

46. James T. Maher, *Radio Music, I Loved You*, 44–45. My thanks to James T. Maher for generously sharing the contents of his unpublished manuscript.

47. Thomas A. DeLong, *Pops: Paul Whiteman, King of Jazz* (Piscataway, N.J.: New Century, 1983), 58.

48. Whiteman and McBride, *Jazz*, 84.

49. Carol J. Oja, "Gershwin and American Modernists of the 1920s," *Musical Quarterly* 78, no. 4 (Winter 1994): 650, 652.

50. Magee, "Before Louis."

51. Max Harrison has explored some of these similarities and cross-influences in "Around Paul Whiteman," *Jazz Monthly*, no. 185 (1970): 4–12.

52. *New York World*, February 17, 1924.

53. Thornton Hagert, liner notes to *An Experiment in Modern Music* (Smithsonian Collection, RO 28, 1981), 9.

54. David Schiff, *Gershwin: Rhapsody in Blue* (Cambridge: Cambridge University Press, 1997), 62.

55. *New York Times*, November 23, 1924.

56. Gilbert Seldes, *The Seven Lively Arts* (New York: Harper, 1924), 97–99.

57. Henry O. Osgood, *So This Is Jazz* (Boston: Little, Brown, 1926), 123, 161.

58. Whiteman and McBride, *Jazz*, 10, 3.

59. Ibid., 20.

60. Quoted in DeLong, *Pops*, 86.

61. Whiteman and McBride, *Jazz,* 257, 155–56.
62. *New York Times Magazine,* March 6 and 13, 1927.

3 SOME LIKED IT HOT

1. Transcribed from recording *Satchmo and Me* (Riverside RLP 12–120).
2. "Louis Armstrong and His Hot Five" can be misleading in that there might literally be a total of five players, including Armstrong. In fact, some of his best-known and most-admired Hot Five sessions, including "Hotter Than That" and "West End Blues," feature a total of six players.
3. *Louis Armstrong in His Own Words,* ed. Thomas Brothers (New York: Oxford University Press, 1999), 130. The "musicians' union" was the all-black Local 208.
4. Louis Armstrong, *Swing That Music* (New York: Da Capo, 1993), 30–32.
5. Brothers, *Louis Armstrong,* 132.
6. Baby Dodds, as told to Larry Gara, *The Baby Dodds Story* (Baton Rouge: Louisiana State University Press, 1992), 72.
7. Frank Tirro, *Jazz: A History* (New York: Norton, 1993), 192.
8. *Satchmo and Me.*
9. Brothers, *Louis Armstrong,* 130–31.
10. Tirro, *Jazz,* 192.
11. Quoted in Joshua Berrett, *The Louis Armstrong Companion: Eight Decades of Commentary* (New York: Schirmer, 1999), 44.
12. Laurence Bergreen, *Louis Armstrong: An Extravagant Life* (New York: Broadway, 1997), 392.
13. Interview with Max Jones, *Melody Maker,* April 8, 1967.
14. Details were kindly provided by Chris Albertson.
15. My thanks to Lawrence Gushee for bringing the announcement of this recital to my attention.
16. Chris Albertson, who was a rather frequent visitor to Hardin's home during her final years and was planning a biography of her, has attested to the accuracy of this information.
17. Brothers, *Louis Armstrong,* 132–33.
18. "Cornet Chop Suey," registration number E580818, is included in "A List of Compositions with a Copyright Assigned to Louis Armstrong," compiled by David Chevan. My thanks to Wayne Shirley of the Library of Congress for bringing this unpublished manuscript to my attention.
19. David Chevan, *Written Music in Early Jazz,* Ph.D. diss., City University of New York, 1997, 306.
20. Dan Morgenstern, "Louis Armstrong," in *The Oxford Companion to Jazz* (New York: Oxford University Press, 2000), 107.
21. Brothers, *Louis Armstrong,* 133.
22. *Chicago Defender,* February 20, 1926.
23. Joshua Berrett, "Louis Armstrong and Opera," *Musical Quarterly* 76, no. 2 (Summer 1992): 216–41.
24. These recollections are in Max Jones and John Chilton, *Louis: The Louis Arm-*

strong Story, 1900–1971 (London: November Books, 1971), 212. "Good for reading" touches on an important literacy factor differentiating the training of Chicago jazzmen from their brethren in New York. As Garvin Bushell has pointed out, "they could read . . . the ones who played the Vendome Theater. Chicago jazzmen had the advantage in those years of having a crack at theater music before New York jazzmen did. They improved their ability that way, and so could read a little better than jazz musicians in the East." *Jazz from the Beginning* by Garvin Bushell as told to Mark Tucker (Ann Arbor: University of Michigan Press, 1988), 25–26.

25. Gunther Schuller, *Early Jazz* (New York: Oxford University Press, 1968), 89.

26. The question is explored in detail in Berrett, "Louis Armstrong and Opera."

27. Martin Williams, *The Smithsonian Collection of Classic Jazz* (Washington, D.C.: Smithsonian Institution, 1973), 20–21.

28. Schuller, *Early Jazz*, 128.

29. *New York Times*, November 23, 1924.

30. Richard M. Sudhalter and Philip R. Evans, *Bix: Man and Legend* (New Rochelle, N.Y.: Arlington House, 1974), 116.

31. *Variety*, September 24, 1924.

32. Quoted in Sudhalter and Evans, *Bix*, 39.

33. Quoted ibid., 192.

34. Quoted in Geoffrey C. Ward and Ken Burns, *Jazz: A History of America's Music* (New York: Knopf, 2000), 154.

35. Quoted ibid.

36. Quoted in Gary Giddins, *Bing Crosby: A Pocketful of Dreams, the Early Years, 1903–1940* (Boston: Little, Brown, 2001), 259.

37. Quoted in Giddins, *Bing Crosby*, 170.

38. A fine example can be heard in Whiteman's recording of "Changes," in a session for Victor on November 23, 1927.

39. Quoted in Thomas A. DeLong, *Pops: Paul Whiteman, the King of Jazz* (Piscataway, N.J.: New Century, 1983), 104.

40. Quoted in Charles Thompson, *Bing: The Authorized Biography* (New York: David McKay, 1976), 21.

41. Ibid.

42. Giddins, *Bing Crosby*, 144.

43. Milton Mezzrow and Bernard Wolfe, *Really the Blues* (New York: Citadel, 1990), 120, 123.

44. Quoted in Ken Murray, "Louis, Bix Had Most Influence on Der Bingle," *Down Beat*, July 14, 1950, 16.

45. Giddins, *Bing Crosby*, 159–60, 162.

46. Ibid., 183–84.

47. Sudhalter and Evans, *Bix*, 477–78.

48. Donaldson is perhaps better known for such songs as "My Blue Heaven," "My Buddy," and "Yes Sir! That's My Baby."

49. Giddins, *Bing Crosby*, 167.

50. George Avakian, liner notes to *The Bix Beiderbecke Story: Whiteman Days,* vol. 3, Columbia CL 846.

51. Krin Gabbard, *Jammin' at the Margins: Jazz and the American Cinema* (Chicago: University of Chicago Press, 1996), 10.

52. Ibid., 12–13.

53. Especially important to the larger discussion here was *Blackbirds of 1928,* with the showstopper of Dorothy Fields and Jimmy McHugh, "I Can't Give You Anything But Love."

54. *Chicago Defender,* November 19, 1927.

55. Giddins, *Bing Crosby,* 228.

56. *Chicago Defender,* September 22, 1928.

57. Bergreen, *Louis Armstrong,* 307.

58. Richard M. Sudhalter, *Lost Chords: White Musicians and Their Contribution to Jazz, 1915–1945* (New York: Oxford University Press, 1999), 828, n. 17.

59. Quoted in Berrett, *Companion,* 77.

60. Quoted ibid., 78.

61. Quoted in Morgenstern, "Louis Armstrong," 112.

62. Audio Companion to *Norton Anthology of African American Literature* (New York: Norton, 1997), 8.

4 UNEASY LIES THE HEAD

1. "Story of Duke Ellington's Rise to Kingship of Jazz Reads Like Fiction," *Pittsburgh Courier,* December 19, 1931. The entire article is reproduced in *The Duke Ellington Reader,* ed. Mark Tucker (New York: Oxford University Press, 1993), 54–56.

2. Much of this paragraph has been adapted from Michael Denning, *The Cultural Front: The Laboring of American Culture in the Twentieth Century* (London: Verso, 1996), xvi–xvii.

3. S. Frederick Starr, *Red and Hot: The Fate of Jazz in the Soviet Union* (New York: Oxford University Press, 1983), 21.

4. "Russian Jazz," *Jazz: The Rough Guide* (London: Rough Guides, 2000), 886–87.

5. Carl Johnson, *Paul Whiteman: A Chronology* (Williamstown, Mass.: Williams College, 1988), 20. The Armstrong quotation is to be found in *Time,* February 21, 1949, 54–55.

6. Quoted in Cameron Crowe, *Conversations with Billy Wilder* (New York: Knopf, 2001), 226–27.

7. Quoted in Thomas A. DeLong, *Pops: Paul Whiteman, King of Jazz* (Piscataway, N.J.: New Century, 1983), 95.

8. Kurt Weill, "Tanzmusik," *Der deutsche Rundfunk* 4 (March 14, 1926): 732, trans. in Kim H. Kowalke, *Kurt Weill in Europe* (Ann Arbor, Mich.: UMI Research Press, 1979), 103.

9. Excerpted from "Goffin notebooks," 1943–44, in Joshua Berrett, *The Louis Armstrong Companion: Eight Decades of Commentary* (New York: Schirmer, 1999), 86.

10. *The 1928 and 1930 Comintern Resolutions on the Black National Question in the United*

States (Washington, D.C.: Revolutionary Review), 1975; http://www.marx2mao. org, 4–5.

11. Charles Edward Smith, "Class Content of Jazz Music," *Daily Worker,* October 21, 1933, 7. In 1939 Smith and coeditor Frederic Ramsey published their landmark work, *Jazzmen.*

12. *New York Times Magazine,* September 12, 1926, 1, 9.

13. Spike Hughes, *Second Movement* (London: Museum Press, 1951), 144.

14. Morroe Berger, Edward Berger, and James Patrick, *Benny Carter: A Life in American Music* (Metuchen, N.J.: Scarecrow, 1982), 1: 336.

15. James Goodman, *Stories of Scottsboro* (New York: Pantheon, 1994), 4.

16. *Daily Worker,* April 19, 1933; James S. Allen, "The Scottsboro Struggle," *Communist* 12 (1933): 437.

17. John Hammond with Irving Townsend, *John Hammond on Record: An Autobiography* (New York: Penguin 1981), 77, 68. Hammond has not been without his detractors. Otis Ferguson, for example, once wrote: "I never saw any holes in his shoes." And Dan Morgenstern has referred to him as someone who "remained the eternal adolescent." See http://www.tnr.com/jazz/hammond.html and http://www.tnr.com/jazz/morgenstern.html.

18. Ibid., 83–84.

19. Louis Armstrong, *Satchmo: My Life in New Orleans* (New York: Da Capo, 1986), 208–9.

20. Ibid., 16.

21. Quoted in Berrett, *Companion,* 80. *Gage, tea, muggles,* and *vipers* are all part of the argot of marijuana and its use. Two of these words inspired such Armstrong numbers as "Muggles" and "Song of the Vipers."

22. Hammond with Townsend, *John Hammond on Record,* 106.

23. Excerpted from "The Satchmo Story," unpublished manuscript, quoted in Berrett, *Companion,* 79.

24. Quoted ibid., 81.

25. Quoted ibid., xiv.

26. Quoted in Samuel B. Charters and Leonard Kunstadt, *Jazz: A History of the New York Scene* (New York: Doubleday, 1962), 131.

27. Margaret Livingston Whiteman and Isabel Leighton, *Whiteman's Burden* (New York: Viking, 1933), book jacket.

28. Buddy Tate, interview with Gary Giddins, Jazz Oral History Project, Washington, D.C., March 1980.

29. Quoted in Berrett, *Companion,* 82–83.

30. Copy on file, Louis Armstrong House and Archives.

31. *Evening Graphic,* October 9, 1931, quoted in Berrett, *Companion,* 84.

32. Sworn before David L. Klein, Notary Public, Kings County, New York, September 22, 1931.

33. Quoted in Ralph J. Gleason, "God Bless Louis Armstrong," *Rolling Stone,* August 5, 1971, 27–33.

34. Max Jones and John Chilton, *Louis: The Louis Armstrong Story* (London: November Books, 1971), 126.

35. Laurence Bergreen, *Louis Armstrong: An Extravagant Life* (New York: Broadway, 1997), 346–47.

36. Max Jones, *Talking Jazz* (New York: Norton, 1988), 136–37.

37. Jones and Chilton, *Louis,* 139.

38. Louis Armstrong–George Avakian rap session of November 11, 1953; transcript in Berrett, *Companion,* 85–86.

39. Quoted in Jones and Chilton, *Louis,* 146–47.

40. Ibid., 148.

41. Berrett, *Companion,* xv; quotations ibid., 9, 14.

42. Armstrong, *Satchmo,* 186.

43. Fuller details are spelled out in the monumental study of Don Rayno, *Paul Whiteman: Pioneer in American Music,* vol. 1, *1890–1930* (Lanham, Md.: Scarecrow, 2003), 50–53.

44. Paul Whiteman, "So You Want to Lead a Band," *Collier's,* September 9, 1939, 52.

45. Details of Whiteman's coronation as King of Jazz and the inscription on the Buescher crown appear in the September 1923 issue of *Talking Machine World.* Further information can be found at http://www.garlic.com/tgracyk/whiteman.htm.

46. Quoted in Berrett, *Companion,* 47.

47. Quoted ibid., 48.

48. Dan S. Ingman, "England's Welcome to Louis Armstrong," *Melody Maker,* August 1932, 2.

49. Hannen Swaffer, *Daily Herald,* July 18, 1932.

50. Robert Goffin, "Hot Jazz," in *Negro: An Anthology,* ed. Nancy Cunard (London: Nancy Cunard, 1934; rpt. Westport, Conn.: Negro Universities Press of Greenwood Press, 1969), 238–39.

51. Hugues Panassié, "Louis Armstrong à la salle Pleyel," *Douze Années de Jazz* (Paris: Editions Corréa, 1946), 121–38; trans. Joshua Berrett in *Companion,* 61–73.

52. http://www.mosaicrecords.com/DisplaySelectionDetail.asp?

53. The Paul Whiteman Collection is housed at Williams College, Williamstown, Massachusetts.

54. Judith Anne Still, Michael J. Dabrishus, and Carolyn L. Quin, *William Grant Still: A Bio-Bibliography* (Westport, Conn.: Greenwood, 1996), 25.

55. Quoted ibid., 45; Still's emphasis.

56. Ibid., 28; Shaw quotation ibid., 8.

57. DeLong, *Pops,* 196.

58. Alain Locke, "Toward a Critique of Negro Music," *Opportunity,* December 1934, 330.

59. Gary Giddins, *Visions of Jazz: The First Century* (New York: Oxford University Press, 1998), 17.

60. Further details can be found in the scripts for the Kraft shows of February 8 and July 26, 1934, in the Special Collections Library, Duke University.

61. Hammond with Townsend, *John Hammond on Record,* 199.

62. Lewis A. Erenberg, *Swingin' the Dream: Big Band Jazz and Rebirth of American Culture* (Chicago: University of Chicago Press, 1998), 121.

63. Ibid., 200.

64. Deems Taylor, foreword to program notes, *The Eighth Experiment in Modern Music,* December 25, 1938.

65. Carl Sandburg, "Jazz Fantasia," in *Twentieth-Century American Poets,* ed. Conrad Aiken (New York: Harcourt Brace, 1944), 73. My thanks to James T. Maher for originally pointing out to me the attribution of *jazzmen* to Carl Sandburg. Communication of July 8, 2000.

66. Editors' introduction to *Jazzmen,* ed. Frederic Ramsey, Jr., and Charles Edward Smith (New York: Harcourt, Brace, 1939), xi.

67. Otis Ferguson, "The Five Pennies," ibid., 223–24.

68. Quoted in *Peace and War: United States Foreign Policy, 1931–41* (Washington, D.C.: 1943), 611. See also *United States Statutes at Large* 55 (1943): 31–32.

69. Remi Nadeau, *Los Angeles: From Mission to Modern City* (New York: Longmans, Green, 1960), 202.

70. Mike Davis, *City of Quartz* (New York: Vintage, 1992), 120.

71. Ted Gioia, *West Coast Jazz* (New York: Oxford University Press, 1992), 4.

72. DeLong, *Pops,* 251.

73. Krin Gabbard, *Jammin' at the Margins: Jazz and the American Cinema* (Chicago: University of Chicago Press, 1996), 179.

74. *Intervals: The Newsletter of David Liebman,* summer 2001, 2. http://www.upbeat. com/lieb/intervals-online/intervals_summer_2001.htm. Additional information from museum guide of the Museum of Jewish Heritage: A Living Memorial to the Holocaust, Battery Park City, New York.

75. Starr, *Red and Hot,* 194–97.

76. Ibid., 127–28.

77. The name was formally changed to New School University in 1997.

78. Leonard Feather, "Goffin, *Esquire,* and the Moldy Figs," in *Reading Jazz,* ed. Robert Gottlieb (New York: Pantheon, 1996), 723.

79. Ibid.

80. This was the original Metropolitan Opera House located at Broadway and 39th Street.

81. DeLong, *Pops,* 268.

82. Vera Stravinsky and Robert Craft, *Stravinsky in Pictures and Documents* (New York: Simon and Schuster, 1978), 373, 648.

83. DeLong, *Pops,* 227.

84. Richard Hadlock, "The New Orleans Revival," in *The Oxford Companion to Jazz,* ed. Bill Kirchner (New York: Oxford University Press, 2000), 308–11.

85. Plot summary paraphrased from Gabbard, *Jammin' at the Margins,* 117–21.

86. *Time,* September 1, 1947, 32; George Hoefer, "Armstrong Pleases Jazz Lovers in Chicago Bash," *Down Beat,* December 3, 1947, 11.

87. Sidney Finkelstein, *Jazz: A People's Music* (New York: Citadel, 1948), 273–74.

88. My thanks to James T. Maher for generously sharing some of this information.

89. *Time,* February 21, 1949, 58.

1. Stanley Dance, *The World of Earl Hines* (New York: Scribner's, 1977), 122. While there is no reason to question the essence of what Hines has to say, most of his freewheeling reminiscences as taped by Dance are unsupported by a properly documented chronology.

2. Quoted by James T. Maher, in personal communication, July 8, 2000.

3. Dance, *The World of Earl Hines,* 122.

4. Garvin Bushell, as told to Mark Tucker, *Jazz from the Beginning* (Ann Arbor: University of Michigan Press, 1988), 112–13.

5. Duke Ellington, *Music Is My Mistress* (Garden City, N.Y.: Doubleday, 1973), 103. Of course, "the piano player" wryly referred to was Ellington himself.

6. Quoted in Mark Tucker, *Ellington: The Early Years* (Urbana: University of Illinois Press, 1991), 117, 186. Tucker also makes the point that the Paul Whiteman tag was by no means exclusive to Duke Ellington. In fact, it was broadly applied, to such black musicians as Dave Peyton in Chicago and George Morrison in Denver, as well as to the white bandleader Jean Goldkette in Detroit.

7. Peyton's complete article is reprinted in *The Duke Ellington Reader,* ed. Mark Tucker (New York: Oxford University Press, 1993), 24–28. It was originally published in *Chicago Defender,* August 27, 1927.

8. "Duke Says Swing Is Stagnant," *Down Beat,* February 1939, 2, 16–17. Also, "Duke Becomes a Critic," *Down Beat,* July 1939, 8, 35.

9. Howard Taubman, "The 'Duke' Invades Carnegie Hall," *New York Times Magazine,* January 17, 1943, 10, 30.

10. *Chicago Defender,* September 22, 1928.

11. Richard Crawford and Jeffrey Magee, *Jazz Standards on Record, 1900–1942: A Core Repertory* (Chicago: CBMR Monographs, no. 4, 1992), v. The Crawford-Magee tabulations of ninety-seven recorded jazz standards, while useful, have to be approached with a degree of caution in that they have depended entirely for their data on Brian Rust's discography, *Jazz Records,* 5th ed. (Chigwell, Essex: Storyville, 1982). As we shall see, Rust's ideas of what constitutes jazz can be somewhat capricious.

12. Quoted in Geoffrey C. Ward and Ken Burns, *Jazz: A History of America's Music* (New York: Knopf, 2000), 210.

13. Richard Sudhalter, personal communication, September 3, 2002.

14. Quoted in John Edward Hasse, program booklet for *The Classic Hoagy Carmichael* (Washington, D.C.: Smithsonian Collection of Recordings, 1988), 5.

15. Quoted in Richard M. Sudhalter, *Stardust Melody: The Life and Music of Hoagy Carmichael* (New York: Oxford University Press, 2002), 23.

16. Hoagy Carmichael with Stephen Longstreet, *Sometimes I Wonder* (New York: Farrar, Straus and Giroux, 1965), 31.

17. Quoted in Sudhalter, *Stardust Melody,* 44, 46, 47.

18. Quoted in Richard M. Sudhalter and Philip R. Evans, *Bix: Man and Legend* (New Rochelle, N.Y.: Arlington, 1974), 72.

19. Sudhalter, *Stardust Melody,* 48.

20. Carmichael with Longstreet, *Sometimes I Wonder*, 63–64.
21. Quoted in Nat Shapiro and Nat Hentoff, *Hear Me Talkin' to Ya* (New York: Dover, 1966), 141–42.
22. Sudhalter, *Stardust Melody*, 70.
23. Ibid., 76.
24. Quoted in Sudhalter, *Stardust Melody*, 107.
25. Herb Sanford, *Tommy and Jimmy: The Dorsey Years* (New Rochelle, N.Y.: Arlington, 1972), 33.
26. Quoted in Sudhalter and Evans, *Bix*, 230.
27. Cited in Hasse, *Classic Hoagy*, 5.
28. Joshua Berrett and Louis G. Bourgois III, *The Musical World of J. J. Johnson* (Lanham, Md.: Scarecrow, 2002), 2.
29. Sudhalter, *Stardust Melody*, 138.
30. Quoted ibid., 130.
31. http://www.mosaicrecords.com/DisplaySelectionDetail.asp? For the record, the actual date of the party was Saturday, August 3, 1929.
32. Thomas A. DeLong, *Pops: Paul Whiteman, King of Jazz* (Piscataway, N.J.: New Century, 1983), 159.
33. Henry Pleasants, *The Great American Popular Singers* (New York: Simon and Schuster, 1974), 151.
34. Patricia Willard interview with Barney Bigard, July 1976, Los Angeles. Material has been drawn from Jazz Oral History Interview on file at the Institute of Jazz Studies at Rutgers-Newark. Reproduced in Joshua Berrett, *The Louis Armstrong Companion: Eight Decades of Commentary* (New York: Schirmer, 1999), 170–71.
35. Laurence Bergreen, *Louis Armstrong: An Extravagant Life* (New York: Broadway, 1997), 433.
36. Quoted in Hughes Panassié, *Louis Armstrong* (New York: Scribner's, 1971), 9.
37. Louis Armstrong, *Satchmo: My Life in New Orleans* (New York: Da Capo, 1986), 188.
38. DeLong, *Pops*, 228–29.
39. This is the lyrical essence of the song as summed up in Will Friedwald, *Stardust Melodies: A Biography of Twelve of America's Most Popular Songs* (New York: Pantheon, 2002), 11. Richard Sudhalter, using metronomic proof, has cogently argued for a more moderate original tempo than what might be suggested by a driving stomp or ragtime piece. Sudhalter, *Stardust Melody*, 108–9.
40. There were apparently several reasons for the rupture, all of them touching on Crosby's alcoholism. He reportedly owed a bootlegger money for a quart of "day-old pop-skull," and Whiteman, having to foot the bill, deducted the amount from Crosby's salary. In addition, there were allegations that Whiteman had humiliated Crosby in front of the band, accusing him of stealing his own liquor. By all accounts, Crosby's sense of hurt over Whiteman's treatment festered until the end of his life. Gary Giddins, *Bing Crosby: A Pocketful of Dreams, the Early Years, 1903–1940* (Boston: Little, Brown, 2001), 214–15.
41. Ibid., 138.

42. For those interested in musical particulars, this is a half diminished ninth chord.

43. Carmichael with Longstreet, *Sometimes I Wonder*, 203.

44. Many of these Whiteman-Armstrong cross-influences were first suggested by Max Harrison in "Around Paul Whiteman," *Jazz Monthly*, no. 185 (1970): 4–12.

45. Walter C. Allen, *Hendersonia: The Music of Fletcher Henderson and His Musicians* (Highland Park, N.J.: Jazz Monographs no. 4, published by Walter C. Allen, 1973), 4.

46. Ibid., 243.

47. Will Friedwald, *Jazz Singing* (New York: Da Capo, 1996), 38.

48. There is no entry for Victor Young in either the 1988 or 2002 edition of *The New Grove Dictionary of Jazz*. He does receive his due in Brian Rust's *The American Dance Band Discography, 1917–1942*, and, even more important, in the monumental *Sixty Years of Recorded Jazz, 1917–1977* by Walter Bruyninckx.

49. Richard Sudhalter, personal communication, January 3, 2003.

50. Quoted in DeLong, *Pops*, 263.

51. Berrett, *Companion*, 78–81.

52. Quoted in Bergreen, *Louis Armstrong*, 360.

53. Berrett, *Companion*, 99–102.

54. Friedwald, *Stardust Melodies*, 144.

55. Quoted ibid., 149.

56. Beiderbecke's last documented performance with Paul Whiteman was at a recording session for Columbia on September 13, 1929. Ill health prevented him from ever rejoining the band, despite offers from Whiteman.

57. Armstrong was to record "Body and Soul" eleven times in the course of his career.

58. Armstrong, *Satchmo*, 46, 86.

59. Crawford and Magee, *Jazz Standards on Record*, x.

60. Friedwald, *Stardust Melodies*, 41.

61. W. C. Handy, *Father of the Blues: An Autobiography* (New York: Macmillan, 1941), 13.

62. Quoted in Leonard Feather, *The Book of Jazz* (New York: Horizon, 1957), 23–25.

63. Handy, *Father*, 80–81.

64. Information about Handy's royalties and his comment about combining ragtime with melody in the spiritual tradition is based on research available at http://bluesnet.hub.org/readings/st.louis.blues.html.

65. Handy, *Father*, 149.

66. Ibid. See also: http://www.basinstreet.com/Programs/BluesEvolution/.

67. Handy, *Father*, 100–102.

68. James T. Maher, *Radio Music, I Loved You*, 44–45. My thanks to James T. Maher for generously sharing the contents of his unpublished manuscript.

69. Presumably lost to posterity are two Whiteman Orchestra performances of "St. Louis Blues" known to have been part of radio broadcasts. They date from September 10, 1929, when Bix Beiderbecke made his last appearance on an Old Gold radio broadcast and Mildred Bailey handled the vocal. The second occa-

sion was the *Camel Pleasure Hour* broadcast of April 13, 1930, which included the singing of Carson Robison.

70. George Avakian, program booklet for *Louis Armstrong Plays W. C. Handy,* Columbia CK 64925, 5.

71. The writer and lyricist James Weldon Johnson (1871–1938) collaborated with his composer brother J. Rosamond Johnson (1873–1954) on such all-black Broadway shows as *The Shoo-Fly Regiment* (1906) and *The Red Moon* (1908). Perhaps their best known song is "Lift Every Voice and Sing."

72. Handy, *Father,* 223.

73. Ibid., 298, 268.

74. An earlier recording from 1926 made by Whiteman in London was never issued.

75. The importance of opera to Armstrong's creative process is explored in depth in Joshua Berrett, "Louis Armstrong and Opera," *Musical Quarterly* 76, no. 2 (Summer 1992): 216–41.

76. Ibid., 225.

77. Harry Dial, quoted in Bergreen, *Louis Armstrong,* 361.

78. Richard M. Sudhalter, *Lost Chords: White Musicians and Their Contribution to Jazz, 1915–1945* (New York: Oxford University Press, 1999), 141–42.

79. Paul Whiteman and Mary Margaret McBride, *Jazz* (New York: J. H. Sears, 1926), 180–82. To clarify, the chorus of "Bananas" has been cobbled together from at least four disparate sources. It begins with what is essentially the opening measure of the Hallelujah Chorus, and follows with quotations from "Bring Back My Bonnie to Me," "I Dreamt That I Dwelt in Marble Halls," and "In an Old-Fashioned Garden." In the case of "Avalon" and its borrowing from Puccini's *Tosca*—specifically, the aria "E lucevan le stelle"—Whiteman neglects to mention that there was a 1921 lawsuit arising from this theft which resulted in an award to Puccini and his publisher, G. Ricordi, of $25,000 in damages and all future royalties. The suit forced the publisher of "Avalon" out of business. Finally, needless to say, what Whiteman naïvely says about copyright of his day has little bearing on the highly complex and litigious world of copyright law and intellectual property rights in the twenty-first century.

80. Roger Lax and Frederick Smith, *The Great Song Thesaurus,* 2d ed. (New York: Oxford University Press, 1989).

81. Berrett, "Louis Armstrong and Opera," 218.

82. Whiteman's central role in the cultivation of middlebrow taste has recently been the topic of a major study. See John Louis Howland, "Between the Muses and the Masses: Symphonic Jazz, 'Glorified' Entertainment, and the Rise of the American Musical Middlebrow, 1920–1944," Ph.D. diss., Stanford University, 2002.

83. Krin Gabbard, *Jammin' at the Margins: Jazz and the American Cinema* (Chicago: University of Chicago Press, 1996), 64.

84. Ibid., 221.

85. *New York Times,* September 19, 1957, 23.

86. At that point, of course, the research of Tad Jones authenticating Armstrong's birth date as August 4, 1901, was some thirty years away.

87. Dan Morgenstern, liner notes to Louis Armstrong, *Chicago Concert, 1956,* Columbia CS 36426.

88. Stefano Zenni, "Peculiarità stilistiche dell'ultimo Armstrong," *Musica Oggi* 21 (2001): 61–73.

6 OUT CHORUS

1. By far the best known example is Harold Evans, *The American Century* (New York: Knopf, 1999).

2. Carol J. Oja, "Gershwin and the American Modernists of the 1920s," *Musical Quarterly* 78, no. 4 (Winter 1994): 650.

3. Joshua Berrett, *The Louis Armstrong Companion: Eight Decades of Commentary* (New York: Schirmer, 1999), 20–23. Compilation of sources culled from Harold Wentworth and Stuart Berg Flexner, *Dictionary of American Slang* (New York: Crowell, 1967), and Louis Armstrong, *Satchmo: My Life in New Orleans* (New York: Da Capo, 1986).

4. Marc H. Miller, *Louis Armstrong: A Cultural Legacy* (New York: Queens Museum of Art, 1994), 15, 46, 112, 113, 197–214.

5. Quoted in Berrett, *Companion,* xiii. Quotation of Wynton Marsalis from *Satchmo,* PBS American Masters series, 1989.

6. Don Rayno, *Paul Whiteman: Pioneer in American Music* (Lanham, Md.: Scarecrow, 2003), 50–51.

7. Thomas A. DeLong, *Pops: Paul Whiteman, King of Jazz* (Piscataway, N.J.: New Century, 1983), 4, 84.

8. Paul Whiteman and Mary Margaret McBride, *Jazz* (New York: J. H. Sears, 1926), 155–56.

9. Ibid., 118–19.

10. Quoted in Berrett, *Companion,* xiv–xv.

11. Joshua Berrett, "Louis Armstrong and Opera," *Musical Quarterly* 76, no. 2 (Summer 1992): 218.

12. Richard M. Sudhalter, *Lost Chords: White Musicians and Their Contribution to Jazz, 1915–1945* (New York: Oxford University Press, 1999), 800, n. 20.

13. Berrett, *Companion,* 139–57.

14. Louis Armstrong to Dizzy Gillespie, July 1, 1959, Louis Armstrong Archive Series, Letters 3, no. 1/10; Dizzy Gillespie with Al Fraser, *To Be, or Not to Bop: Memoirs* (Garden City, N.Y.: Doubleday, 1979), 295–96.

15. Billy Taylor, "Negroes Don't Know Anything About Jazz," as reprinted in Lewis Porter, *Jazz: A Century of Change* (New York: Schirmer, 1997), 202–7.

16. Archie Shepp, "An Artist Speaks Bluntly," *Down Beat,* December 16, 1965. Reprinted in Porter, *Jazz,* 212–15.

17. *New York Times,* December 19, 1995.

18. A major and thoroughly damning review of Collier's book is Dan Morgenstern's piece, "Louis Armstrong: An American Genius," which originally appeared in the *Annual Review of Jazz Studies* 3 (1985). It has since been reprinted in *Reading Jazz,* ed. Robert Gottlieb (New York: Pantheon, 1996), 1034–41.

19. Quoted in Geoffrey C. Ward and Ken Burns, *Jazz: A History of America's Music* (New York: Knopf, 2000), 130, 117–18, 231.
20. Quoted ibid., 109.
21. Quoted ibid., 101.
22. Sudhalter, *Lost Chords,* 821, n. 21
23. David Hadju, "Wynton's Blues," *Atlantic Monthly,* March 2003, 46.
24. PBS telecast of December 19, 2001.

GENERAL INDEX

affidavit, Whiteman supporting Armstrong, 116–18, 148

Afrocentrism, xii–xiii, 204–6

Albert, Mayann (mother of Armstrong), 20–21, 35

Albertson, Chris, 219 n.16

Alexandria Hotel, 18

All Things Considered, 205–6

Ambassador Hotel, 19, 37

"Ambassador Satch," 146–47, 191

"The American Century" and jazz, 196–97

American Federation of Musicians, 117, 148

American Tobacco, 89

Anderson, Marian, 135

animal dances and early jazz, 9–11; and fascination with the exotic, 10; and primitivism, 10; and psychology of sex, 10

Ansermet, Ernest, 53

Armstrong, Louis: as "actor and musician," 71, 114, 171, 177, 199; baptismal records and correct birthdate, 21; bowel function and, 112; commitment to public, xiv, 71, 113–14, 152, 177, 196, 199; deposition in U.S. District Court, 117–18; earnings, 121; family history of slavery, 21; feature films, 203; first interracial ensemble, 96; inclusiveness of musical taste and religion, 22–24,

113–14, 199, 200, 215 n.40; influences visual arts and modern lingo, 197; interest in opera, 22, 77, 200; little interest in money and managing a band, 121, 122, 177–78, 197; marijuana use, 112–13, 171–72; modernism and traditionalism, 203–4; poised for international stardom, 97–98; scat and, 83–84; sharing nickname of "Pops" with Paul Whiteman, xi, 196; squalor of New Orleans birthplace, 20–21; surrogate fathers and families, 22–25, 106, 198; trumpet as talisman, 24–25, 125, 177–78, 197; work ethic, 24, 122, 200

Armstrong All Stars, 145, 146, 183

Atlantic City, 19, 37

Atlantic City (film), 191

Avakian, George, 183–84

Bailey, Mildred, 84, 98, 127–28, 149, 160–63, 189

Baker, Josephine, 127

Bannet, Louis ("the Dutch Louis Armstrong"), 138–39

Barbarin, Isidore, 29

Barbarin, Paul, 182

Barbary Coast "blues" of Whiteman, 1; casualty of moral crusade, 9; and hot jazz, 2

Bargy, Roy, 149

cross-influences of Whiteman and Armstrong, 53, 62, 168, 199, 218 n.51

Cunard, Nancy, 126

Daily Worker, 107, 109

Damrosch, Walter, 217 n.10

dance band business: virtual monopoly (pre-1919) of Creole and black musicians, 19–20

Dandridge, Dorothy, 191

Davis, Peter, 25, 122

De Rose, Peter, 84

DeSylva, Buddy, 104, 137

Dickerson, Carroll, 78, 81, 94, 96

Dodds, Baby, 43–44

Dodds, Johnny, 71

Donaldson, Walter, 58, 86

Dorsey, Jimmy, xiii, 87, 156, 187

Dorsey, Tommy, xiii, 87, 137, 156, 168

Downes, Olin, 64

Dreamland Café, 32–33, 68

DuValle, Reg, 153

Dvořák, Antonín, 73

Early, Gerald, xi–xii

"Ear" vs. "eye" musicians: black-Creole tensions in New Orleans, 28–30

Ebony, 136

Edgewater Beach Hotel, 161

Eisenhower, Pres. Dwight, 192–93

Ellington, Duke, xi, xiv, 41, 134, 209; assessment of Whiteman, 150, 225 n.7 and 8

Ellison, Ralph, 97

Encyclopedia Britannica, 38–39

Ernst, Hugh C., 59

Esquire, 141

Europe, James Reese, 11–12, 181

Evans, Gil, 209

An Experiment in Modern Music: Aeolian Hall (Feb. 12, 1924), 41, 55, 59–62, 217 n.10; Second Experiment (Dec. 29, 1924), 64; Fifth Experiment (Jan. 25, 1933), 170, 175; Sixth Experiment (Dec. 15, 1933), 98, 130; Eighth Experiment (Dec. 25, 1938), 118, 132, 134

Fairmont Hotel, 18

Farrell, Charlie, 94

Faubus, Gov. Orval, 192

Feather, Leonard, 140–41, 172–73

Finkelstein, Sidney, 147

First Esquire All American Jazz Concert, 141, 143, 173

Fleischmann's Yeast Hour, 89

Fox, Ed, 149

Frank Sebastian's Cotton Club, 112–13

"From Spirituals to Swing" concert, 132–34, 145

Fulton, Jack, 170–71, 177

Gabler, Milt, 145

Gade, Jacob, 182

Gaiety Theater Building, 52

Galli-Curci, Amelita, 77

Gauthier, Eva, 58

Geddes, Norman Bel, 56

Gennett, 35, 52, 80–81, 155

Gershwin, George, 41, 58, 60

Giddins, Gary, 83

Gilbert, John, 94

Gillespie, Dizzy, 204

Gingrich, Arnold, 141, 173

Glaser, Joe, 73, 95, 105–6, 134, 166

Goffin, Robert, 126, 140–41, 173, 216 n.64

Goldfield, Harry, 90

Goldkette, Jean, 41, 87, 156, 165

Goodman, Benny, 132, 146, 151

Gorman, Ross, 56

Granada Café, 94, 151

Grand Terrace, 149

Great Depression and segregation, 99–100

The Great Gatsby, 38, 55

Green, Abel, 80

Green, Johnny W., 175, 176

Griffith, D.W., 11
Grofé, Ferde, xiii, 12, 16, 56, 64, 66, 87, 175, 208; sectional choirs used by, 35, 41

Hall, Jim, 205–6
Hammerstein, Oscar, 176
Hammond, John, 108–11, 112, 132–34, 145, 147, 222 n.17
Handy, W. C., 11–12, 47, 178–85; as "black Rockefeller," 178, 227 n.64; money and birth of American composer, 179–80
Handy and Pace, 47
Hanson, Howard, 130
Hardin, Lil, 41–43, 44–46; academic studies in classical music, 73–74; copyright feud with Armstrong, 72–73; first meeting with Armstrong, 43; nurtures early solo career of Armstrong, 68–75, 168; presented in solo recital, 73–74; Tirro observation, 71;
Harlem Renaissance, 39–40, 48, 96–97
Hasse, John Edward, 153
Hawkins, Coleman, 49, 62, 110
Hazlett, Chester, 87
Hearst, William Randolph, and Methodists, 9
Henderson, Fletcher, xiii, 41, 46, 47, 48–49, 110, 151; Armstrong's time with, 49–52, 181; farewell party for Armstrong, 54; as "Ivy League prom king," 50; Whiteman's admiration for, 49
Herbert, Victor, 58, 60
Herman, Woody, 146
Hickman, Art, 15; and saxophone sonority, 16
Higginbotham, J. C., 182
High Society (film), 191–93
Hill, Edward Burlinghame, 58
Hindemith, Paul, 58
Hines, Earl, 76, 94, 149
Hobson, Wilder, 147
Holiday, Billie, 137–38, 145–46, 173

Hope, Bob, 174
Horne, Lena, 138
Hot Five and Hot Seven, 41, 69–74, 76–78, 94, 168, 219 n.2
Hughes, Spike, 108

Immerman, Connie, 106, 117, 148
Immigration Act (1924), 38
"inside the strain," 49–50, 86
International Labor Defense (ILD), 110–11
Invisible Man, 97
"Ivy League Marxists," 147, 205

jazz: bicoastal view, xiii; challenges of defining it, xi–xiii; first appearance of "jazz" in print, 15; lack of uniformity in early spelling, 13–14; overlapping terminology, 14–15
Jazz (Whiteman-McBride), 5–6, 55, 56–58, 65–67
jazz and "folk character," 104–5
jazz and popular music: Armstrong and Whiteman as twin fathers, xi–xii, xiv; making "a lady out of jazz," 217 n.10
jazz as proletarian music, 100, 106–11, 132–34, 147; and resolution of 100th U.S. Congress, 206
Jazz at Lincoln Center, 206–8, 210–11
jazz biopics, 189–90
Jazz Classique Orchestra (Whiteman), 17
Jazzmen, 135–36, 141, 145
"jazzmen," origin of, 224 n.65
The Jazz Singer (film), 86, 93, 98, 130
Johnson, James Weldon, 185
Johnson, J. J., 209
Johnson, William, "Bunk," 145
Jolson, Al, 91, 98, 130–31
Juvenile Protective Association, 44

Kaganovich, Lazar, 139–40
Kapp, Jack, 169
Karnofsky family, 23–25
Katscher, Robert, 104

Kenton, Stan, 209
Keppard, Freddie, 31
Kern, Jerome, 58
"King of Jazz," xiii; Duke Ellington as, 99; legal protection of title, 123; Whiteman's coronation as, 123, 223 n.45
King of Jazz (film), 89–93, 99, 130, 160, 188, 191
Kirk, Andy: early training under Wilberforce Whiteman, 3
Kraft Music Hall, 98, 130
Ku Klux Klan, 38, 148, 158

"laboring of American culture," 100–101
Lafayette Theater, 52
Lambert, Scrappy, 86
Lambertville Music Circus, 194–95, 203
Landry, Art, 18
Lane, Eastwood, 64
Lang, Eddie, xiii, 90, 96, 156, 168
Lanin, Sam, and His Orchestra, 47
Lawrence, Gertrude, 176
League of Composers, 58
Lee, Spike, 10
Lenin, Vladimir Ilyich, 101
Leoncavallo, Ruggero, 186
Lewis, John, 204, 209
Lewisohn Stadium, 184
Lincoln Gardens, 34, 35, 37, 42, 118, 155
Liszt, Franz, 175
Little Rock, Arkansas, 192–93, 203
Livingston, Fud, 129
Locke, Alain, 39, 130
Lombardo, Guy, 94–95, 150–51, 177
Lopez, Vincent, 58
Lorillard Company, 89
Lott, Eric, and minstrelsy, 10–11, 214 n.20
Lovano, Joe, 205–6
Luce, Henry, 196
Lucky Strike, 89
Lunceford, Jimmie, early training under Wilberforce Whiteman, 3

Maher, James T., 151–52, 157
Malneck, Matty, 83
Mana-Zucca, Mme, 64
Marable, Fate, 111
Mare Island, 17–18
Marsalis, Wynton, 197, 206–8, 209–11
Marshall Plan, 147
Mason, Daniel Gregory, 59
Melody Maker, 120, 121
Memphis Cotton Carnival, 185
Memphis Police Force, 119
Mercer, Johnny, 137, 146
Mezzrow, Mezz, 84
microphone design, 93–94
Middleton, Velma, 183
Milhaud, Darius, 10, 55, 58, 126–27
Millay, Edna St. Vincent, 40
Million Dollar Theater, 82–83
Mills, Florence, 92–93
Mills Music, 166
Monkey Trial, 39
montage of jazz notables, 190–91
Morgenstern, Dan, xii, 193, 206, 208
Mozart, Wolfgang Amadeus, 74
Murrow, Edward R., 184
"Muscular Christianity," 5–6
musicians in common, xiii, xiv, 11–12, 47, 52, 80, 82–86, 87, 90, 93–95, 96, 98, 101, 127–28, 134, 137, 149, 156, 158–60, 160–63, 168, 174–75, 178–85, 187, 189, 199
"The Mussolini of Ragtime," 102–3

National Association of Talking Machine Jobbers, 19
Negro: An Anthology, 126
Newman, Ernest, 66
New Masses, 133
New Orleans (film), 145–46, 173
New Orleans revival, 144–45
New Orleans Rhythm Kings, 154
New School for Social Research, 140–42, 173
New Yorker, xii–xiii
"noble lie" (Plato's *Republic*), xii

Okeh, 52, 95

Old Gold broadcasts, 89, 128–29

Oliver, King, xiii, 27–28, 31–35, 198; on cat swinging a lead, 197; Creole Jazz Band, 37–38, 81; frustrating white competition, 43–44; paranoia and pride, 44–46; problems with musicians union, 33; telegram to Armstrong, 34–35

O'Meally, Robert G., 97

Original Dixieland Jazz Band, 12, 53, 61, 101, 185–86

Ory, Edward "Kid," 27, 31, 71

Osgood, Henry O., 65, 135

Pacific theater and defense industry, 136–37

Page, Hot Lips, 134

Palais Royal: orchestra, 12, 37; clientele, 37, 55;

Paley, William S., 89

Palmer Raids, 106

Panama-Pacific International Exposition, 2

Panassié, Hugues, 126–27, 140–41

Parish, Mitchell, 166

Parker, Charlie, 77

Paul Whiteman Record Club, 144

"Paul Whiteman" tag crossing racial boundaries, 46, 150, 225 n.6;

Pearl Harbor, 136

Pekin Café, 32

Peyton, Benny, 101

Peyton, Dave, 49, 208

The Philadelphia Story (film), 191

Philco Radio Hall of Fame, 171

Pingitore, Mike, 56, 87, 90

Piron, Armand J., 29–30, 216 n.53

Pittsburgh Courier, 99

"playing away from the score," 69, 76

Plessy vs. Ferguson, 20

Powell, Adam Clayton, 136

"prescriptive" score, 74

Prohibition, 40

Puccini, Giacomo, 228 n.79

"race records," 38, 47

Ramsey, Jr., Frederic, 135, 147

Rank, Bill, 165

Ravel, Maurice, 59

Razaf, Andy, 97

Records for the Millions, 144

Redman, Don, xiv, 41, 49, 62, 187, 208

"Red Summer" (1919), 20, 38

Reverend Satchelmouth, 84

Rhapsody in Black and Blue, 138

Rhapsody in Blue (film), 143–44, 188, 202–3

Rhythm Boys, 82

Rinker, Al, 83

Robeson, Paul, 136

Robichaux, John, 29

Robinson, Fred, 94

Robinson, Jackie, 136

Robinson, Perry, 205

Robison, Willard, 85

Rockwell, Tommy, 95–96, 106, 116–17, 148, 166

Rodgers, Richard, 176

Rogers, Joel Augustus, 40

Rolfe, R.A., 89

Rollins, Sonny, 206

Roosevelt, Theodore, 5

Roseland Ballroom, 46–47

Rosner, Eddie, 139

Royal Albert Hall, 102–3

Rudd, Roswell, 205

Runyon, Damon, 12–13

Saar, Louis Victor, 73–74

Sandburg, Carl, 135, 224 n.65

Satchmo (nickname), 125

Satchmo: My Life in New Orleans: core of solid common sense, 21–22, 111–12

Satchmo the Great, 184

Satie, Erik, 72

Savoy Ballroom, 94, 95, 96, 130

Schlesinger, Arthur M., xii

Schoenberg, Arnold, 58, 104

Schreker, Franz, 104

Schuller, Gunther, 76–77, 209

Scott, Howard, 48–49
Scottsboro Nine, 108–9
Secrest, Andy, 163, 177
Seldes, Gilbert, 59, 64–65, 135
Selmer, Henri, 125
The Seven Lively Arts, 64–65
Shaw, Artie, 134, 209
Shepp, Archie, 205
Singleton, Zutty, 76, 94, 151
Sissle, Noble, 48
Small's Paradise, 54
Smith, Bessie, 98, 110, 127–28, 181–82
Smith, Charles Edward, 107–8, 135
Smithsonian Collection of Classic Jazz, 206
Smithsonian Jazz Masterworks Orchestra, 206
"sock time," 154
So This Is Jazz, 65
Sousa, John Philip, 58
Southern Pacific Railroad, 31
Stearns, Marshall, 147
Still, William Grant, xiv, 48, 98, 128–30, 175, 209
Stokowski, Leopold, 130
Straus, Simon William, 19
Stravinsky, Igor, 55, 59, 209
Streckfus Steamboat Line, 165
Streisand, Barbra, 193
Strickfaden, Charles, 129
Strong, Jimmy, 94
Sudhalter, Richard, 95, 152, 187, 201–2, 209
Sullivan, Ed, 118
Sunset Café, 81, 84, 105–6
Sweet 'n' Low, 174
Swing That Music, 141
symphonic jazz, 10, 16, 41, 58–59, 78–80, 82, 150, 170, 175, 178, 184–85, 199, 209

Tait's Restaurant, Whiteman fired from, 16
Tate, Buddy, 116

Tate, Erskine, "Little Symphony," 75–76
Taylor, Billy, 204–5
Taylor, Deems, 62–63, 134
Tchicai, John, 205
Teagarden, Jack, xiii, 96, 98, 134, 164–65
Teplitsky, Leopold, and Russian jazz, xiv, 101
"Third Stream," 209
Time, 99, 146, 147
Tivoli Theater, 102
Trade Union Congress, 102
transcontinental journeys of Armstrong and Whiteman, 36; defining trajectories in jazz history, 36
Trent, Jo, 84
Trianon Ballroom, 43, 118
Trumbauer, Frank, xiii, 85–87, 101, 129, 156
Turner, Richardson ("Dick"), 80
"Twenty-One," 174
"Twenty Questions," 174

Uncle Tom's Cabin, 176

Van Doren, Charles, 174
Venuti, Joe, xiii, 87, 90, 96, 156

Waller, Thomas, "Fats," 96–97
Waters, Ethel, 98, 127, 138
Weill, Kurt, 105
West Coast and early jazz musicians, 30–31, 33–34
White, George, *Scandals of 1922*, 58, 90, 143
Whiteman, Elfrida Dallison (mother of Paul) and oratorio, 5
Whiteman, Paul: acquiring "foreign flavor," 56; alumni of his band, xiii, xiv, 151; boosterism, music, and economics, 198; and California hotel circuit, 16; commitment to public, xiv, 55–56, 91, 150–51, 152, 178, 188, 196, 199, 201; concerts as "productions,"

INDEX OF MUSICAL TITLES